D1591073

THE ESOTERIC COMEDIES
OF CARLYLE, NEWMAN, AND YEATS

THE ESOTERIC COMEDIES
OF CARLYLE, NEWMAN, AND
YEATS

STEVEN HELMLING

The right of the
University of Cambridge
to print and sell
all manner of books
was granted by
Henry VIII in 1534.
The University has printed
and published continuously
since 1584.

CAMBRIDGE UNIVERSITY PRESS
Cambridge
New York   New Rochelle   Melbourne   Sydney

Published by the Press Syndicate of the University of Cambridge
The Pitt Building, Trumpington Street, Cambridge CB2 1RP
32 East 57th Street, New York, NY 10022, USA
10 Stamford Road, Oakleigh, Melbourne 3166, Australia

First published 1988

Printed in Canada

Library of Congress Cataloging-in-Publication Data
Helmling, Steven, 1947–
The esoteric comedies of Carlyle, Newman, and Yeats / by Steven
Helmling.
p.   cm.
1. English literature – 19th century – History and criticism.
2. Comic, The, in literature.   3. Carlyle, Thomas, 1795–1881.
Sartor resartus.   4. Newman, John Henry, 1801–1890. Apologia pro
vita sua.   5. Yeats, W. B. (William Butler), 1865–1939. Vision.
I. Title.
PR468.C65H38   1988   88-1065
820'.9'008 – dc 19   CIP

British Library Cataloguing in Publication Data
Helming, Steven
The esoteric comedies of Carlyle, Newman,
and Yeats.
1. Prose in English. Carlyle, Thomas,
1795–1881. Critical studies   2. England.
Catholic Church. Newman, John Henry,
1801–1890. Works. Critical studies
3. Poetry in English. Yeats, W. B. (William
Butler), 1865–1939. Critical studies
I. Title
828'.808

ISBN 0 521 36165 6

To the memory of my parents,
who gave me my sense of what's funny:
Bob,
whose humor might change
from apoplexy to high mirth several times an hour;
and the witty, teasing
Eddo –
because she either was, or was not, Irish

CONTENTS

ACKNOWLEDGMENTS

I WANT TO THANK my teachers and friends at Rutgers. In addition to the members of my dissertation committee, Thomas R. Edwards, George Levine, and Richard Poirier, I am grateful to Fred Main and Barry Qualls. I first wrote about "esoteric comedy" in a seminar on Yeats led by Carol Smith, then further in a paper on Newman in a course on Victorian nonfiction taught by George Levine. (More specific, but no less extensive, debts to the work of George Levine are documented in the notes to my chapters on Carlyle and Newman.) George Kearns read early drafts of the Carlyle and Newman chapters with care above and beyond the call of duty, and even of friendship. And I remain especially grateful for the encouragement and the example of Paul Fussell. In fairness to my teachers, I should add that I was (and am) a willful student, and anyone who objects to any of the things I think I have learned should not blame them.

At Rutgers I was lucky, too, in my out-of-the-classroom friends, and any roundup of the usual suspects would certainly include Georgia Jackson Cowart, David Cowart, Joe Esposito, Mary Fran and Bill Karanikolas, Richard Lavenstein, Susan Nash, John Beldon Scott, and Olivia Smith.

At the University of Delaware and environs, I am grateful for the friendship of Ellen and Drury Pifer, Lynda Schmid and David Lamb, Bill and Chris Homer, Ceal Phelan and Peter DeLaurier, Linda Henderson and Harvey Price, Fiona Dejardin, Neal Van Duren, Maggie Andersen and Richard Rosenfeld; and for the strong collegial support of Jerry Beasley, Heyward Brock,

Acknowledgments

Phil Flynn, Barbara Gates, Jay Halio, Leo Lemay, Don Mell, and Jeannie Walker. And I want to thank one of my oldest teachers and friends, Frank Nisetich of the Department of Classics at the University of Massachusetts at Boston.

I also want to thank A. Walton Litz and Denis Donoghue. Neither has read a word of *Esoteric Comedies,* but both encouraged me on a project whose beginnings coincided with a late phase of this one, and theirs is the sort of encouragement that has a way of exceeding its object. And finally I thank the anonymous "Reader A," who first reviewed the manuscript for Cambridge University Press and whose suggestions for revision helped enormously.

At Rutgers, I was the recipient of a four-year University Fellowship while writing my dissertation; and the Delaware Humanities Forum helped support a late phase of revision during the 1984–5 academic year. I am grateful to both institutions for their support.

But I owe most, of course, to my wife Patricia Leighten. Her work on avant-garde art movements in Europe has been a stimulating complement to my own in Anglo-American modernism; even more important, her loving and sympathetic intelligence kept me going through many a day when, like Bartleby the scrivener, I preferred not to.

For permission to quote the facsimile *Critical Edition of Yeats's "A Vision" (1925),* ed. George Mills Harper and Walter Kelly Hood, I am grateful to Macmillan Publishers Ltd. For permission to quote other works of Yeats, I am grateful to A. P. Watt Ltd., on behalf of Michael B. Yeats and Macmillan London Ltd.; and to Macmillan Publishing Company for permission to quote from W. B. Yeats's *A Vision* (copyright 1937 by William Butler Yeats, renewed 1965 by Bertha Georgie Yeats and Anne Butler Yeats), *The Variorum Edition of the Poems of W. B. Yeats,* ed. Peter Allt and Russel K. Alspach (copyright 1916, 1918, 1919, 1924, 1928 by Macmillan Publishing Company, renewed 1944, 1946, 1947, 1952, 1956 by Bertha Georgie Yeats), and *The Autobiography of William Butler Yeats* (copyright 1916, 1936 by Macmillan Publishing Company, renewed 1944, 1964 by Bertha Georgia Yeats). I am also grateful to the Hugh Lane Municipal Gallery of Modern Art in Dublin for permission to reproduce

Acknowledgments

Max Beerbohm's cartoon, "Mr. W. B. Yeats Presenting Mr. George Moore to the Queen of the Fairies." An earlier version of Chapter 3 appeared under the title "Yeats's Esoteric Comedy" in the *Hudson Review,* vol. 30, no. 2 (Summer 1977), and I am grateful to the editors for permission to revise and reprint.

INTRODUCTION

ESOTERIC COMEDY AND "THE GYMNASTICS OF TALENT"

❧❧❧

I do not press the skepticism of the materialist. I know the quadruped opinion will not prevail. 'Tis of no importance what bats and oxen think. The first symptom I report is, the levity of intellect; as if it were fatal to earnestness to know much. Knowledge is the knowing that we can not know. The dull pray; the geniuses are light mockers. How respectable is earnestness on every platform! but intellect kills it. Nay, San Carlo, my subtle and admirable friend, one of the most penetrating of men, finds that all direct ascension, even of lofty piety, leads to this ghastly insight, and sends back the votary orphaned. My astonishing San Carlo thought the lawgivers and saints infected. They found the ark empty; saw, and would not tell, and tried to choke off their approaching followers by saying, "Action, action, my dear fellows, is for you!" Bad as was to me this detection by San Carlo, this frost in July, this blow from a bride, there was still a worse, namely the cloy or satiety of the saints. In the mount of vision, ere they have yet risen from their knees, they say, "We discover that this our homage and beatitude is partial and deformed: we must fly for relief to the suspected and reviled Intellect, to the Understanding, the Mephistopheles, to the gymnastics of talent."

– Emerson, "Montaigne: or, the Skeptic"

A CLASSIC, according to Mark Twain, is a book everyone wants to have read but nobody wants to read. Whether or not they are classics in this or any sense, Carlyle's *Sartor Resartus*, Newman's *Apologia Pro Vita Sua,* and Yeats's *A Vision* often seem books more honored than read. As different as they are in many ways, each offers a kind of wisdom in response to a culture-wide crisis of faith and belief – but by the time Yeats published *A Vision* (1926: revised 1937), not only the

1

wisdom but the crisis, too, seemed to most readers laughably old-fashioned. Twentieth-century culture has not been patient with books whose partisans recommend them as repositories of paraphraseable and excerptable wisdom. The New Criticism inaugurated a style of attention to literature not as thesaurus of important truths but as enactments of variously interesting stances toward the world, and a specifically anti-Victorian bias once seemed an indispensable component of "modernist" sensibility.

Not until the 1950s – the 1953 publication of John Holloway's *The Victorian Sage* was the watershed – were New Critical assumptions about reading and writing brought to bear on texts like *Sartor Resartus* and the *Apologia,* with startling results. Readers became readier to locate the interest of such books less in the logic of their arguments or positions than in their surprises of rhetoric and tone, and to regard their obscurities and difficulties not as regrettable authorial oversights a helpful criticism should redeem, but rather as mazes deliberately placed in the reader's path by writers entirely calculating and self-conscious about their literary means. In these elaborate difficulties lay the heart not only of the author's matter but also of the reader's pleasure, and thus a new phase of appreciation of these "classic" writers began.

But the antihistorical and antibiographical bias of the New Criticism, then of *la nouvelle critique,* necessarily missed the audacity of these writers and these writings vis-à-vis their original audiences, for whom the question (and the distortion) of "the classic" did not arise: an audience that read *Sartor Resartus* as an anonymous lampoon in a humor magazine, that read the *Apologia* in the heat of a bitter personal controversy, that read (or chose not to read)[1] *A Vision* at a self-consciously "disillusioned" time, when allegiances were in full pendulum swing from "last Romantics" to a tough-minded modernism. None of these books assumes a passively receptive audience; on the contrary, Carlyle, Newman, and Yeats are acutely aware that their projects involve designs upon the reader that most readers will resist as eccentric or irrelevant or worse – a resistance each contrives to make not only the object but also the subject of his rhetorical play. The result in each case, full of jokes, irony, and paradoxes about wisdom and folly, is an oddly unforthcoming apocalypse, a devious and teasing revelation as often occulted as disclosed.

Hence "esoteric comedies." At first I thought of these books as "comedies" simply because each was, in unexpected ways, humorous, and "esoteric" because each agitated themes and vocabularies – Carlyle's Germanic transcendentalism, Newman's idiosyncratic theology, Yeats's gyres and cones – that (their authors know full well) will strike most readers as recondite, arcane, and at least a little absurd. If some aura of the esoteric is implicit in the conviction that to read is to be initiated into an experience, rather than argued into a position, such a view of literary experience is relevant not only to the way we should read *Sartor Resartus,* the *Apologia,* and *A Vision,* but to the way Carlyle, Newman, and Yeats wrote them. These books aim not to explain a doctrine but to involve us in the activity of wresting illumination from bafflement. They instruct us, if obliquely, in how to read them, thus implicitly criticizing or correcting whatever habits of "reading" (interpreting, understanding) we had before and suggesting that if our reading is sufficiently sympathetic, generous, and intelligent, we will gain some access to the author's sense of things far more vibrant and alive than a mere expository report could offer.

I assume then, as John Holloway does in *The Victorian Sage,* that in writers like these, what matters is "to discover in detail what the methods are whereby the sage gives expression to his outlook" and "exactly where, in his writing, we may trace what re-creates for the reader the sage's somehow esoteric insight."[2] But Holloway's emphases differ from mine about as a sage differs from a comedian. Holloway's word "sage" comports all too readily (especially when modified by "Victorian") with just that sense of cultural legitimacy and custodianship that Mark Twain dislikes about the "classic." Of course, Holloway acknowledges that the figures he calls "sages" often act less as spokesmen of and for their culture than as critics and even adversaries of it, but my special focus is on their willingness to express their opposition by recourse to poses distinctly unsagelike. Carlyle, Newman, and Yeats have each sized up, with great shrewdness, the materialist, rationalist, prosaically "common sense" age they inhabit; each has observed that the age's complacencies (which make the sage a supererogatory figure) are lucklessly entoiled in the age's anxieties (which make the sage a figure devoutly to be looked for), and each is ready to make great and witty play with this contradiction. Each could play the sage when it pleased him, but I am interested in those moments when an adversary stance becomes something more ambiguous, more irresponsible, more alienated, more impatient of what is expected and thus more self-indulgent, more at liberty than is compatible with the pose of the high-toned preachifier, the earnest wise man, or the physician to an age – all roles whose prerogatives are secured only at the intolerable cost of contracting to address the age in the age's terms rather than one's own. I am interested in those moments when sagely poses are parodied or inverted or laid aside, and we hear instead the accents of the mock sage, the mock fool, or even the mock "common man," talking of esoteric matters that the common reader will regard as foolish, in tones mock pompous, mock silly, or mock sensible.

Genre and Antigenre

I hope it goes without saying, given the heterogeneity of these three writers and these three books, that I do not propose "esoteric comedy" as a *genre*. It might, indeed, more accurately be called an antigenre, for one of its motives is to expose and criticize the semblance of naturalness and thus immutability that generic (and other) conventions encourage, in literature and elsewhere. It is no accident that, generically considered, each of these esoteric comedies is a maverick. *Sartor Resartus* is notoriously unclassifiable generically, so much so that its chief use to Northrop Frye, in his *Anatomy of Criticism,* is as an embarrasment to all the precedent theories of genre Frye wishes to overthrow.[3] Newman's *Apologia* might seem, generically, the most straightforward of the three, yet it holds in tension motives – of frank spiritual confession on the one hand, of all-out polemic on the other – whose generic incompatibility it seems to insist on. And *A Vision* is framed by conflicting accounts of how the text came into existence, which complicate how we read it and how seriously we take it – and lest we miss the point, Yeats lets us know that he is unsure himself how seriously to take it.

In each case, the equivocal generic status of the text is deliberate, and highly self-conscious: The genre question is posed repeatedly (and in exasperated despair of an answer) in the text of *Sartor Resartus* itself by The Editor; and again in the baffled

4

comments – "*Is* the work a translation?" – from critics that Carlyle included in the "Testimonies of Authors" he appended to the first English edition of 1838.[4] Newman, more deviously, so disposes genre cues – confessional and polemical, earnest and sarcastic, candid and "reserved" – as to set them at odds with one another.[5] As for *A Vision,* most critics are content to accept Yeats's instruction and call it a "sacred book" – a deference that is part polite lip service to a great poet's folly, part the convention whereby scholars of early modern writing follow early modern writers in talking not of "genre," which assimilates the individual work to others it resembles, but of "form," as if every individual work is sui generis. In *A Vision,* Yeats's high purple is so self-conscious, his touches of self-parody so broad, as to leave us uncertain whether his "sacred book" is an example of its genre or a parody of it, much as we debate whether *Ulysses* is an epic or a mock epic. In any case, isn't there something anomalous in the very notion of "the sacred book, generically considered"? – since it seems evident (if paradoxical) that the sacred book generically aspires to transcend all genres. (Thus does Yeats's most retrograde-seeming work fulfill a modernist criterion.)

As a theorist of genre, Northrop Frye does not let himself off his own hook, and when his project obliges him to find *Sartor Resartus* a place in his generic scheme, he assigns it to the discursive, intellectual, satiric genre, or genre complex, he calls – with how self-conscious an eye on his own book's title? – "anatomy."[6] Frye's scheme is generative, implying a sort of genealogical or familial relation between contiguous categories, so it is interesting that "anatomy" is flanked on one side by autobiography and "confession," as an example of which Frye cites the *Apologia,* and on the other by a family of forms Frye calls "encyclopaedic," instancing, among others, *A Vision.*[7] Thus, although Frye is one of our most influential theorists of comedy, it is in connection with "anatomy" that he has most to tell us about esoteric comedy. The "anatomy" (or "Menippean satire") "deals less with people as such than with mental attitudes"; it "presents people as mouthpieces of the ideas they represent"; it "sees evil and folly . . . as diseases of the intellect, as a kind of maddened pedantry"; it "presents us with a vision of the world in terms of a single intellectual pattern." The Menippean satirist, "dealing with intellectual themes and attitudes, shows his exuberance in intellectual ways, by piling up an enormous mass of erudition about his theme," and lampoons pedantry by parodying the jargon of a *"philosophos gloriosos"* figure.[8] All of these formulations are suggestive, at various points, for the esoteric comedy of Carlyle, Newman, and Yeats – especially the last, since Carlyle often satirizes particular Enlightenment and Utilitarian philosophers, and Newman often rebuts skeptics and agnostics by parodying their language and tone. Yeats, too, an autodidact who failed his university exams, often affects a fussy, mock-pedantic tone.

Esoteric Comedy and Eighteenth-Century Satire

Sartor Resartus, the *Apologia,* and *A Vision* thus resemble, in positing various sorts of foolishness – generic miscues, parodic mockery, ironic personae – that the reader must "see through," much of the best of eighteenth-century satire. But there is a crucial, indeed, "epistemic" difference: The extravagant nonsense of, say, *A Tale of a Tub* or *Tristram Shandy* satirizes extravagance and nonsense with the aim of disposing you to reject their claims as laughable, whether contemptibly so (Swift) or benignly so (Sterne), and thus to keep you firmly in touch with some implicit canon of shared reasonableness and common sense. Their comedy is affirmative, then, but what it affirms is the reverse of "esoteric." If the great eighteenth-century writers are Lockean in their psychology as in their epistemology, the post-Romantic esoteric comedians avow themselves heirs rather of Idealist philosophers: in Carlyle's case, the German transcendentalists, and in Newman's and Yeats's, Bishop Berkeley. Indeed, if there is an eighteenth-century esoteric comedian, it is Berkeley himself, airily – and in the name of "common sense" – dismissing the existence of matter. His *Three Dialogues* approach esoteric comedy in mobilizing an almost Voltairean wit, a relentlessly ironic *écrasez l'infame,* against the irrational and obstinate superstition that matter *does* exist.[9]

Carlyle, Newman, and Yeats offer provocations more of Berkeley's sort than of Swift's. In *Sartor Resartus,* the *Apologia,* and *A Vision,* your assent is solicited to propositions "common sense" will protest, by voices that seem to make a point of indulging and exaggerating every appearance of eccentricity or crankery that opportunity presents. Teufelsdröckh's inspired ravings, New-

6

man's deft theological hair splitting, Yeats's spirit communicators and interpenetrating cones suggest at first glance "partial" minds astride just such hobbyhorses as it was Swift's particular business to ridicule. In fact, read anachronistically, there are passages of *A Tale of a Tub* that seem to satirize Carlyle, Newman, and Yeats: There is astrological foolery of just the sort *A Vision* is built on, and the Romish sophistries of "Peter" are all too suggestive of Newman's elaborate casuistries. As for Carlyle, he makes much, in *Sartor Resartus,* of the clothing metaphor's Swiftian credentials, but his seriocomic uses of that metaphor are altogether different from Swift's. When the speaker of *A Tale of a Tub* cheekily asks,

Is not Religion a *Cloak,* Honesty a *Pair of Shoes,* worn out in the Dirt, Self-Love a *Surtout,* Vanity a *Shirt,* and Conscience a *Pair of Breeches,* which, tho' a Cover for Lewdness as well as Nastiness, is easily slipt down for the Service of both.[10]

– we recognize that, yes, Swift is satirizing hypocrisy; but he is satirizing also the self-regarding "wit" of this speaker, who traffics in such threadbare clichés as the immemorially tired clothing metaphor apparently under the apprehension – such is the vanity of the half-learned – that it is a smart and original aperçu of his own. Carlyle's project, more conflictedly, aims both to satirize and to redeem everything he can make "Clothes" suggest.

As writers, Carlyle, Newman, and Yeats operate differently from Swift not because of any antipathy to him – quite the reverse is true, especially for Carlyle and Yeats – but because their age is so fundamentally different from Swift's. If Swift can satirize eccentricity as a danger to the common sense of his preindustrial age, Carlyle, Newman, and Yeats must satirize the common sense of an emerging mass culture that can only regard their kind of intellectual and imaginative independence of mind as eccentric or worse. Their insistent hobbyhorsing is a quixotic gesture of opposition to a prevailing "common sense" that had come to mean almost the reverse of Swift's large-minded conception of a shared humane tradition. Indeed, by the time of Carlyle and Newman, the rhetoric of "common sense" had been assimilated to just the materialist and positivist habits of mind that

Swift was almost prophetic in identifying as humanism's fated historical antagonist. A century after Swift, humanism like his had itself become "esoteric," "sense" like his had ceased to be "common," and judging from the baffled responses to Swift throughout the nineteenth century, his comedy had ceased to be understood, let alone enjoyed.

If Carlyle, Newman, and Yeats are extravagant in their crankery, it is perhaps partly because they have the advantage of Swift's example, which demonstrates that even in Swift's own time, appeals like his could not very effectively be addressed to "common sense." The reception of *A Tale of a Tub,* for example, was not at all what Swift had expected, as the "Apology" that prefaces the 1710 edition makes clear. Swift had assumed that "Men of Wit and Tast" could not fail to get his point, and although the 1710 "Apology" makes as if to straighten out a mere minority of misguided readers, it is clear that the public's "Wit and Tast" have failed Swift, that he must explain his explanation, that although his satire had aimed to affirm central and elevated values, he had seemed to many readers of good will to be doing precisely the opposite: had seemed a crank as eccentric as, perhaps indistinguishable from, the *Tale*'s supposed author, blathering scurrilously well beyond the bounds of polite discourse. To so mistake one's age as to mistake oneself as a spokesman for the age's central values is a pathos the esoteric comedian's deliberate crankery aims *not* to incur.

Esoteric Comedy as Protomodernist

Although two of these authors are firmly Victorian, and the other only ambiguously "modern," it was as a student of twentieth-century modernism that I first read and then resolved to write about these books. *Sartor Resartus,* the *Apologia,* and *A Vision* struck me, much against my expectation, as works that were, in some manner I wanted to explain to myself, protomodernist. First of all, the insistence on arcane interests, and the tendency of these to become private myths, seemed an important continuity between Carlyle's Germanism, Newman's Romanism, and Yeats's occultism, on the one hand, and, on the other, Joyce's conflations of *Thom's Dublin Directory* with Vico, Pound's syntheses of neo-Platonism, Senator Benton, Antonine maritime

8

law, and whatnot, and the curriculum in anthropology, comparative religion, and Continental literature proposed in the notes to *The Waste Land.*

But more important were issues of literary technique and effect: how to write, how to read. *Ulysses, The Waste Land,* the *Cantos:* these, too, were works you learned to read only by reading them; they were, indeed, the works that had set me to pondering the implications of such a possibility. Like the masterpieces of modernism, *Sartor Resartus,* the *Apologia,* and *A Vision* (as we have noted) aspired to mix or transcend genre, to summon, then distort (often to the breaking point), and thus implicitly criticize, conventions of literary address – a gesture in which more general conventions of thought, language, and social conduct seemed also to be implicated. That "criticism of life" might be undertaken not in the form of analysis and statement but as a function of an acutely and self-consciously critical sort of writing and reading of literature seemed also a very "modernist" assumption. In Carlyle, Newman, and Yeats, as in Joyce, Pound, and Eliot, "style" seemed to be conceived as not merely ornamenting but somehow constituting "content." Each asserted and delighted in (as an affront to all varieties of literal-mindedness) its own fictiveness, implying thereby that an apprehension of fictiveness, rather than of fact, is the beginning of all wisdom. What seemed most interesting about them could not be located without the concept of "persona," even when – especially when – their authors addressed us in the first person. (Each seemed simultaneously to raise and dismiss questions about authorial "sincerity.")

Difficulty

And like the masterpieces of modernism, these books were willfully and self-consciously *difficult,* and advertised their difficulty as an index (and a criticism) of the insufficiency of ordinary habits of discussion and understanding, as well as a challenge to the fit audience, though few – that citizenry of "the selecter world," that "high fellowship" Meredith associates with the "Comic Spirit"[11] – willing to depart from conventional habits of mind for at least the length of a book. Surrounded by an increasingly materialist culture dedicated to the Baconian program of placing all

9

wits upon a level,[12] Carlyle, Newman, and Yeats would each applaud Blake's haughty avowal that "that which can be made Explicit to the Idiot is not worth my care." Each aims to incite his readers to unwonted intellectual and imaginative exertions, and holds, like Blake, that "what is not too Explicit" promotes that end "because it rouzes the faculties to act."[13]

If this difficulty is self-conscious, like Blake's, it is much more ironic and devious than his. The difficulty of *Sartor Resartus,* for example, is incessantly reiterated, even exaggerated, by a voice within the text, "The Editor," whose professed aim is to remove such difficulties for us: *His* difficulties initially compound, rather than alleviate, our own, until his interpretations become a sort of ironic counterprompt, so systematically wrong in their readings as to constitute at last a reliable index of how *not* to read *Sartor Resartus.* If Carlyle's text seems to insist on its own difficulty, lest we miss it, Newman's ploy is the reverse: to be blandly (ironically) unconfiding about the difficulty of what he well knows to be difficult matters indeed. His "History of My Religious Opinions" (the *Apologia*'s subtitle) contrives repeatedly to suspend us between the promptings of the admirably lucid sound of his narrative (the "History") and the provokingly recondite casuistries (the "Religious Opinions") whose development he traces in such matter-of-fact tones. And Yeats? His habitual pose in *A Vision* is mock naïve: He is an ordinary person like ourselves, reporting spiritual visitations that perplex him as much as us. The whole project is so beset with "difficulties" that malevolent beings called "Frustrators" are invoked to explain them; if they and the other "Spirit Communicators" whose disclosures *A Vision* reports solicit less than your full assent, Yeats knows what you mean: "I can but answer that if sometimes, overwhelmed by miracle as all men must be when in the midst of it, I have taken [such disclosures] literally, my reason has soon recovered."[14]

Self-referentiality

The persistent self-referentiality of all this is another "protomodernist" symptom. *Sartor Resartus* is a difficult text purporting to transcribe the transactions of an expert reader with a difficult text; the comedy of misreading, and metamisreading that results is as complicated as anything in Borges. An oddly similar effect is often secured by Newman, in the numerous passages in which he defends controversial texts written by an earlier self, with whose position he may no longer agree but whose polemical energy and verbal-intellectual ingenuity he endorses in ways that bear on how the *Apologia* itself should be read; as C. F. Harrold has noted, one of the things unique to the *Apologia* among Newman's works is its bold way of announcing its strategies even as it deploys them.[15] As for Yeats, the two editions of *A Vision* (1925, 1937) present essentially the same "esoteric system"; only their introductory frames differ, but both introduce the system in ways to emphasize rather than attenuate the difficulties of interpretation and evaluation the system and its presentation should raise. All three books contrive to keep before the attention of the reader-interpreter the problematic of interpretation itself.

Textuality

Another quasi-modernist (and esoteric) thing about these comedies is a feature best designated by a postmodernist word, "textuality." *Sartor Resartus,* the *Apologia,* and *A Vision* all exploit fully and knowingly the inscrutabilities of the printed page; each is conceived and composed, from first word to last, as "text." Present-day apostles of "text" commonly speak as if they have discovered a principle rather than a vocabulary, but for Carlyle, Newman, and Yeats, "text" is old news. They are acutely aware of manipulating words to alternately summon and void seeming presences in the silent spaces of print, and they are entirely self-conscious about it; they know that the imperturbable poker face of a carefully composed page will abide no question. What I have written, I have written. *Sartor Resartus* had its origins in a period when Carlyle was suffering a severe writer's block; the break came when Carlyle saw several numbers of a new humor magazine and toyed with the idea of writing something for it. "*Literature*" has nothing to do with this," he observed (he who entertained, and was the victim of, such daunting ambitions toward "*Literature*"), "but Printing has."[16] *Sartor Resartus,* uniquely among Carlyle's works, is founded on conflicting personae (a device dependent on the printed page) and presents itself as a mock book review, thus making possible varied parodic and satiric effects at the expense of a genre whose conventions (indeed, whose whole existence)

11

arise entirely from the technology of printing – and also at the expense of an intellectual milieu that mistakes its culturally determined conventions (not only conventions of reading) for the unalterable outcome of a "natural" order of things.

If for Carlyle "Printing" is a liberating disguise, for Newman and Yeats it is an infintely extensible theater in which to dramatize a highly performative sense of the self and its masks. Newman was invariably meek and mild in person, and regarded himself as congenitally incapable of "enthusiasm" or other strong affect, but he becomes an "Achilles" in print (the image is his own), a polemicist of ferocious and inspired zeal – to many, indeed, a fanatic. His *Apologia* makes a fine art of exploiting the incongruences between his genre's obligations to confessional sincerity and the ironies intrinsic to being "sincere" in public print, and for an audience in large part hostile and suspicious. (And while composing the *Apologia*'s public masks of sarcasm and hauteur, the private Newman was "constantly in tears, and constantly crying out with distress.")[17] As for Yeats, his sense of the gap between his private human frailties and the "antithetical," highly artificial public poses of his "written speech" (as he calls it)[18] generates ironies central to all his utterance and an explicit theme in much of it, from "Adam's Curse" on. A persistent implication in each of these esoteric comedies is that such ironies may be most potent where they are least acknowledged.

To all of this *A Tale of a Tub* again provides an instructive contrast. Simultaneously a masterpiece of textuality and an indictment of it, Swift's *Tale* makes writing itself, especially writing for the printing press, both symptom and cause of all the forms of "modern" madness Swift means to satirize. The supposed author of *A Tale of a Tub* recurs frequently to the special prerogatives attaching to his status *as writer,* and the manifest incoherence and lunacy of his performance, exuberantly festooned with all the trappings of the printed book (headnotes, footnotes, marginalis, prefaces, dedications, apologies, even amusingly extensive lacunae, marked with row upon row of asterisks), link the vanity of authors to the insanities of an age.[19] A lone hack, scribbling in a garret, too easily blows away in a self-generated wind, which is to say that the communion of a solitary mind with pen and paper is a virtual prescription for irresponsibility and weirdness – especially when the finished product will be conveyed anonymously through a technological medium to an audience unknown in all but its hunger for sensation. There is even an ironic sense in which Swift's recognition that the solitary, musing, fitfully "inspired" activity of writing can lend a crazy courage to properly timid minds is validated in the careers of Carlyle, Newman, and Yeats. What Swift perceives as a threat to civil sanity, Carlyle, Newman, and Yeats raise, through sheer intellectual and imaginative audacity, to an activity ingeniously subversive of "sanities" whose canons of public hygiene they experienced as oppressive.

Parody

A central instrument of this project is *parody* – parody of all the languages prevailing in the literary-intellectual-journalistic environment, parody of literary genres (book review, spiritual autobiography, mystic handbook) – as a way of suggesting the need for discriminations that can separate the genuine from the spurious, the superficially apparent from the obscurer actual, the plausible but false from the incredible but true. Here, in the deployment of the "low" devices of parody to high "critical" purpose, is another affinity between esoteric comedy and modernism – and a rationale for using the word "parody," as I have had to do throughout this study, in all its modern and postmodern senses. Until historically recent times, "parody" meant something quite precise – verbal imitation for purposes of ridicule – and was deemed a low and trivial form of humor. But by 1934, Ezra Pound would identify, as one of literature's "critical" functions, "criticism by exercise in the style of a given period."[20] Pound was summing up a tendency that had been growing since Cervantes (in English, since Swift) to make parody the instrument of more than joking perception. Pound had particularly in mind Flaubert and Joyce, whose practice enlarged radically the uses of parody. In both authors, parodic "imitation" extends beyond verbal mannerism to embrace and conflate broad cultural archetypes (*Liebestödt,* Odysseus myth) and local media forms (pulp fiction, newspaper formats). Nor is the motive so simply to deflate: If *Madame Bovary* parodies the sort of fiction that has corrupted its heroine, the result is parody that transcends or sublimates its original, mocking it, so to speak, from above rather

13

than below, thus reversing the usual direction of parodic energy, so that parody of a "low" original attains to "high" art. Nor is mocking *resemblance* essential: If *Ulysses* parodies the *Odyssey,* it is parody whose dissimilarity from its original is most of its comic point.

The lesson of modernism and of postmodernism seems to be that as archetype becomes cliché, mimesis becomes parody – which is why, with the emergence of mass technologies of communication, parody has assumed increasing importance, until by now it seems an indispensable element not only of literary utterance but of any expression that aspires to sophistication. We now take for granted that in a media-saturated milieu, flooded by images and stereotypes that preempt the possibilities and the prerogatives of mere human beings, parody must be the condition of all relations of the self with culture – a strategy of resistance, defiance, attack, satire, but also of appropriation and adjustment, of critical accommodation as well as contemptuous rejection. The struggle of the self for autonomy from the images and idealizations by which culture would determine it is a salient concern of modernism, and it underwrites much of the verbal imitation and formal novelty of Joyce, Pound, Eliot, and others. Their high-culture anguish turns jokey when extended to popular culture – hence the divide between the modernism of yesterday and the postmodernism of today – but in any case, we are speaking of a diversity of literary responses to the emergence of a mass culture, from Swift's satire of print technology till now.

Hence the continuing importance of Swift. Swift seems very much a "modern" in parodying not mere verbal mannerism, but the forms and formats of a new technology (printing) and their effects on public language and consciousness. But the esoteric comedians come later in the emergence of a mass culture, and their recourse to parody is more modernist than Swiftian in motive and spirit. Swift's purposes are wholly, and harshly, satiric. He is isolating something he despises and ridiculing it to the advantage of other things he values. A century and more later, such discriminations are not so easily made, the tensions between the self and the surrounding culture are more conflicted, and parody becomes a means of participation, however equivocal or ironic, in the forms and themes of the social imagination at large.

14

Thus Carlyle, Newman, and Yeats parody the discourses of their contemporaries and the conventions of their literary genres in part to contravene them, but also in part to redeem them. Their parody is a more devious means to the end Wordsworth proclaims in the 1800 preface to *Lyrical Ballads:* to alter the "formal engagement" between writer and reader according to which the writer is "contracted" to "gratify certain known habits of association."[21] Carlyle, Newman, and Yeats mean, like Wordsworth, to challenge, not "gratify," their audience's "known habits of association"; and they mean not merely to change old habits for new, but to make their readers conscious of the force of habit itself in channeling (and diminishing) intellectual-imaginative-affective powers of perception and response. Their parody of verbal styles, generic conventions, and decorums of literary address acts to expose the unconscious operation of convention itself to the scrutiny of conscious reflection: The aim is to suggest the limitations and the arbitrariness of regnant conventions, conventions of reading, of understanding, of imagining, and what they preclude our seeing or entertaining as possibilities outside them. Their ambition is apocalyptic, in the modern, secular way: to change how we see.[22] The esoteric comedian intends that this "making conscious" of the unconscious force of convention should act as Shelley said poetry does: to "purge[ ] from our inward sight the film of familiarity which obscures from us the wonder of our being."[23]

Irony, the *Eiron,* and Self-parody

In posing their alternative possibilities, Carlyle, Newman, and Yeats (especially the two latter, who write *in propria persona*) resort to another strategy definitive of esoteric comedy, the Socratic pose of the *eiron,* the wise man who enlightens others by playing the fool with them. It is a pose with a number of uses. It preempts the rejection of those who will dismiss an esoteric interest – Germanic philosophy, Romish casuistry, automatic writing, and spiritualism – as foolish. It adds piquancy to the ironic triumph of the seeming fool over conventional wisdom, even as it disvalues the triumph, since the willfulness and artificiality of the fool mask advertise the indifference of the esoteric comedian to convincing his audience. ("I took no trouble to convince," writes Yeats in a poem about *A Vision,* "Or seem plausible to a man of sense.")[24] And it witnesses the willingness of the esoteric comedian to sacrifice dignity or respectability in behalf of the "foolish" thing he believes: He is a fool for his ideas, much as one might be a fool for love.

The pose of the *eiron* turns out to be, again, a vehicle of parody: parody of his critics, his supposed "superiors," whose point the *eiron* distorts satirically in pretending to rehearse or understand it, but also (and here is another element definitive of esoteric comedy), *self*-parody. The *eiron* poses of Carlyle, Newman, and Yeats are partly a response to caricatures of themselves or their projects already circulating in the great world. The young Carlyle, for example, aspires to a cultural role, introducing German transcendentalism to England, already preempted, and bungled, by Coleridge – an embarrassment Carlyle negotiates in the figure of The Editor, a caricature of the inept enthusiast. But The Editor is also a caricature of British skepticism and in that guise, too, turns out to be a parodic vehicle for impulses genuinely Carlyle's own. In like manner, Teufelsdröckh both exemplifies and parodies Carlyle's "prophetic" ambitions.

Carlyle's self-parody emanates from diffidence and encodes profound conflict between his Calvinist self-distrust and his enormous ambition. Newman feels no such diffidence, and no such conflict, and part of his ferocity is his awareness that he addresses an audience that thinks he *should* feel these things and has vented its moralism in reductive judgments about who Newman is and what he is about. So Newman explicitly designs his *Apologia* to redeem the caricature version of himself – "a scarecrow which is dressed up in my clothes"[25] – that Kingsley has set up and attacked. Throughout the *Apologia* Newman mockingly caricatures all the caricature Newmans (Newman-the-Jesuit, Newman-the-fanatic) that public discourse has generated, and often in a way to emphasize their contradictoriness (Newman-the-wizard-of-guile, Newman-the-gullible-dupe). Newman's self-parodies express his contempt for the various public misperceptions of him, even as he turns these parodies into vehicles for his own expression – as if to tell his critics that even their caricatures are better than they are.

Yeats's self-mockery is a genial and teasing pose of nonchalance vis-à-vis an audience whose newly fashionable contempt for "Traditional sanctity and loveliness"[26] elsewhere, in other "moods," sends him raving. Yeats knows from a lifetime of experience that his project will be treated reductively, contemptuously, and sarcastically by his self-consciously "modern" audience. Since the 1890s his occultism had been the stuff of jokes and gibes and of caricatures in the most literal sense: cartoons in the newspapers, by Max Beerbohm and others. The author of *A Vision,* attempting to introduce the waste-land world of post-Great War disillusion to his esoteric system, is "Mr. W. B. Yeats Presenting Mr. George Moore to the Queen of the Fairies" all over again. The esoteric comedian's self-parody, in effect, parodies the parodies that have preceded him, the caricatures and stereotypes with which an unreceptive milieu has armed (or blinded) itself against possibilities it prefers not to entertain.[27]

Esoteric Comedy and the Decorums of Self-assertion

But the esoteric comedian's penchant for self-parody is more than an incidental feature of a larger penchant for parody in general. The esoteric comedian's parody mocks the homogenized and standardized canons of public discourse enforced by an emerging mass culture, but his self-parody responds to another system of constraints as well, the literary (and other) decorums attending the new moral "sensibility" that overtakes English culture in the eighteenth and nineteenth centuries, bringing with it a new diffidence about self-assertion in any form, and especially the self-assertion of an ambitious writer. The new psychologies ensuing on the Reformation (Luther, Pascal, Hobbes) made "the self" an object of new moral scrutiny and new moral distrust, and transformed a traditional Christian rhetoric of self-abnegation into the congenital self-accusation that attends non-Latin Europe's shift from shame culture to guilt culture.

At the same time, the "new science" banished all supernatural sanctions for imagination (inspiration, the Muses, "Thus saith the Lord"), locating its sources so firmly in the self that any writer's claim for "imagination" was necessarily a claim first for the writer's own insight or wisdom. The Protestant attack on authority entailed distrust of any self-aggrandizing ambition, including those of authors, and especially those of the satirist or the prophet who presumes to operate as judge or critic. Among the conse-

"Mr. W. B. Yeats Presenting Mr. George Moore to the Queen of the Fairies." Courtesy of the Hugh Lane Municipal Gallery of Modern Art, Dublin.

quences for literature was a reduction of, or diffidence about, what claims writers might credibly make for imagination and for their own powers of vision and prophecy.

These are among the reasons that Milton's assumption of the mantle of prophecy could not be emulated after him: Neither Milton's *grandezza* nor its sanctioning "Heavenly Muse" was tenable in a climate shaped by Descartes, Hobbes, and Locke – not to mention Addison and Steele.[28] The post-Milton poet with "prophetic" ambitions assumes (in ways the work of Harold Bloom has illuminated) all but prohibitive burdens. Blake's bardic pretensions helped keep him a marginal figure until Yeats discovered him, while Wordsworth's display a palpable diffidence in adapting the Miltonic note to a plain-man middle style. Wordsworth's "levelling" muse (in Hazlitt's phrase)[29] is egalitarian and universalizing in ways quite foreign to Milton, who imagines his fit audience, though few, as part "classic" elite, part remnant elect. Yet even Wordsworth's earnest other-directedness seems tainted by excessive presumption to (of all people) Keats, who disvalued the older poet's "egotistical sublime" in favor of a "poetical Character" that properly "has no self."[30] (The conflictedness of Keats's own Miltonic ambitions is traceable in the aspirations first essayed in *Hyperion,* then recanted in *The Fall of Hyperion.*)

So in the century and more between Milton and these poets, with the Miltonic aspiration to prophecy seemingly unviable, the moralizing impulses of imaginative writers find expression elsewhere – in satire preeminently, whose most potent eighteenth-century practitioners targeted precisely the sort of presumption that Milton's imaginative grandiosity might seem to exemplify. Swift, for example, has really no other subject; while Pope, more conflictedly, demonstrates, only a generation after Milton, that the Miltonic *ore rotondo* cannot be emulated except as Pope emulates it, parodically – a gesture, notice, which discounts not Milton's accomplishment, but Pope's own. As a moralist, Pope disclaims prophetic pretensions in favor of the humbler prerogatives attaching to the "low" genre of satire; yet to many of Pope's contemporaries, Pope's moralism seemed self-aggrandizing and vain, his righteousness the more despicable as a hypocritical *self*-righteousness – and these judgments increasingly implied an indictment applicable to satire generally. In the

19

midcentury generation, consider the conflicted moral impulses of righteous self-assertion and guilty self-accusation in Samuel Johnson, a "satirist *manqué*" (as Walter Jackson Bate calls him),[31] whose aversion to his fellow Tories, Swift and Pope, was constant and (suggestively) vehement. After Johnson, William Cowper, considering his options as poet and moralist in *The Task*, explicitly disavows "the satyric thong" (the punitive and sadistic image itself tells why); while in *Charity*, Cowper worries that even "St. Patrick's dean / Too often rails to gratify his spleen" and proceeds to picture the satirist as a psychotic thrill killer:

> Most sat'rists are indeed a public scourge;
> Their mildest physic is a farrier's purge;
> Their acrid temper turns, as soon as stirr'd,
> The milk of their good purpose all to curd.
> Their zeal begotten, as their works rehearse,
> By lean despair upon an empty purse,
> The wild assassins start into the street,
> Prepar'd to poignard whomso'er they meet. . . .
>   All zeal for a reform, that gives offense
> To peace and charity, is mere pretence:
> A bold remark; but which, if well applied,
> Would humble many a towering poet's pride.[32]

Cowper's haste to apologize for his own "bold remark," even in the service of so worthy a project as humbling pride, exemplifies perfectly the decorum of diffidence that increasingly after Milton enjoins poet, prophet, or satirist to judge not, that he be not judged. As the "age of sensibility" proceeded, Swift and Pope increasingly seemed disagreeable personalities, and satire an unamiable undertaking. It is telling that the one nineteenth-century writer to declare an affinity with Pope-the-satirist, Byron, nevertheless produced satire differing from Pope's most immediately in the extent of Byron's irony *at his own expense.*

"Amiable Humour"

This shift in sensibility had profound consequences for the theory and practice of humor. Comedy had, classically, been reckoned one of the lower motives of art. The best that could be said for it was that it instructs by negative example, condemning bad things by holding them up to ridicule: If we look up to the heroic figures of tragedy as ideals or models of virtue, we look down on the figures of comedy as examples of what to avoid. But in the eighteenth century, the age of burgeoning "sensibility," the classical justification for comedy, as a solicitation to morally proper feelings of superiority, was increasingly seen as involving the temptations of vainglory – here the *locus classicus* was Hobbes's definition of laughter as *"Sudden Glory"*[33] – and therefore morally troublesome. Laughter involved a dangerous moral physiology, and hence the story Stuart Tave tells in *The Amiable Humorist,*[34] the transformation of humor into something harmless, charitable, well-intentioned, good-hearted, "nice." The esoteric comedian's deployment of humor in general, and of self-parody in particular, seems very much a period emanation of this ideal of amiability: If making fun of things can seem vainglorious, an obvious way to make it "amiable" is to make fun of yourself, too.

But for the esoteric comedian, the mask of "amiability" is a cover for a critique of the surrounding society at once deeply subversive and vastly ambitious. Carlyle, Newman, and Yeats put themselves self-consciously against the grain of their culture, offering themselves as exemplars of moral and imaginative alternatives to the presuppositions of the surrounding society, alternatives their milieu has ruled out, has constructed itself to resist. Their projects involve a kind of presumption that their audiences will find in itself suspect; the *eiron* mask helps disguise this presumption and make it more palatable, but it does not attenuate the comprehensiveness of the esoteric comedian's indictment of materialist, bourgeois, "modern" culture. "Prophecy" is an explicit (if anxious) ambition of the young Carlyle, as the *Two Note Books* spanning the composition of *Sartor Resartus* demonstrate. Likewise Yeats, who in youth self-consciously modeled himself on Blake and Shelley, and in old age dared hope that his accomplishment might yet rival Dante's. Newman's apocalypticism is the most covert or muted of the three, servitor as Newman is of an institution that reserves all apocalyptic prerogative to itself. And Newman's moral elbow room is further circum-

scribed by the need to mount an *Apologia* (i.e., a defense) against
the entire range of a complexly factionalized religious milieu: not
only against Broad and Low Church Anglicans like Kingsley, but
also against Dissenters in one direction, High Church Anglicans
in another, and even, most obliquely, against the hierarchy of
Newman's own Church, which so distrusted his Idealist (rather
than the orthodox Thomist and Realist) cast of mind; it is perhaps this conflicting multiplicity of constraints that makes Newman's "humour" seem the least "amiable," the least accommodating of the three. Carlyle and Yeats each smilingly offers his
apocalypse to an audience he knows will resist it; Newman more
bristlingly asserts that his only real audience is God, that ultimately he is indifferent to how he is judged outside the narrow
society of those "two and two only luminously self-evident
beings, myself and my Creator."[35] Newman offers his apocalypse
with a take-it-or-leave-it air; his byword (I have made it the title
of my chapter on Newman) is "Hippoclides doesn't care." His
party-of-one pose is shared by Carlyle and Yeats, but in texts
other than *Sartor Resartus* and *A Vision,* even as Newman
expounds his psychology of faith more accommodatingly in texts
other than the *Apologia.* The point is that for all three, "amiability" has its limits. At some point, accommodation with the
reader ceases, and the esoteric comedian asserts, with Blake, that

A Riddle or the Crickets Cry
Is to Doubt a fit Reply[36]

From "Amiability" to "Wit"

The limits of amiability are partly a matter of cultural climate as
well as of individual temperament. The domestication of wit,
humor, and comic impulses generally from the potentially dangerous, subversive, and explosive forces they are into something
tamer, more polite, less challenging, and therefore more congen-
ial to the moral and social style of the new bourgeois gentility that
came with the Industrial Revolution is a story that ends, for
Stuart Tave, with Carlyle. The sequel is the countermovement
narrated by Robert Bernard Martin in *The Triumph of Wit.* Martin rehearses Tave's theme in a chapter called "The Dangers of
Laughter" and proposes the triumph of "wit" as representing,

against the decorums of amiable "humour," the very different "Claims of the Intellect." As Martin explains:

> Humour [i.e., the ideal of "amiability"] had nearly total sway in the nineteenth century until the late 1860s. . . . Wit and intellectual comedy had been universally agreed upon as arrogant, cold, and unpoetic, but when they had almost disappeared in practice the suspicion grew that they might be a cool refreshment from the sticky and unrelieved sentimentality of what had been passing as comedy.

This countermovement in favor of a sharper, more "intellectual," more "critical," and demanding "wit" was necessary, Martin writes, "if comedy was to pull itself out of the sentiment in which it had been wallowing, and if it was to represent anything like the totality of man's nature."[37] Certainly the intellectualism and esotericism of *Sartor Resartus,* the *Apologia,* and *A Vision* issue from just such motives.

But "wit" and "amiability" are not easily separated, either in esoteric comedy or, as Martin demonstrates, in Victorian theories of comedy. The "triumph of wit" begins, Martin writes,[38] in efforts to explain wit as an effect of "incongruity," arising from a sense of surprising disproportion, so transgressing expectation as to produce laughter – an explanation whose oblique but obvious motive is to redeem wit from the moral taint of superiority feeling, thus making it more amiable. Even in Meredith, whom Martin presents as the culmination of the triumph of wit, a similar conflictedness is visible: Meredith asserts comedy's "sunny malice" and makes mock of the sentimental and the dull, but the ideal of amiability nevertheless persists in his reiteration that "contempt is a sentiment that cannot be entertained by comic intelligence." The categories seem to find their fruitful and necessary conflation in Meredith's characterization of comedy as "humanely malign."[39] I would not have anyone suppose that Carlyle, Newman, or Yeats wrote according to a theory, but esoteric comedy may be said to negotiate the "dangers" of the superiority theory in a way to produce effects referable to the incongruity theory: The concession to amiability that produces self-parody and exaggerated *eiron* poses also generates a cognitive dissonance between our amusement at the *eiron*'s eccentricity and the manifest wit and power – at least self-assurance – of his rhetoric and his vision. Is this a figure we can feel very safe laughing at? He seems a crank, yet his vision is grandiose – and often enough his laughter seems to be very much at *our* expense. Here is esoteric comedy's distinctive twist on the figure Frye calls the *"philoso-phos gloriosos"*: Carlyle, Newman, and Yeats often indulge the pedantry and jargon of their "esoteric" interests in a fashion to appropriate the comically alienated role of the *philosophos glo-riosos* to themselves and to find in it a vantage from which to satirize the "common sense" of the rest of the culture.

In short, if the esoteric comedian's wit is "amiable," even his amiability frequently bears the sting of wit – a wit whose motives are adversary to the whole cultural surround. To call *Sartor Resartus,* the *Apologia,* and *A Vision* "comedies" is not to miti-gate the seriousness or the scope of their subversive ambitions. The esoteric comedian may be regarded as an avatar of Lionel Trilling's "opposing self," an alienated onlooker possessed of an "intense and adverse imagination of the culture in which it has its being." The range of this opposition, Trilling explains, is noth-ing less than the whole of culture,

> not only to [the surrounding culture's] achieved works of intellect and imagination but also to its mere assumptions and unformulated valuations, to its habits, its manners, and its superstitions. The modern self is characterized by certain powers of indignant perception which, turned upon the unconscious portion of culture, have made it accessible to conscious thought.[40]

Developing his theme, Trilling summons the imagery of the prison house in Wordsworth and Dickens, but the agon of self and culture the esoteric comedian stages is a spectacle rather witty than melodramatic. To the pathos of unsung struggle, stoic long suffering, and likely defeat, they propose the comic alterna-tive of a kind of intellectual-imaginative triumph, however eccentric, qualified, or ironic. Yeats used to pronounce that "in farce, the soul is struggling against a ridiculous object: in comedy, with a removable object: in tragedy, with an irremovable object."[41] This polished *mot* nicely suggests Yeats's sense of the "opposing" or (Yeats's word) "antithetical" self's destiny being

24

defined in the objects it opposes, and it reminds us that not all such struggles are comic. But it also indicates esoteric comedy's air of smiling nonchalance vis-à-vis an adversary conceived as altogether within the powers of wit, mind, and humor to defeat, or "remove."

The adversary is, of course, the materialist, utilitarian, positivist, rationalist, post-Enlightenment mind-set of mass bourgeois culture, a habit of mind that saw human action as the passive reflex of pain–pleasure mechanisms, which, because they are "natural," we can master only (in the Baconian formula) by obeying.[42] If, as satirists, Carlyle, Newman, and Yeats "make difficulties" for the complacencies of the materialist world view, as prophets they offer deliverance from its anxieties: Their mission in the impoverished landscape of modernity – Arnold's "darkling plain," Eliot's "waste land" – is to announce the sovereignty of mind over a world of "natural" compulsion and unfreedom. The regnant materialism of the age had produced an "iron time / Of doubts, disputes, distractions, fears," complained Matthew Arnold, and "had bound / Our souls in its benumbing round."[43] Against the cause-and-effect world picture of a nature desacralized and a humanity assiduously remaking itself in nature's automatized image, the esoteric comedian proclaims (in Carlyle's words) a "Gospel of Freedom" and affirms the power of mind to transcend the cause-and-effect "universe of death" reified in the inventions of science and technology. "Our life is compassed round with Necessity," writes Carlyle-Teufelsdröckh; "yet is the meaning of Life itself no other than Freedom, than Voluntary Force."[44] Against a world picture that looks inescapably determined, that seems to dictate a sort of stoic acquiescence, the esoteric comedian finds sources of energy within the shaping power of the mind and turns these to the uses of freedom.

Comedy

This last point touches on my largest reasons for calling these works "comedies." I have suggested many of the smaller ones already: Their ironic fooling generates all sorts of incidental satire – though there is of course (almost) no question of belly laughs – at the expense of progress and the promises of materialist science and technology. They so manage their effects as to exploit the ironies of a "comic apocalypse": All apocalypses are "comic" in the conventional Christian sense of promising deliverance from this-worldly travail and illusion, but Carlyle, Newman, and Yeats recognize that any apocalypse within their means to incite cannot be for everybody, and their comic strategy entoils transcendental vision in elaborate, often fussy and pedantic-sounding discursiveness[45] – with results that answer to Carlyle's sense of the universe as an "open secret," Newman's insistence on "economy" in intellectual matters, Yeats's lifelong conviction that "the knowledge of reality is always in some measure a secret knowledge."[46] If esoteric comedy needs a motto, a sentence from *Sartor Resartus* that Yeats revered might serve: "In a Symbol, there is concealment and yet revelation."[47] Esoteric comedy contrives just this effect of "concealment and yet revelation," an apocalypse that half discloses, half occludes its visionary prospect. And each makes some show at last of drawing back the curtain it had, if only fitfully, drawn away, and we end uncertain, the esoteric comedian himself ends uncertain, whether we have witnessed the rending or merely the trembling of the veil.

The apocalyptic or transcendental ambitions of esoteric comedy distinguish it quite sharply from comedy-as-usual. Comedy is usually deflationary in motive; it means to puncture pretense, overextravagance, and high flying of all sorts. In the nineteenth-century English novel, for example, comedy characteristically operates in just this way to confront high idealizations of various kinds with human and social circumstances they cannot master – an operation undertaken on behalf of progress, modernity, and a more honest acceptance of human nature, as against outworn manners, mores, dogmatisms, or superstitions whose rigidities an advanced age dismisses with a laugh. As Meredith puts it, "the basis of the comic" is "an esteem for common sense."[48]

But esoteric comedy promotes a very uncommon sort of sense, and its arcane interests and claims to visionary power involve just the sort of hobbyhorsing that comedy-as-usual would seek to deflate. Their "spiritual" motives align them with older worlds of vision and faith that modernity dismisses as laughable. If the comic norm appeals to the classical "superiority theory," esoteric comedy comports with the sense of "comedy" indicated in medieval Christian usage, which stresses (as Northrop Frye notes) themes not of social integration, but of salvation[49] – though here, too, esoteric comedy fuses motives usually regarded as generically incompatibile: a witty social humor of jokes and irony, on the one hand, and, on the other, the soberer comedy of ultimate transcendence that apocalypse generically implies beyond the veil, as in the *Commedia* of Dante or the book of Revelation.

But if "salvation" has a quasi-religiose sound, the Egypt from which esoteric comedy proposes deliverance is as secular as anyone could wish. Carlyle, Newman, and Yeats address, and redress, their era's anxiety that the boons of science and progress must entail the disappearance of much that the supposed beneficiaries would prefer not to part with: a politics founded on something more than self-interest (Carlyle), a religion that need not shrink before intellect into timid sentiment (Newman), poetic imagination and literary power undaunted by modern "disillusion" (Yeats). The testimony of these three writers amounts to an affirmation and a demonstration that ideas matter, that they have consequences for good and ill, that they are powerful.

They are powerful because, as Carlyle puts it, "ours is a fictile world; and man is the most fingent of creatures"; "the very Rocks and Rivers" of material reality "are, in strict language, *made* by our outward Senses"; likewise, "the Inward Sense" constructs "all phenomena of the spiritual kind."[50] Yeats, too, declaring that "Civilization is hooped together . . . By manifold illusion," pictures the human project as a ceaseless "ravening through" and "uprooting" of illusory meanings.[51] The esoteric comedian's enterprise thus anticipates what Roland Barthes has called "The Structuralist Activity," which

> highlights, the strictly human process by which men give meanings to things. . . . of course the world has never stopped looking for the meaning of what is given it and of what it produces; what is new is a mode of thought (or a "poetics") which seeks less to assign completed meanings to the objects it discovers than to know how meaning is possible, at what cost and by what means. Ultimately, one might say that the object of structuralism is not man endowed with meanings, but man fabricating meanings, as if it could not be the *content* of meanings which exhausted the semantic goals of humanity, but only the act by which

these meanings, historical and contingent variables, are produced. *Homo significans:* such would be the new man of
structuralist inquiry.[52]

Barthes's essay dates from 1964, well before the present "opposition" between structuralism and deconstruction had been "constructed." Granted, Carlyle, Newman, and Yeats are keen "to
assign completed meanings to the objects [each] discovers," but
their esoteric comedy enacts (it is no anachronism to say) a
"deconstruction" of the materialist world picture as prelude to
the "construction" of alternatives answering better to their
desire. If the archmaterialist Bacon had pictured the progress of
knowledge as a beelike accumulation of facts and truths, esoteric
comedy answers, with a young philosopher writing in 1915, that
it is not truths we accumulate, but interpretations; and *"interpretation,"* writes T. S. Eliot in the conclusion to his dissertation,
"involves an act of faith":

> if you wish to say that only those truths which can be dem-
> onstrated can be called true, I will acquiesce, for I am as
> good a materialist as anybody; but though materialist, I
> would point out what a little way such truths bring us. For
> materialism itself is only an interpretation.[53]

In like fashion, Carlyle, Newman, and Yeats, with remarkable
consistency, although in very different ways, rebut materialism
with the witty stroke that materialism itself is "only" an interpretation, an idea, a fiction, and one whose peculiar (and dangerous) power springs from the widely held delusion that it is not a
mere idea, but "the truth." Their analysis of the sorrows of materialism comports with Shelley's perception of the irony by which
"man, having enslaved the elements, remains himself a slave."
In the contrary axiom that "all things exist as they are
perceived,"[54] they locate, as Shelley does, the intellectual-
imaginative power that can restore humanity to its birthright of
freedom.

They proclaim, and they exemplify, a "Gospel of Freedom"
meant to hearten those who, convinced of materialism's "truth"
but unhappy about it – a widespread Victorian, and modern,
complaint – suppose they can retain the emotional benefits of

religion and literature only by contriving not to think about them. On the contrary, it is precisely in mindful activity that Carlyle, Newman, and Yeats look for their ironic and eccentric consolations: They concede nothing to the resigned conviction that ignorance is bliss, but look instead to the very agent that many of their contemporaries were ready to blame for the age's malaise, "to the suspected and reviled Intellect, to the Understanding, the Mephistopheles, to the gymnastics of talent." The comedy that they locate there involves the reversal of all sorts of presuppositions its readers were expected to bring to it. It parodies the "natural"-seeming conventions of literature to expose those conventions as given by culture and thus to challenge a whole world view of what is "natural" and therefore immutable and what is fictive and therefore within the power of human decision to change. It exposes the materialist world picture, which had claimed to banish as mere fictions the belief systems of the past and to replace them with certain fact, as itself a belief system and a fiction. And if materialism had exposed old faiths as fictions and therefore untenable, esoteric comedy retorts that to participate in a fiction, and knowingly, is a finer and grander thing than mere acquiescence in "fact" – with the implicit corollary that by their fictions, ye shall know them. It presents points of view it acknowledges to be eccentric, it emphasizes and indulges their eccentricity, then ensures that eccentricity triumphs over a prevailing but more limited and limiting common sense. And it inverts comedy itself, deploying its usually deflationary devices to elevating, "transcendental" purpose, and turns irony from "infinite negation" to an affirmation that might as well be called infinite.

I should conclude with some remarks on the limitations of this book. My special focus – on the most eccentric moments of the most eccentric books of three most eccentric careers – exerts on this study a centrifugal pressure away from any semblance of balance or judiciousness. Like Swift's "inspired" hack, I have doubtless been alone with my theme too long and have not managed to state my case without overstating it. There are long stretches of all three books devoid of the comic self-consciousness I am calling "esoteric comedy": for example, the heart of Book 2 of *Sartor,* which narrates the earnest and anguished Teufelsdröckh's

29

"conversion" from "Everlasting No" to "Everlasting Yea," or the pathos and high purple of the passages in the *Apologia* describing Newman's childhood, his illness in Sicily, his farewell to Oxford. (These are the passages that anthologists for a century and more have chosen to represent these texts.) Likewise many of the more sublime pages of *A Vision* – though to my ear the gaiety and humor of Yeats's artificiality always suggest a delightedly self-spectatorial consciousness.

And of course "esoteric comedy" is a phrase of my own; it is nowhere to be found in the writings of Carlyle, Newman, or Yeats. None was a theorist of comedy, and none felt much obliged, whether as writer or as intellectual, to formulate theories of any kind. The arguable exception is Carlyle: Stuart Tave quite properly adduces Carlyle's essays on Richter[55] as exercises in the theory of "amiable humour"; and it is a commonplace that The Editor's portrait of Teufelsdröckh in the chapter of *Sartor* called "Characteristics" is an idealized image of the Richterian "amiable humourist." But the Richterian Carlyle is retailing Richter's ideas, not elaborating his own; and in any case, the comedy of *Sartor Resartus* is profoundly at odds with "amiable" theory, on the score both of its daunting and elaborate difficulty, and of its often quite grim adversions, as ferocious and unsettling as anything in Swift, to war, capital punishment, and other "characters" of human depravity.

Another thing I am *not* saying here is that there are consequential transactions of "influence" between these writers. Carlyle and Newman pointedly ignored each other. Yeats's occasional faint praises of Newman's prose do not suggest a large acquaintance with his writing. As for Carlyle, the young Yeats agreed with his friend Arthur Symons that *Sartor Resartus* was a "sacred book of the arts"; and in *Ireland after Parnell* (1922), he remembered Carlyle as "the chief inspirer of self-educated men [i.e., like himself] in the 'eighties and early 'nineties."[56] But by the time he came to write *A Vision* Yeats regarded both Carlyle and Newman as incomplete men, and both figure in *A Vision* as types of transitional phases between better-balanced ones. Carlyle, assigned to Phase 7, exemplifies too "objective" a regard for public opinion; and Newman's "abstraction" is indicated by his assignment to Phase 25, along with (provocatively) Luther and Calvin. Yeats's dealings with Carlyle might profitably be considered by the light

30

of Harold Bloom's "anxiety of influence" – for example, when Yeats criticizes Carlyle's use of the "personalities of history" as mere "metaphors in a vast popular rhetoric, for the expression of thoughts that seeming his own were the work of preachers and angry ignorant congregations"[57] – which sounds (narcissism of small differences?) motivated by an anxiety to distinguish the historical fantasia of Carlyle's *Heroes and Hero-Worship* from Yeats's own, in *A Vision* itself. (Though I would concede Yeats's point about Carlyle generally, *Heroes* does not seem to be the work of Carlyle's on which to base a charge of insufficient idiosyncracy.) But whatever the extent of Yeats's oedipal relations with Carlyle, they are not part of my subject in this book.

In some ways, what I am arguing here might not seem at all "new." On Carlyle, for example, everyone has always recognized that *Sartor Resartus* is a work of "humour," and in "reading" The Editor as Teufelsdröckh's comic butt rather than his exemplary disciple and convert, I am reverting to an assumption taken for granted in discussion of Carlyle from his own time until just a generation ago. Likewise, Newman's powers as an ironist are old news, and Yeats's frequent jokiness in *A Vision* has been noted before. But others have been content to take these as, in each case, incidental features of an oeuvre whose proper concerns lie elsewhere. The humor, irony, jokes, and comedy of these writers have been regarded as epiphenomena of style rather than stuff and substance of each writer's vision. (Often, despite avowals to the contrary, the assumption seems to be that "comic" impulses cannot be acknowledged without detracting from the "seriousness" of the writer. The supposed incompatability of "serious" with "comic" motives is one of the generic preconceptions esoteric comedy means to confound.) I have tried here to relate the moment-by-moment pleasures of these texts to the profoundest motives they spring from, with the ambition (which does not seem to me at all a modest one) of changing your reading of these books and your image of each of these writers.

Sartor Resartus, the *Apologia,* and *A Vision* are usually condescended to (or more rarely, but worse, idolized) as aspiring to a "wisdom" that cold-eyed moderns will no longer entertain; what previous accounts of them seem to me to miss is their own awareness of the difficulty of achieving and transmitting "wisdom" in an age that puts "wisdom" in quotation marks. These

31

three writers are as conscious as anyone (more conscious than most) that they live in a skeptical age, an age especially skeptical of projects like their own. And all of them had lived the agon of skepticism out in their own lives. All three were of a powerfully skeptical temperament, against which their own efforts to "construct" a faith had to contend, long before they contended with the mere public, and this skepticism is enacted in the comedy of these three books: Teufelsdröckh's skepticism of institutions collides with The Editor's skepticism of Teufelsdröckh; Newman examines the claims of rationalism as fastidiously as a Gibbon examining second-century theology, till Charles Kingsley himself protests Newman's "seemingly sceptic method"; Yeats agrees that the disclosures of spirits are hard to account for and then proceeds to retail them. The predicament of wisdom in an age of common sense is what esoteric comedy acknowledges and negotiates, as Emerson (in the epigraph from "Montaigne: or the Skeptic" above) suggests all "gymnastics of talent" in our age must.

Hence my contention that much, if not all, of what these books have to offer in the way of "wisdom" may best disclose itself to the eye that reads them less as works of wisdom than as works of wit. But I had better repeat that I do not mean to imply that comedy is all: Obviously there is much more to say about these writers than I say here; for each of them, comedy has its limits, in ways the individual chapters take up at length. But though I do not claim that their comedy tells us all there is to know about Carlyle, Newman, and Yeats, I am persuaded that an account of any of them that leaves it out leaves out something essential, because I assume – and the following pages in effect test the assumption – that a writer's characteristic ways of disposing language provide the most useful handles on the motives and intentions shaping the larger motions of the oeuvre and the career. Accordingly, my method in what follows is to read several passages very closely, then to consider how the varieties of comedy operative there help us find our way into the largest issues these writers open – for themselves, and for us.

1

THE "THAUMATURGIC ART OF THOUGHT"

CARLYLE'S *SARTOR RESARTUS*

. . . we are but fettered by chains of our own forging, and which ourselves can break asunder. This deep, paralysed subjection to physical objects comes not from Nature, but from our own unwise mode of *viewing* Nature.

– Carlyle, "Signs of the Times"

All language but that concerning *sensual* objects is or has been figurative. Prodigious influence of metaphors!

– Carlyle, *Two Note Books*

The structuralist stance, as well as our own attitudes assumed before or within language, are not only moments of history. They are an astonishment rather, by language as the origin of history. By historicity itself.

– Jacques Derrida, "Force and Signification"

CARLYLE, said one of his disciples, led us into the desert and left us there. This famous remark sums up what seems – and seemed to the Victorians themselves – a peculiarly Victorian fate. Of course, it is a peculiarly Carlylean fate as well, for the first man Carlyle led into the desert was himself, and no one was more conscious than he that his wanderings there followed no pillars of cloud or fire and promised no Pisgah or Canaan. Ambitious to lead and prophesy, but ambivalent about his fitness to do either, Carlyle often insists that he is a mere observer and commentator, a critic of culture rather than one of its Heroes: not the charismatic figure who leads us into the desert, merely the reporter who informs us that the desert is where we have somehow, here and now, arrived.

Such ambivalence is everywhere in Carlyle's writing: in his theory of the Hero, whose role, directly contrary to that of other Romantic heroes, is curiously self-abnegating ("to conform to the Law of the Whole, and in devout silence follow that" [*Works,* 5:56]);[1] in his intensely self-conscious "anti-self-consciousness theory," as Mill called it;[2] in the rebel distinctiveness – some call it "affectation" – of his exhortations to obedience and conformity; in the self-assertiveness of his insistent demand for "self-annihilation." Eric Bentley remarks that Carlyle's vision of change and "becoming" is nevertheless emphatically *not* a vision of "progress." George Levine finds a peculiarly Carlylean state of arrest at "the boundaries of fiction" (and of much else) enacted in Carlyle's prose style, in which, however agitated and volatile, "all the energy circles about a still point of spiritual truth and never gets outside the circle." Philip Rosenberg, considering Carlyle's fascination with the French Revolution, perceives that "incomplete revolution" is the "paradigm" of Carlyle's most vigorous thought, characteristically expressed "in books and essays that stop just short of consummation."[3]

The gibe current in Carlyle's own day, that he rants earsplittingly in praise of silence, suggests that even at its most trifling, response to Carlyle has acknowledged that his peculiar power has its springs in the tension of enormous contradictions. There are other authors whose writing enacts a drama of irresistible forces playing upon immovable objects; it is the special pathos of Carlyle that he so readily shifts roles in this self-generated agon, from combatant to referee, in order to proclaim his own defeat. With more imaginative freedom he might have been one of the great prophets of Romanticism; with more rigor of intellect, one of the great critics of it. Instead, he becomes a disheartening, sometimes quite unattractive figure of defeat, stoic and bleak at best, reactionary and irrational at worst, all the gentleness and humanity of the man willfully twisted in the writing – because emotion must be summoned to authenticate utterance, and the more insecure the thing uttered, the coarser the emotion – into bitterness, self-righteousness, and punitive resentment. Such is the accepted judgment of Carlyle, and I do not mean to challenge it, beyond observing that its very harshness is testimony enough that Carlyle's critics today, like his disciples a century ago, speak out of the sort of disappointment that attends the frustration of only the keenest enthusiasms.

The responses Carlyle's writing arouses (both of expectation and of disappointment) are as potent as they are for us because Carlyle himself experienced them so profoundly. In *Sartor Resartus* Carlyle feels and communicates these excitements as nowhere else in his work, sounding the master theme – the sovereignty of mind, of "the grand thaumaturgic art of Thought" (118), over a universe that looks inescapably determined – that, though it would always govern his thinking and writing, would never again appear in his work with such hopeful and extravagant conviction.

Sartor Resartus is generally recognized as Carlyle's first mature work, the first in which everything promised by the power and energy of the style sustains and is sustained by a correspondingly buoyant and confident treatment of themes ("Work," "Wonder," the burdens of "Self") whose coloring in later work is decidedly darker. I follow other commentators of the past thirty years in finding *Sartor*'s interest and value not in its detachable aphorisms or homilies, but in the dialectic (dialogue) Carlyle orchestrates between Diogenes Teufelsdröckh's *Die Kleider, ihr Werden und Wirken,* and The Editor, whose self-appointed task it is to introduce, excerpt, sort out, discuss, and finally judge the Teufelsdröckhian text. What my account hopes to add is an awareness of this dialectic as *comic* in a variety of senses: an awareness that it is, most immediately, funny and ironic in its presentation of The Editor's persistent miscomprehension of Teufelsdröckh's motives and meanings and that this comedy, at once satiric and affectionate, deploys varieties of subversive humor profoundly at odds with the preachier, more didactically upbeat course the book traces (figured in Teufelsdröckh's own autobiographical passage from "Everlasting No" to "Everlasting Yea") from doubt and negation to belief and affirmation, from the sarcasm and "Descendentalism" of Book 1 to the "Symbols," "Organic Filaments," and "Natural Supernaturalism" of Book 3. Tracing such a course, arriving at such affirmations, *Sartor Resartus* may be called, in a conventional sense, a comedy; but I hope to illuminate a more devious esoteric comedy whose locus is the play of language and figure, especially in Book 1, *Sartor*'s often neglected first third, written earlier than the rest of the book and (I will argue) out of very different motives and ambitions. Book 1's climactic discourse on "Metaphors" is usually treated, if at all, as a prefiguration, a tentative first version, of Book 3's celebration of "Symbols"; I hope to show that it in fact diverges profoundly from the latter doctrine, implying a radically different epistemology and a radically different construction – even a "deconstruction" – of the book's central preoccupation, the culture–nature question. To ask what in the human condition is to be assigned to "nature" and what to "culture" (or "custom," to use *Sartor*'s usual word) is to ask what in political and social arrangements is susceptible to a collective shaping will. Book 1's "Metaphor" and Book 3's "Symbol" differ so radically in the answers they imply to these questions as to be irreconcilable.

Culture and Nature

Sartor is the most conflicted, as well as the most comprehensive and suggestive, of Carlyle's many treatments of the culture–nature theme, but what all *Sartor*'s conflicting positions share is a determination to make the reader conscious that there is a difference between culture and nature, whether to assert the primacy of culture over nature, as in Book 1, or, as in Book 3, the reverse. If "custom" is what we can alter and improve in our condition, and "nature" is what we must resign ourselves to endure, then to enlarge the scope of custom at the expense of nature must be the ambition of a revolutionary "thaumaturgic art of Thought" (118); such is the program of *Sartor*'s Book 1, which argues that nature is not the condition, but the creature, the result, of the "culturally" given codes by which we ourselves constitute it; such is the good news of Book 1's climatic revelation that "all [is] but Metaphor" (73). But in Book 3, Carlyle seeks to confer on culture a transcendental aura of sanctity by grounding it, via his doctrine of "Symbols," in nature. If "Symbol" leads to "Natural Supernaturalism," Book 1's "Metaphor" leads just as inexorably to a sort of "Cultural Supernaturalism."

But there is irony in this as in all Carlyle's projects. In Book 1, Carlyle means to reveal and celebrate culture as the product of a collective imagination, and thus as a kind of unconscious work of art. But before this collective project can be celebrated, it must be redeemed from the unconsciousness in which its true charac-

36

ter is hidden; and the means Carlyle has chosen for this work of "making the unconscious conscious" are unremittingly, and often quite harshly, satiric. In Book 1, "clothes" are chiefly a metaphor for custom, for use-and-wont, for all that is mistaken for "natural" because it is (something very different) customary; in Book 1, accordingly, Teufelsdröckh's project is not to retailor a threadbare world – this is the task reserved for Book 3 – but rather to denude it of "adventitious wrappages" so that (to cite the names of two of Book 1's crucial chapters) "The World in Clothes" can stand naked and revealed as "The World Out of Clothes": "The beginning of all Wisdom," says Teufelsdröckh, "is to look fixedly on Clothes . . . till they become *transparent*" (67). Thus laid bare, the human world can "*transcend* the sphere of blind Custom, and so become Transcendental" (259); the recognition that what had seemed to belong to nature really belongs to culture makes culture, and cultural self-consciousness, the agents of cultural renewal and redemption, or *Palingenesia,* to use Teufelsdröckh's word. But Carlyle's ambivalence about self-consciousness is great; his satiric relish for his denuding project registers a deep and abiding distrust of culture; and so when he reverts to an ideology of "Nature" in Book 3, his celebration of culture is virtually lost in his admonitions against it, and his exalted apocalypse thus reads all too disconcertingly like a debunking exposé. Carlyle's Enlightenment education acquainted him with the long tradition of political thought that cherishes custom as the "second nature" that validates social order; such has been the defense of culture against metaphysical critiques of it since the time of Socrates. But for Carlyle, custom's powerfully illusory second nature is just what is wrong with it, because it leads us to mistake the adventitious circumstances of the surrounding culture for immutable "natural" arrangements: In this way, as Teufelsdröckh proclaims, "Custom doth make dotards of us all" (259).

"Difficulty" and the "Active Reader"

It is to subvert that habit-induced "dotard" condition that Carlyle elaborates his ironic, parodic, and self-consciously difficult esoteric comedy. I will have more to say later about metaphor and symbol, culture and nature, and the transformations Carlyle's rhetoric compels upon the issues they raise as *Sartor* proceeds from Book 1 to Book 3. But it is of the essence of Carlyle's esoteric comedy that it confronts us with these matters, poses them as problems for us, in more immediate ways: in the very tone and texture and conflicting genre cues that buffet the reader from the very first page. As a lifelong rebel against his intellectual milieu, Carlyle characteristically sought to "make difficulties" for the complacent materialism of his age: portraying the mundane as miraculous, the strange as familiar, the received wisdom as folly, and so on. But in *Sartor Resartus,* uniquely among his works, Carlyle's way of making difficulties for a stodgy public is to write a calculatedly difficult book.[4] Even the astute and generous Emerson protested its obscurity and wondered if some sort of explanatory program might not be appended to the text: "At least in some of your prefaces," he urged, "you should give us the theory of your rhetoric."[5] Had Carlyle written such a preface, I suspect he would have followed the example of Swift, whose satires typically have multiple prefaces, each proffering an "explanation" that only complicates things more. (This is arguably the effect of the amusingly uncomprehending "Testimonies of Authors" with which Carlyle sardonically prefaced *Sartor*'s belated first English edition in 1838.)

But something like a Carlylean justification of *Sartor*'s difficulty is implied in his 1828 essay, "Goethe's *Helena.*" Carlyle acknowledges that Goethe's *Helena* makes heavy demands on the reader, but so far from apologizing for this as a vitiating defect, Carlyle defends it as a particular virtue:

> The reader is kept on the alert, ever conscious of his own active coöperation. . . . We love [*Helena*] the more for the labor it has given us: we almost feel that we ourselves had assisted in its creation. And herein lies the highest merit of a piece, and the proper art of reading it. . . . [Goethe's] words are so many symbols, to which we ourselves must furnish the interpretation; or they remain, as in all prosaic minds the words of poetry ever do, a dead letter. (*Works,* 26:149–50)

To call reading an "art" is to stress its social, culturally contingent character and thus to contest the model implicit in materialist thinking, according to which reading would be only a special case of the "natural" act of perception, inert "object" (the printed page) impinging on passive "subject" (the gentle reader). That "the proper art of reading" entails "active coöperation" between reader and text is a proposition entirely relevant to *Sartor Resartus;* it is the difficulty of this task that generates much of the comedy of the book, as The Editor struggles mightily but for the most part vainly to understand the text (Diogenes Teufelsdröckh's *Die Kleider*) he is offering to explain to an audience consisting largely, as he well knows, of just such "prosaic minds" as will have least patience with it. In *Sartor Resartus* as in "Goethe's *Helena*" the spectacle of an earnest reader struggling with a difficult text is noble and comical at the same time:

> *Helena,* like many of Goethe's works, by no means carries its significance written on its forehead . . . on the contrary, it is enveloped in a certain mystery, under coy disguises, which, to hasty readers, may be not only offensively obscure, but altogether provoking and impenetrable. Neither is this any new thing with Goethe. Often has he produced compositions . . . which bring critic and commentator into straits, or even to a total nonplus. (*Works,* 26:148)

For "Goethe" and *"Helena"* in this passage, substitute "Carlyle" and *"Sartor Resartus,"* and the result is a proposition about *Sartor Resartus* that Carlyle would have welcomed; substitute "Teufelsdröckh" and *"Die Kleider,"* and the result reads like any of the numerous passages in *Sartor* itself in which The Editor rehearses his long-suffering exasperation with the Teufelsdröckhhian "straits, or even . . . total nonplus" from which he proposes to deliver his readers, but often enough cannot extricate himself.

Like Goethe's *Helena, Sartor Resartus* is designedly a book you must exert yourself to understand; you cannot sit back and let *Sartor* "just hit you," as you can (and indeed *must;* what choice do you have?) with other, more typically Carlylean masterpieces *(The French Revolution, Past and Present),* in which Carlyle aims to be a spellbinder, holding you enrapt and entranced. In *Sartor Resartus,* by contrast, and especially in Book 1, the characteristic action is spell-*breaking:* The Editor interrupts Teufelsdröckh's rhapsodies constantly, and always –

whether fussily begging to differ or happily seconding with enthusiasm – in such a way as to shatter the Teufelsdröckhian spell. Teufelsdröckh, too, routinely breaks his own spells, orchestrating startling juxtapositions of high-rolling transcendentalisms with (sometimes quite grimly) satiric "Descendental" ironies. Deliverance from the "thrall" of "old-clothes" customs and habits is one of the master themes of Carlyle's whole career, but in *Sartor Resartus* Carlyle has found the literary means to enact this theme, whereas elsewhere his project is rather to deliver us from pernicious thralldoms by binding us to others he deems wholesomer – "Work," "Silence," "sincere idolatry," and so on. The program for "the proper art of reading" announced in "Goethe's *Helena*" assigns the reader a larger, more "active" role and explicitly connects it with issues that go beyond the literary:

> Continuance of passive pleasure . . . is here [i.e., in reading], as under all conditions of mortal existence, an impossibility. Everywhere in life, the true question is, not what we *gain,* but what we *do:* so also in intellectual matters, in conversation, in reading, which is more precise and careful conversation, it is not what we *receive,* but what we are made to *give,* that chiefly contents and profits us. True, the mass of readers will object; because, like the mass of men, they are too indolent. (*Works,* 26:150)

Reading in its noblest form, then, is not a "passive pleasure" for the indolent, but a form of "Work" (The Editor calls it "self-activity" – odd phrase – and adds that it is "the best effect of any book" [28]) and therefore but a special case, and thence also an emblem, of that active and inquiring spirit Carlyle regards as the proper disposition vis-à-vis "all conditions of mortal existence."

But this imperative of our condition – that we try to understand it – is one Carlyle regards as not even remotely fulfillable, though it necessarily entoils us in a labor simultaneously exalted and absurd:

> . . . ever, from time to time, must the attempt to shape for ourselves some Theorem of the Universe be repeated. And ever unsuccessfully: for what Theorem of the Infinite can the Finite render complete? (*Works,* 28:25)

Carlyle's Sartor Resartus

Carlyle is profoundly ambivalent about the whole project of "understanding": The impossibility of it sometimes makes him despair, sometimes yields a grim satisfaction at the (virtually universal) spectacle of human arrogance laid low. But in *Sartor,* this theme of the human will to understand, fatally entoiled in overwhelming mysteries, is rendered comic – despite the *Schadenfreude* of many "Descendental" passages – because the earnest and sincere will to understand redeems, finally, the human incapacity to do so. In *Sartor Resartus,* it is at last both funny and admirable that all The Editor's efforts to know are ultimately bamboozled, if only by his own restless inability to stay satisifed with the answers he contrives to his own questions.

Self-referentiality

Take the notion that "reading" is a metaphor for the project of understanding generally; add a sense of both activities as comically limited; then consider the Swiftian (even Borgesian) self-referentiality and archbookishness of *Sartor's* esoteric comedy. Like a play with multiple plots, *Sartor Resartus* superimposes multiple enactments of the comedy of understanding and misunderstanding, reading and misreading, playing itself out – a comedy whose pincers at last converge upon the reader, whose own reading ("active" or not?) it puts in question. First, there is Diogenes Teufelsdröckh's *Die Kleider,* a text full of wit and solemnity, pathos and humor, satire and transcendentalism: an effusion (and in part a history) of Herr Teufelsdröckh's effort to understand the human condition. Then there is The Editor, thoughtful, sympathetic, and interested, but fundamentally common-sensical, who has assumed the difficult task of understanding Herr Teufelsdröckh's book, sifting its gold from its dross, selecting and arranging excerpts of each, all properly labeled and accompanied by explanatory comment, elucidation, summary, rejoinder, commendation, criticism, whatever. Then there is the reader, implicit throughout, in whose behalf The Editor has undertaken such labors: a member of the great magazine-reading public (*Sartor* was initially conceived and written designedly for *Fraser's*), not uncurious, but with decidedly limited patience and imagination, whom The Editor alternately humors, teases, cajoles, challenges, exhorts. Call this personage

41

"the mock reader" to distinguish him (for he is surely male) from the "active reader" whom the author (not the ostensible author, The Editor, but the [originally anonymous] Carlyle) hopes to locate and address, even – so great is his ambition – to create: a reader better disposed to "the proper art of reading." The active reader must "see through" the miscues The Editor offers to the mock reader and in the process see that The Editor is a mock reader of a sort, too. The Editor's transactions with *Die Kleider* provide "readings" that, although certainly "active" (even hyperactive), the active reader must see are misreadings; and thus the whole activity of reading, of interpreting, of making sense and order out of difficult materials is one to which the reader is made both witness and self-conscious participant. At every point, the text provides a model of reading (Teufelsdröckh reading the world, The Editor reading Teufelsdröckh, the mock reader reading The Editor in the fashion The Editor expects) by which, and against which, the actual active reader must measure his or her own responses.

Genre: Parody, Hoax, "Hum"

The first "difficulty" such a reader would confront, paging through *Fraser's Magazine* in November of 1833, is generic: What *kind* of writing is this anonymous piece called *Sartor Resartus?* As I wrote in my introduction, critics began asking the genre question about *Sartor* even before it was published, but I know of none who has noticed that The Editor asked it first or has pondered what that circumstance might import for the whole enterprise of "determining" the genre of a book like this. Call this the first instance of comic self-referentiality in a text that persistently raises about itself questions that the active reader should be asking anyway: questions raised, ironically, in the miscomprehending form in which they occur to The Editor and receiving the comically wrong answers he contrives to them.

Sartor's genre, then. From the very first page, *Sartor* hints incessantly (and quite heavy-handedly) that it is something other than it appears. Only the laziest or most foolish reader (it would seem) could miss seeing that *Sartor Resartus* is not what it purports to be, a long book review-essay of the sort that was a staple of magazines of the period; to mistake *Sartor Resartus* in that way would be as absurd as to mistake the cheeky *Fraser's Magazine* for such sedate and solemn reviews as the *Edinburgh* or the *Quarterly*.[6] Yet there was no shortage of readers who erred in just this way, readers for whom Herr Teufelsdröckh, *Die Kleider,* and The Editor seemed plausible enough to be genuine. Carlyle always protested that he meant no one to be fooled and, toward those who were, would only (like the disingenuous prankster) profess astonishment that anyone could really have fallen for his utterly transparent jest. Yet the legions of the hoaxed contained not only hasty "common readers," but Fleet Street professionals; the "Testimonies of Authors" appended to *Sartor'*s 1838 English edition pillories the book's more witless reviewers simply by quoting them without comment – and they are amusing reading. One of them argues his conclusion that "no such [person] as Professor Teufelsdröckh . . . ever existed" (320) at such length and with such fine prosecutorial zeal as to seem himself, finally, to be pulling the reader's leg. In a letter to Emerson (April 29, 1836), Carlyle made play of being uncertain whether this gentleman had stupidly missed *Sartor'*s satire or wittily compounded it: "Either a *thrice*-plied quiz (Sartor's "Editor" a *twice*-plied one); or else opening on you a grandeur of still Dulness rarely to be met with on Earth." And again almost a year later (February 13, 1837): "Since the Irish Bishop who said 'there were some things in *Gulliver,* on which he for one would keep his belief *suspended,*' – nothing equal to it, on that side, has come athwart me."[7]

Carlyle's protestations of surprise at such gullibility sound quite sincere, but he had ample warning that some readers would be fooled when, during the long effort to get *Sartor* printed, the publisher John Murray rejected the manuscript on the advice of an "expert" who ended his report with the query "*Is* the work a translation?" (319). It is notable that this evidence that even an "expert" might be hoaxed did not prompt Carlyle to alter his text to forestall such mistaking; indeed, his only known revision was the change of his hero's name from "Teufelsdreck" (a common name at the time for asafoetida, a potent herbal laxative) to "Teufelsdröckh" – which looks calculated rather to increase than diminish the professor's plausibility, to make him seem more "real," less obviously a fictional character with a grossly and satirically suggestive name.[8]

Carlyle's asperities toward the hoaxed show a forgivable relish, but of course *Sartor* would have failed of its purpose if it had hoaxed everybody. It appears that most readers read *Sartor* as a parody of a book review-essay – such parodies were, indeed, a staple of *Fraser's* – but readers whose responses to the proffered cues went no farther than to detect the parody would remain misled if they took *Sartor* for no more than elaborate trifling of the typical *Fraser's* kind. Carlyle hopes, of course, for the reader who can discern that there is more – but what? – to *Sartor Resartus* than mere humor-magazine foolery. Granted that *Sartor* is not a hoax, that it is meant to be "seen through," still, what it is about is hardly obvious or transparent. From the very first page, *Sartor Resartus* advertises ulterior motives, but ambiguously. The accents of irony and humor are everywhere in Chapter 1, satirizing the Enlightenment's "Torch of Science," as well as the avidity of projectors and scribblers whose "Rush-lights and Sulphur-matches" have sent their feeble illumination into every "cranny or doghole in Nature or Art," yet have produced "little or nothing of a fundamental character . . . on the subject of Clothes." The tone ranges from the *faux-naif* –

> . . . to many a Royal Society, the Creation of a World is little more mysterious than the cooking of a dumpling; concerning which last, indeed, there have been minds to whom the question, *How the apples were got in,* presented difficulties. (4)

– to something altogether darker –

> Man's whole life and environment have been laid open and elucidated; scarcely a fragment or fibre of his Soul, Body, and Possessions, but has been probed, dissected, distilled, dessicated and scientifically decomposed. (4–5)

The suggestion of these passages is of a satire on the pretensions of science, at moments very much in the manner of Swift:

> Our Theory of Gravitation is as good as perfect: Lagrange, it is well known, has proved that the Planetary System, on this scheme, will endure forever; Laplace, still more cunningly, even guesses that it could not have been made on any other scheme. (3–4)

And the reader who supposed that *Sartor Resartus* was to be some such jesting and reactionary lampoon on the self-congratulation of "progress" could reflect that *Fraser's* was just the vehicle for it.

But the following paragraph deploys a rhetoric that Tory "common sense" will join Enlightenment progressivism in distrusting, a rhetoric of inner versus outer, of secrecy and concealment, of the mysterious noumena beneath misleading phenomena:

> How then comes it, may the reflective mind repeat, that the grand Tissue of all Tissues, the only real Tissue, should have been quite overlooked by Science, – the vestural Tissue, namely of woolen or other cloth; which Man's Soul wears as its outmost wrappage and overall; wherein his whole other Tissues are included and screened, his whole Faculties work, his whole Self lives, moves, and has its being? (5)

The chapter goes on to appeal for support to a quarter most Englishmen will regard with skepticism: "Germany, learned, indefatigable, deep-thinking Germany" (6). The ensuing panegyric on German speculativeness at the expense of British pragmatism resonates in a way to pique John Bull prejudices no less than the too hasty credence of the speculative and intellectually adventurous avant-garde, self-regardingly steeped in things German, Coleridgean, and transcendental.

These observations are meant to indicate the degree to which the text before us is of an unusually agitated sort. Changes in tone, especially considering the multifold prejudices of the book's original audience, make decisions as to the author's meaning – even the question, Is the author to be identified with "The Editor of these sheets" who introduces himself at the chapter's close? – problematic, at least for every active reader. There is enough irony and ambiguity to make any reader, of whatever predilections, feel solicited and satirized by turns so swift and so dizzying as to seem almost simultaneous. Such agitation keeps "the proper interpretation" in question: keeps it at once urgent and at the same time in abeyance. Any hope of an interpretation in the sense of a portable, paraphraseable "meaning" must be renounced in favor of a more arduous *project* of interpretation –

a demanding, difficult, and perhaps finally inconclusive *activity*. Hence *Sartor*'s most significant deviation from the conventions of the genre it parodies: In a "real" book review, the reviewer writes after reading and digesting, whereas the presiding fiction of *Sartor Resartus* is that The Editor is writing, considering, and reconsidering his conclusions as they occur to him in the process of reading *Die Kleider.*[9] Often, for example, he postpones judgment on some important crux until presently unavailable "Biographical Documents" arrive. (When these "documents" do arrive, of course, so far from answering earlier questions, they pose altogether new ones, becoming yet another text The Editor must decipher.)

So recognition that *Sartor Resartus* is not a hoax, but a parody and something more, raises a characteristically Carlylean problem: that things can be *more* mysterious, *harder* to interpret and understand, when you "know" what they are than when you do not. The humor and the difficulty of *Sartor's* prose, and the play it makes with the possibility of hoax, are calculated to entoil us in something more careful and deliberate than the hasty and inattentive reading-as-usual endemic to a print-saturated milieu. The reader hoaxed by a parody has been misled by a cunningly counterfeited set of conventions and the habit of responding to these conventionally, that is, unthinkingly. But what of uncounterfeited conventions and the varieties of intellectual and imaginative "habit" they encourage? Custom and convention are collective human contrivances, not "natural" at all, though longstanding "use-and-wont" can make them seem so. Hence, observes The Editor in *Sartor*'s first chapter, the curious blindness of Science to the whole issue of Clothes:

> [Philosophers hitherto have erred in] regarding Clothes as a property, not an accident, as quite natural and spontaneous, like the leaves of trees, like the plumage of birds. In all speculations they have tacitly figured man as a *Clothed Animal;* whereas he is by nature a *Naked Animal;* and only in certain circumstances, by purpose and device, masks himself in Clothes. (5–6)

The Editor here is cautioning us against habitual ways of thinking and seeing, lest we unthinkingly suppose that *cultural* "acci-

dents" (note this philosophical language) are *natural* "properties" – a mistake on the same order as mistaking a parody for the
real thing.

Which is to say that this prose is enacting its themes, at one
remove: We are being told that we must see through appearances
that have been endorsed by habit and custom if we are to see the
more difficult truth behind them, and we are being told this by a
text that is itself notably difficult and in ways that hint broadly
that it, too, must be "seen through." Indeed, in case we miss the
point, the difficulty of the text quickly becomes an explicit theme,
reiterated and even exaggerated constantly by The Editor, who,
although he assures us that his whole purpose is only to ease our
encounter with Herr Teufelsdröckh and his wild notions, nevertheless harps so insistently on the difficulties as to make the text
seem more daunting than it is.

The Editor: The "Active" Misreader as Stooge

And so it is as an earnestly self-conscious but unwittingly comic
exemplar of commitment to the activity of the "proper art of
reading," doggedly but for the most part ineffectually working to
achieve "active cöoperation" with the difficult text before him,
that The Editor figures in *Sartor Resartus*.[10] He is the primary
device of *Sartor*'s reflexive esoteric comedy of reading and meta-
reading. It is he who raises all the issues we have just traversed –
difficulty, genre, hoax, "hum" – lest we miss them. And his frequent animadversions on *Die Kleider* spotlight precisely the features of the text – its disorder, obscurity, extravagance, labored
ingenuity – that any reader, active or not, might complain of. But
whereas The Editor raises the right issues, his disposition of them
usually leaves something to be desired. He has read *Die Kleider*
many times, he tells us, keeping at it despite an initial "disqui-
etude" – but with ironic results:

> ... now the Volume on Clothes, read and again read, was
> in several points becoming lucid and lucent ... but, in spite
> of all that memory and conjecture could do, more and more
> enigmatic; whereby the old disquietude seemed fast settling
> into fixed discontent. (11)

The Editor pronounces *Die Kleider* "a very Sea of Thought, neither calm nor clear," where the reader must become a sort of "pearl diver," learning to sift the "sea wrack" in order to find the "true orients" (10); indeed,

> It were a piece of vain flattery to pretend that this Work on Clothes entirely contents us; that it is not, like all works of genius ... a mixture of insight, inspiration, with dulness, double-vision, and even utter blindness. (28)

This sounds like a registration of minor annoyances – *Die Kleider*'s "genius" is conceded, and its faults compared to sunspots, lost, for any ordinary eye, in brilliance – but as The Editor continues his survey of his subject's "Characteristics," impatience gets the upper hand of admiration, and the sun metaphor gives way to another, more deflating and comical, that expresses The Editor's exasperation:

> ... the Book ... too often distresses us like some mad banquet, wherein all courses had been confounded, and fish and flesh, soup and solid, oyster-sauce, lettuces, Rhine-wine and French mustard, were hurled into one huge tureen or trough, and the hungry Public invited to help itself. To bring what order we can out of this Chaos shall be part of our endeavour. (34)

The contrast between these two metaphors registers The Editor's manifest inability to mediate between the extremities of his response – whence the comedy of his luckless "endeavour": For a critic aspiring to authoritative judgment, The Editor's relations with his subject are curiously unsettled. In short, for all his stress on the difficulty of the work of reading and understanding, The Editor figures in *Sartor Resartus,* ironically, as an exemplary misreader (in the pre-Harold Bloom sense) and misunderstander. His efforts to mediate between us and Teufelsdröckh afford us instead opportunities to measure the Teufelsdröckhian text against The Editorial interpretation, with the comical result that The Editor's derelictions soon come to function as an ironic counterexample to the attitude of mind Teufelsdröckh exemplifies, and his "readings" of Teufelsdröckh commence to serve as textbook lessons in how *not* to read Teufelsdröckh. In a book about the necessity of "seeing through" phenomena to the noumena they conceal, the pretenses of The Editor are the first and the most consistent feature of the text that we must see through.

And in a book so concerned with difficulty, seeing through The Editor is almost too easy – easier, certainly, than elucidating the elaborately reflexive and self-referential "textuality" that results from Carlyle's manipulation of his comic stooge. Consider, for example, The Editor's unavailing struggles to order Teufelsdröckh's disorder. The Editor is sworn "to bring what order we can out of [Teufelsdröckh's] Chaos" (34), yet his reiterated complaints about *Die Kleider*'s "almost total want of arrangement" and its paucity of "true logical method and sequence" (34) ring only too true of his own book as well; his *Sartor Resartus* manages less to order Teufelsdröckh's chaos than to reproduce it, so that *Die Kleider*'s hodgepodge disorder is, ironically, replicated in the very process supposed to sort it all out. The Editor's tussle with Teufelsdröckh is clearly an unequal one, and only the more comical because it is The Editor's own unhappy complaints about Teufelsdröckh's "Chaos" that so insistently advertise his manifest failure to subdue it.

More complicated is the issue of genre: As we have seen, *Sartor Resartus* contrives to make its own genre quite problematic. (Indeed, scholars are still arguing about it.) The active reader must see first that *Sartor* is not a book review, but a parody of a book review, then recognize that it is something much more than that as well; and these recognitions involve the further recognition that "the proper art of reading" is not a "natural" activity, but a highly socialized operation governed by culturally given codes of interpretation and response to such things as genre cues. The same issues are raised again when The Editor attempts (unsuccessfully) to determine *Die Kleider*'s genre. He quotes Teufelsdröckh's own announcement on the matter:

> "As Montesquieu wrote a *Spirit of Laws,*" observes our Professor, "so could I write a *Spirit of Clothes;* thus, with an *Esprit des Lois,* properly an *Esprit de Coutumes,* we should have an *Esprit de Costumes.*" (35)

Teufelsdröckh's punning and word play here glance, again, at the culture–nature question, whimsically (which is not to say unseriously) connecting "law" with "custom" and thence with "costume" and pressing the incongruence of small things with great that sustains the passage's wit. "Wit," in case anyone can have missed it, is further advertised to any reader with enough French to be reminded in the course of reading the word *esprit* three times in one sentence that "wit" is one of its meanings. Having conjured this mock comparison with Montesquieu, Teufelsdröckh goes on in mock-modest tones to dismiss it, but in terms that make *L'Esprit des Lois* sound like an intellectual fantasia, in contrast to *Die Kleider*'s own scrupulous sobriety – in terms, that is, that exactly reverse the characters of the two books. The passage carries on with witty sallies on the trope of a Divine Tailor wielding his fashionable Scissors according to a "Cause-and-Effect" philosophy insouciantly at odds with all its known Enlightenment versions; but such a science, Teufelsdröckh avers, is beyond his (or any merely human) capacity: No "Cause-and-Effect Philosopher" can explain, nor can he himself, "not why I wear such and such a Garment, obey such and such a Law; but even why I am *here,* to wear and obey anything!" This self-admonition proves (of course) entirely ironic, for these are precisely the sorts of question Teufelsdröckh *does* mean to take up. By the same token, when Teufelsdröckh, aping the accents of the modest and scrupulous *philosophe,* affects to renounce any such ambition –

> Much, therefore, it not the whole, of that same *Spirit of Clothes* I shall suppress, as hypothetical, ineffectual, and even impertinent: naked Facts, and Deductions drawn therefrom in quite another than that omniscient style, are my humbler and proper province. (36)

– he is, ironically, announcing exactly the program (adherence to "naked Facts," etc.) that his book does *not* undertake. Likewise again with the remark on style, which promises to eschew "omniscience": "Omniscience" is precisely the effect of full-throated Teufelsdröckh-ese.

No one should know these things better than The Editor, veteran (as he advertises himself) of many rereadings of *Die Kleider.*

Carlyle's Sartor Resartus

Yet all of this mock renunciation The Editor takes at face value, observing that despite this "prudent restriction," Teufelsdröckhian subject matter "too often lie[s] quite beyond our horizon" (36). In short, The Editor consistently mistakes every twist and turn of Teufelsdröckh's witty, ironic, and playful announcement of *Die Kleider*'s genre: Where Teufelsdröckh playfully invokes Montesquieu, The Editor expects *Die Kleider* actually to be a sober, *philosophique* Montesquieuan inquiry. (Treacherously, indeed, Teufelsdröckh does write, and The Editor quotes, passages of speculation on the origins of clothing and morals that evince just the sorts of interest and reflection that one finds in Montesquieu, Diderot, Voltaire, and Rousseau.) The *coutumes-costumes* word play goes right past The Editor; and even Teufelsdröckh's pledge concerning "naked Facts" does not deter The Editor from a too literal response (indeed, the reverse; he takes it hook, line, and sinker) notwithstanding that "naked" is almost too obviously a charged word when we are talking of "clothes." In mistaking *Die Kleider*'s genre in this way, in missing Teufelsdröckh's wit and so failing to grasp how the text's playfulness qualifies its genre claims, The Editor is committing an error cognate to that of the reader hoaxed by *Sartor*'s own parodic games into taking too literally, too much at face value, its look of being a book review.

But not only is The Editor's sense of genre too literal; it is also too fastidious, as is audible in his contemptuous metaphor of the "huge tureen or trough" into which Teufelsdröckh's insights have been indiscriminately dumped. Obviously Teufelsdröckh hopes for a reader who will be exhilarated by his book's rhetorical, tonal, and associative leaps; alas, The Editor is no such reader. A good deal of his indignation with *Die Kleider* expends itself in behalf of a desire to tidy up the book's mess, to sort out the various kinds of writing in it, in order to commend some and reprove others. He admires passages of "concentrated and purefied Learning" and genuinely "Philosophic reflections" (39) but is made uncomfortable by Teufelsdröckh's wit – when indeed he is even aware of it. Teufelsdröckh's irony and satire are comparable in incisiveness and moral seriousness to Swift's, but The Editor routinely deplores such passages as exhibiting an "idle wire-drawing spirit" in which "a tone of levity, approaching to conventional satire, is too clearly discernible" (43); at length he coins the word "Descendentalism" (65) to distinguish such passages from the sublime flights of "Transcendentalism" that he so prefers. This effort to disjoin satire from uplift accurately forecasts the responses of Carlyle's readers for the next century and a half; if Teufelsdröckh often aspires to a Swiftian moral wit, The Editor is tellingly "Victorian" *(avant la lettre)* in his high-minded aversion to a Swiftian angle of vision – and thus, again, an inadequate guide to and reader of the Teufelsdröckhian apocalypse.

The Editor's impulse to sift what he likes in *Die Kleider* from what he dislikes is both misguided, since if it succeeded it would rob Teufelsdröckh of his most characteristic effects, and futile, since The Editor cannot succeed in it anyway. What Teufelsdröckh has joined together, no man – or at least not The Editor – can put asunder: What better emblem of that "Fact" (to give the word its proper Carlylean emphasis) than the professor's own name? "Diogenes Teufelsdröckh," which means something like "God-born Devil-dung," manages to conflate the most radically opposed categories available to a fideistic imagination, and thus encodes all that sense of oxymoron and paradox that is the essence of Teufelsdröckh's vision and the bane of The Editor's. Teufelsdröckh's character, The Editor finds, presents the same sort of bafflements as Teufelsdröckh's book: "Certainly a most involved, self-secluded, altogether enigmatic nature, this of Teufelsdröckh!" (32) he exclaims, unable to decide whether Teufelsdröckh is "a very seraph" or a malignant "incarnate Mephistopheles":

A wild tone pervades the whole utterance of the man . . . now screwing itself aloft as into a Song of Spirits, or else the shrill mockery of Fiends; now sinking in cadences, not without melodious heartiness, though sometimes abrupt enough, into the common pitch, when we hear it only as a monotonous hum; of which hum the true character is extremely difficult to fix. Up to this hour we have never fully satisifed ourselves whether it is a tone and hum of real Humour, which we reckon among the very highest qualities of genius, or some echo of mere Insanity and Inanity, which doubtless ranks below the very lowest. (31–2)

Note that the ambivalence registered in such paired contraries as seraph–fiend or genius–insanity (or inanity) is here connected with "Humour," a quality The Editor honors as "among the very highest qualities of genius" but for which (as with genre, irony, tone, and *Die Kleider*'s other literary properties) he exhibits little aptitude. Humor, of course, has been one of *Sartor*'s pervasive features from page one, the most immediate and insistent cue to its ulterior purposes; and as we have seen, The Editor can serve as humorist when these purposes (Carlyle's) require it. But here they require that he appear as exemplary solemn ass, with fatuous sobriety commending humor, and – here Carlyle contrives another small feat of textual self-referentiality – deploying, three times in a short space, the word "hum," as if oblivious to its colloquial sense. In Carlyle's day, "hum" was connected with "humbug" and suggested practical jokes, legpulls, hoax, or even swindle. (That twice- or thrice-plied "quiz" whose indignant exposé of *Sartor* in the *North American Review* Carlyle included in his "Testimonies of Authors" uses the word in just this sense, pronouncing *Sartor Resartus* "in plain English, a *hum*" [321].) When The Editor notes Teufelsdröckh's "monotonous hum" and observes that "of [this] hum the true character is extremely difficult to fix," he unwittingly implies about Teufelsdröckh and *Die Kleider* questions that active readers will already have asked about *Sartor Resartus* and its (real) author.

"Seeing through Clothes"

In his manifest ineptitude at "seeing through" the subtleties of style and language in which Teufelsdröckh's meanings are (to recur to an ancient metaphor) "clothed," The Editor unwittingly reveals himself as unfit for the very project of "seeing through" the culturally conditioned codes and structures of tradition for which "Clothes" are Teufelsdröckh's central metaphor. Of course, The Editor's inability to get the stable fix he wants on Teufelsdröckh's meanings is a function not only of his slowness of mind, but of Teufelsdröckh's resolute efforts to defeat any such reduction of his vision to the usual kinds of sense. Carlyle sets The Editor and Teufelsdröckh at such programmatically crossed purposes in order to draw a sharp contrast between a conventional literal-mindedness that he regards as peculiarly susceptible to the errors and delusions of the prevailing materialist world picture and the sort of intellectual-imaginative freedom that he sees as the only possible agent of that cultural gestalt's redemption.

This issue is most insistently – even repetitiously – drawn in The Editor's invariably and comically uncomprehending response to Teufelsdröckh's figurative language in general and to his protean and promiscuous play with the clothing metaphor itself in particular. The whole book springs from the clothing metaphor; both Teufelsdröckh's title *(Der Kleider)* and Carlyle's *(Sartor Resartus)* advertise this and imply as well that the active reader of this text within a text within a text (Teufelsdröckh's within The Editor's within Carlyle's) will require a literarily sophisticated awareness of metaphor's uses as an evocative and argumentative device. Such an awareness is, needless to say, sorely lacking in The Editor, whose literal-minded readiness to mistake literary cues at face value has consistently misled his understanding of the book he has appointed himself to explain; for him, *Die Kleider* really is a book *about* clothing. The Editor's misreadings of Teufelsdröckh – taking literally what is meant figuratively, and vice versa; taking seriously what is meant humorously, and vice versa – provides a virtual *omnium gatherum* of the fallacies of literal-mindedness and functions as a running ironic counterexample, and hence a kind of prompt, to the "proper" reading Teufelsdröckh and Carlyle expect from readers wittier than The Editor. The Editor's programmatic failure to get it right comically underscores the Carlylean-Teufelsdröckhian point that mistaking culture for nature, mistaking a world picture for reality, mistaking metaphorical for factual statement, mistaking irony for straightforwardness are all cognate errors.

Metaphors are provisional, amenable (unlike facts) to variation and revision; hence Teufelsdröckh's delight in the exploitable ambivalences of metaphor and The Editor's unavailing efforts to "rationalize" such ambivalences away. In Teufelsdröckh's usage, the clothing metaphor is peculiarly and richly unstable. Clothes are an outward surface, an appearance, covering a naked reality beneath – in Kantian language, a phenomenon enclosing a noumenon – yet it is *in* the phenomenon, the outward covering, that Teufelsdröckh contrives to make the clothing metaphor – as emblem and evidence of "spirit," culture, and other specifically human (i.e., non-"natural") properties – locate the noumenal. Hence Teufelsdröckh's delight in the contradiction announced in the titles of two (structurally) crucial chapters of *Sartor*'s Book 1, "The World in Clothes" and "The World Out of Clothes." Teufelsdröckh's "palingenetic" project figures as, on the one hand, an affair of *seeing* clothes, looking at them, attending to them, because we have been too used to taking them for granted, as "natural," and thus have stopped seeing them for what they are and, on the other hand, as an activity of *seeing through* clothes, through appearances, to the "naked" reality they both conceal and adorn, both deny and shape. To trace the career of Teufelsdröckh's clothing metaphor through the transformations allowed, or rather incited, by the tension between these two rhetorics, of the naked and the clothed, is to glimpse not only how grandiose were the young Carlyle's hopes about the power of mind to remake and redeem the dead letter of the world as we find it, but also how specifically political was his confidence, how insistently he imagined "the world" and its problems as historical, and how ambitious was the scope of what in the historical and political situation he took to be amenable to revolutionary change. It is also, of course, to monitor The Editor's well-intentioned but comically inadequate struggle to follow where Teufelsdröckh would lead – itself finally a hopeful emblem of a world desirous, however little capable, of change.

The clothing metaphor makes its advent in *Die Kleider* (and thus also in *Sartor Resartus*) in the chapter called "The World Out of Clothes," where Teufelsdröckh recalls a period of youthful dejection in which it seemed that all philosophies and metaphysics were futile, that "what we on Earth call Life" was only "the Somnambulism of uneasy Sleepers" (54), that "our ME [is] the only reality; and Nature . . . but the reflex of our inward Force" (55). The outward universe seemed a lifeless, mechanical show, inward reality a vain and irredeemable solipsism. "It was in some such mood . . . that I first came upon the question of Clothes" (56). He remembers reflecting on the nakedness of his horse, which, apart from the trappings of his human rider, *wears* (note the ambivalence of the naked–clothed figure) the natural clothes of his own body: The horse is "his own sempster and weaver and spinner, nay his own bootmaker, jeweller, and, man-milliner" (56); by contrast, Teufelsdröckh abruptly realizes (and with

shock) that his own human apparel is not organically living, but
creepily dead:

> While I – good Heaven! – have thatched myself over with
> the dead fleeces of sheep, the bark of vegetables, the entrails
> of worms, the hides of oxen or seals, the felt of furred beasts;
> and walk abroad a moving Rag-screen, overheaped with
> shreds and tatters raked from the Charnel-house of Nature,
> where they would have rotted, to rot on me more slowly!
> (56)

The diction of the passage – "entrails of worms" and so forth –
implies a grotesque, even disgusting, assessment of the "clothed"
animal's much vaunted superiority to the naked ones. "Day
after day, I must thatch myself anew," observes Teufelsdröckh,
sketching a picture of the human condition as an obsessive self-
shrouding in dreck and death, an unremitting expenditure of living
energies to keep the ever decomposing mantle in some sort of
repair:

> Day after day, I must thatch myself anew; day after day, this
> despicable thatch must lose some film of its thickness; some
> film of it, frayed away by tear and wear, must be brushed-
> off into the Ashpit, into the Laystall; till by degrees the
> whole has been brushed thither, and I, the dust-making,
> patent Rag-grinder, get new material to grind down. O
> subter-brutish! vile! most vile! (56)

This compulsive toil, grown habitual and automatic, induces a
stupefaction that destroys the sense of wonder ("let but a Rising
of the Sun, let but a Creation of the World happen *twice,* and it
ceases to be marvellous, to be noteworthy, or noticeable" [57]),
and of all this, says Teufelsdröckh, clothes are the outward and
visible sign – which being the case, off, off, ye lendings:

> For my own part, these considerations, of our Clothes-
> thatch, and how, reaching inwards even to our heart of
> hearts, it tailorises and demoralises us, fills me with a cer-
> tain horror at myself and mankind . . . Nevertheless there is
> something great in the moment when a man first strips him-

self of adventitious wrappages; and sees indeed that he is naked, and, as Swift has it, "a forked straddling animal with bandy legs"; yet also a Spirit, and unutterable Mystery of Mysteries. (57)

Teufelsdröckh's wit here generates a suggestive excursus on themes of culture and nature, spirit and matter, life and death – yet The Editor's response to the passage is only a bathetic anxiety lest the "courteous reader" indignantly take Teufelsdröckh as an advocate of nudism:

> The Editor himself, on first glancing over that singular passage, was inclined to exclaim: What, have we got not only a Sansculottist, but an enemy to Clothes in the abstract? A new Adamite . . . ? (57–8)

The Editor feels it incumbent upon him to rebuke any such attitude ("Consider, thou foolish Teufelsdröckh, what benefits unspeakable all ages and sexes derive from Clothes" [58]), as if Teufelsdröckh really *were* "a new Adamite," zealously advocating, like that early Christian sect, a return to prelapsarian habits of dress, or undress. (The Editor even goes so far as to observe, in triumphant refutation of Teufelsdröckh's "Adamitism," that Teufelsdröckh himself goes about *fully dressed*.) The Editor thus assumes the role of defender of all that Teufelsdröckh means not only to satirize but also, as the mention of the Sansculottes reminds us, to indict and change.

But after four hundred words or so, all passion spent, The Editor begins to see light and now wants to assure us that Teufelsdröckh is no crusader in behalf of nakedness: "Nowise, courteous reader! The Professor knows full well what he is saying" (59) – but as usual, The Editor understands less than full well what the Professor is saying, as his paraphrase of Teufelsdröckh's revolutionary point makes comically clear:

> If Clothes, in these times, "so tailorise and demoralise us" [The Editor is here quoting Teufelsdröckh's own phrase from the passage above], have they no redeeming value; can they not be altered to serve better; must they of necessity be thrown to the dogs? (59)

The Editor at last divines Teufelsdröckh's point, that clothes *can* be altered and made to serve better; what he has missed is the figurativeness of Teufelsdröckh's language, which makes clothing emblematic of social arrangements, political institutions, collective myths, indeed, every supervention of "culture" upon "nature." For Teufelsdröckh, it is this ensemble of history and custom that, "reaching inwards even to our heart of hearts ... tailorises and demoralises us, [and] fill[s] me with a certain horror at myself and mankind." The Editor's fussy prudishness blinds him to Teufelsdröckh's Swiftian insight, just as his literal-mindedness prompts him to suppose that Teufelsdröckh's subject really is clothing and nothing more.

Accordingly, there is something richly ironic about The Editor's relief at finding that on the subject of clothes, Teufelsdröckh holds proper views after all. The "courteous reader" will be gratified to hear that so far from Adamitism, Teufelsdröckh is one to whom "the utility of Clothes" is "altogether apparent" (60); nay, Teufelsdröckh discerns "the more recondite and almost mystic qualities," even "the omnipotent virtue of Clothes," and as proof The Editor cites the following very uplifting passage as Teufelsdröckhian testimony to "the benefits unspeakable all ages and sexes derive from Clothes":

"You see two individuals," [Teufelsdröckh] writes, "one dressed in fine Red, the other in coarse threadbare Blue: Red says to Blue, 'Be hanged and anatomised'; Blue hears with a shudder, and (O wonder of wonders!) marches sorrowfully to the gallows; is there noosed-up, vibrates his hour, and the surgeons dissect him, and fit his bones into a skeleton for medical purposes. How is this; or what make ye of your *Nothing can act but where it is?* Red has no physical hold of Blue, no *clutch* of him, is nowise in *contact* with him: neither are those ministering Sheriffs and Lord-Lieutenants and Hangmen and Tipstaves so related to commanding Red, that he can tug them hither and thither; but each stands distinct within his own skin. Nevertheless, as it is spoken, so is it done: the articulated Word sets all hands in Action; and Rope and Improved-drop perform their work.

"Thinking reader, the reason seems to me twofold: First,
that *Man is a Spirit,* and bound by invisible bonds to *All
Men;* secondly, that *he wears Clothes,* which are the visible
emblems of that fact. Has not your Red hanging-individual
a horse-hair wig, squirrel-skins, and a plush-gown; whereby
all mortals know that he is a JUDGE? – Society, which the
more I think of it astonishes me the more, is founded upon
Cloth.["] (60)

For the "thinking reader," the irony here – a hanging as exem-
plum of the communal ties that ("O wonder of wonders!") bind
"Man" to *"All Men"* – is grim, and it compounds the irony that
The Editor misses the irony, the grimness, and the moral. He has
cited the passage, remember, as reassuring evidence of Teufelsdröckh's reverent regard for "the omnipotent virtue of Clothes."
He naïvely takes at face value Teufelsdröckh's sarcastic pretense
of drawing an exalted conclusion *("Man is a Spirit")* from the
ghastly spectacle he has just described. The Editor's readiness to
enjoy the conclusion while shutting his eyes to the evidence here
seems a type of fatuous optimism; and his taking (mistaking) an
irony at face value is implicated in an all too familiar variety of
moral failure.

Teufelsdröckh and Carlyle address (and assume) a reader
morally and otherwise more alert than The Editor to the multi-
farious ways in which the refinements and differentiations clothing registers (both encodes and elicits) in our culture can also
"tailorise and demoralise us." "You see two individuals," the
passage begins – but we see not individuals, not people at all:
What we see are clothes, a "fine Red" ceremonial robe condemning "threadbare Blue" mufti. The clothes here, as in the "clothes-
as-dreck" passage above, are emblematic of all that is mere custom and use-and-wont: all, in short, that is taken (even by poor
"threadbare Blue") as beyond question or change. But if in the
earlier passage the clothes were dead, the naked body beneath
was still alive; here it is the clothes that are alive and potent in
the scene. The human beings are mere objects, automata,
impelled through a routine determined not by their judgments or
volitions, but by their "adventitious wrappages," their clothes,
and what the clothes are emblems of, the social structure, given

and apparently unchangeable, in which all, the judge, the hangman, and the condemned, figure as mere replaceable parts moving predictably and without protest always within the same limited set of possibilities. A further irony is that the antimaterialist Teufelsdröckh presents this protest in a scene of judicial action where the social "mechanics" of pleasure and pain, punishment and reward are (to the utilitarian eye) most undeniably displayed. The scene as Teufelsdröckh presents it defies the principle of Newtonian mechanics according to which "nothing can act at a distance." *Quod erat demonstrandum: "Man is a Spirit."*

All of this irony, as we have seen, is lost on The Editor, who cites this passage as wonderfully high-minded stuff. The Editor can only view with alarm, however, Teufelsdröckh's next changes on the theme of the naked and the clothed, a vision of the grand pomps of state with all the assembled dignitaries at a stroke, "as by some enchanter's wand," denuded of their finery and left stark naked at their stations. At this spectacle, "I know not whether to laugh or weep," confesses Teufelsdröckh; but The Editor is decidedly not amused: "Who is there now," he indignantly demands, "that can read the five columns of Presentations in his Morning Newspaper without a shudder?" (61) When Teufelsdröckh conjectures that the apparition of the emperor without clothes (as in the child's fable) would result in the dissolution, "in wails and howls," of "the whole fabric of Government, Legislation, Property, Police, and Civilised Society," The Editor protests that the satire is simply too harsh: "Hypochondriac men, and all men are to a certain extent hypochondriac, should be more gently treated" (61–2). As Teufelsdröckh continues, suggesting (inter alia) that every "Scarecrow," as "Clothed Person," should enjoy the traditional liberties of an Englishman, "considering his high function (for is not he, too, a Defender of Property, and Sovereign armed with the *terrors* of the law?)," The Editor can only groan in antiphonal complaint: "Unhappy Teufelsdröckh ... Art thou the malignest of Sansculottes, or only the maddest?" (62–3).

If the clothing metaphor suggests the non-"natural" properties that, both for good and ill, characterize and distinguish the "human," it also affords Teufelsdröckh-Carlyle a means of inquiring what is dead and makes for death, what is alive and makes for life, in the human situation. Riding his "naturally" dressed horse, Teufelsdröckh presents human (i.e., artificial, non-"natural") clothes as dreck, contrasted with the living human body. In the execution scene, clothes appear as spectrally alive, usurping the prerogatives of their human wearers (and with the power, indeed, of transforming living bodies into dreck, as the passage reminds us by emphasizing the postexecution fate of the corpse of "threadbare Blue"); in the satirical "emperor's-new-clothes" passages, clothing figures as the *primum mobile* of a complex social mechanism that would self-destruct without it. Teufelsdröckh next proceeds to yet another variation on his theme, this time bringing together the classes and the masses, a king and a wagon driver, or "Carman," in a state of democratic undress; here the naked body itself is denuded of spirit and made to appear not as a living thing, but as a mere empty costume, compounded of dreck and devoid of life:

> ... dissect them with scalpels [i.e., a king and a wagon-driver] ... the same viscera, tissues, livers, lights, and other life-tackle, are there: examine their spiritual mechanism; the same great Need, great Greed and little Faculty; nay ten to one but the Carman, who understands draught-cattle, the rimming of wheels, something of the laws of unstable and stable equilibrium, with other branches of wagon-science, and has actually put forth his hand and operated on Nature, is the more cunningly gifted of the two. Whence, then, their so unspeakable difference? From Clothes. (64)

The organs and "life-tackle" of the body, and the "spiritual mechanism" as well, here seem mass-produced bits of apparatus, while clothes appear to be a mechanical contrivance, externally applied, for imposing artificial distinctions on a population that "natural" distinctions would order very differently. Clearly audible is Teufelsdröckh's disdain for any egalitarianism founded on such a vision of equality as the dissecting knife might open; but just as clearly the effete king who owes his dominion over the wagon driver to his mere clothes also has Teufelsdröckh's contempt. (Here, at least, The Editor does not miss the irony of Teufelsdröckh's pretending to praise clothes for their noble function of concealing the king's inferiority to the workman.)

All of this satire, so grim, so uncomforting, so hard on "Hypo-

chondriac man," prompts The Editor to coin a word worthy of
Kenneth Burke:

> The grand peculiarity of Teufelsdröckh is, that with all this
> Descendentalism, he combines a Transcendentalism, no
> less superlative; whereby if on the one hand he degrade man
> below most animals . . . he on the other, exalts him beyond
> the visible Heavens, almost to an equality with the Gods.
> (65)

To "degrade man below most animals" (the substance of the Victorian indictment against, e.g., Swift): that were "Descendentalism" indeed, and never mind its precedents going back to Homer and the Bible. No, The Editor prefers the other tendency in Teufelsdröckh, his "Transcendentalism," which "exalts [man] beyond the visible Heavens" – like this, for example:

> "To the eye of vulgar logic," says [Teufelsdröckh], "What
> is man? An omnivorous Biped that wears Breeches. To the
> eye of Pure Reason what is he? A Soul, a Spirit, and divine
> Apparition. Round his mysterious ME, there lies, under all
> those wool-rags, a Garment of Flesh (or of senses), contex-
> tured in the loom of Heaven." (65)

– and so forth. In such passages ("unhappily too rare," sniffs The Editor), Teufelsdröckh's "high Platonic Mysticism" opens "a whole inward Sea of Light and Love" – though The Editor goes on to complain (with an "alas") that "the grim coppery clouds soon roll together again, and hide it from view" (66). But the point is that this Teufelsdröckhian "Transcendentalism" entails a variation on the nakedness theme that The Editor can, at last, approve: "The beginning of all Wisdom," writes Teufelsdröckh, "is to look fixedly on Clothes . . . till they become *transparent*" (67); and The Editor sees in this exercise of x-ray vision a prospect of "Wonder, the basis of Worship" (67) as an effect of *seeing through* the dreck of habit and custom to a consciousness of "universal Wonder . . . the only reasonable temper for the denizen of so singular a planet as ours" (67).

Carlyle's Sartor Resartus

Teufelsdröckh's unremittingly dialectical, ironic, and paradoxical vision, his insistence on the doubleness and conflictedness of things, even the near indecency of his frequent recourse to the theme of nakedness, here become acceptable to The Editor because they open the issue of the mere appearance versus the "Transcendental" reality. "Nothing that [Teufelsdröckh] sees but has more than a common meaning, but has two meanings," The Editor wonderingly explains, apparently forgetting that till lately this had been his chief theme of complaint against Teufelsdröckh. But no more; Teufelsdröckh's "double meanings" now inspire The Editor to some transcendentalizing of his own:

> For matter, were it never so despicable, is Spirit, the manifestation of Spirit: were it never so honourable, can it be more? The thing Visible, nay, the thing Imagined, the thing in any way conceived as Visible, what is it but a Garment, a Clothing of the higher celestial Invisible, "unimaginable, formless, dark with excess of bright"? (66–7)

A few pages later The Editor quotes Teufelsdröckh himself to the same effect:

> All visible things are emblems . . . Matter exists only spiritually, and to represent some Idea, and *body* it forth. Hence Clothes, as despicable as we think them, are so unspeakably significant. (72)

Again we have the conflation of clothes and body ("clothing" exists to "*body* [something: the body itself?] forth"), and again Teufelsdröckh does not hesitate to turn his metaphor reflexively inside-out: Not only are clothes necessarily "emblematic," but "on the other hand, all Emblematic things are properly Clothes" (73). Clothing, appearance, matter, the body, are all emblems of spirit, and the figure of speech is volatile enough to be compelled in all directions. Clothes cover the body? According to Teufelsdröckh, the body itself is only "A Clothing or Visible Garment for that divine ME [the soul] . . . [Man] is said also to be clothed with a Body" (73).

63

Esoteric Comedies

The Thaumaturgic of "Metaphor"

The Editor's recognition that with Teufelsdröckh "everything has more than a common meaning, but has two meanings," approaches the valuable insight that literal meanings are "transcended" in Teufelsdröckh's rhetoric, but seems mistakenly to assume that these second meanings resemble the first ones in being unitary and stable, *one* of only *two* possible meanings. Of course, Teufelsdröckh's usage is altogether airier than that. The instability of Teufelsdröckh's metaphors, their happy way of meaning too many things at once, can look like a failure of clarity or analysis – and it is as evidence of just such failure that The Editor usually takes (or mis-takes) them. But Teufelsdröckh's cavalier way with metaphor is altogether deliberate and self-conscious – anything but unwitting – and the kaleidoscopic shifting of reference and implication that Teufelsdröckh compels upon his metaphors sets meaning against meaning in a fashion to ensure that construing (or constructing) one meaning entails de-construing the last, and finally a sort of deconstruction of meaning itself – a strategy the text calls attention to so insistently (via the ironic device of The Editor's almost invariably uncomprehending complaints) as to argue that "meanings" are compliant in considerable degree to our will, that what a thing "means" matters less, finally, than what *we* mean. The "palingenetic" motive of this project should be evident: not only to free our (imagined) world of outdated meanings and to encourage the invention of new meanings in place of old, but more, to encourage an awareness of the fictiveness of meaning itself. Teufelsdröckh's mercurial wit locates the life of things in the play of the living spirit, conscious (and self-conscious) that it does not merely perceive, but actually constitutes, the meanings of its experience, rather than in the dead letter of "facts" such as Thomas Gradgrind deems to aggregate a universe, or metaphors mistaken for fact by a literal-mindedness like The Editor's.

Teufelsdröckh's profuse and dialectical efflorescences of metaphor, then, are meant finally less to enforce certain meanings than to encourage a figurative, imaginative, meaning-making (and -unmaking) activity of mind. It is as an example of just the sort of stodginess Teufelsdröckh means to unsettle that Carlyle has contrived The Editor's habits of literal-mindedness – includ-

64

ing his expectation that like "facts," metaphors shall have stable
and unitary meanings assigned to them. The Editor is a device,
not a "character," and a lifelike consistency (such as we find
oftener in fiction than in life) is not to be expected from him. But
if there is consistency in Carlyle's presentation of him, beyond
the evident program that he should exhibit every possible way of
misunderstanding Teufelsdröckh, it is that his misunderstandings generally spring from a too literal-minded response to things.
As we have seen, he routinely mistakes fancies for propositions,
irony for plain speaking, metaphors for facts, and so on. Even the
"Transcendental" passages of Teufelsdröckh's that he most
admires he evidently takes as statements that are "true" in some
more naïve sense than Teufelsdröckh intends, as if their "truth"
were an affair of established meanings licensing assurance and
repose, rather than a desideratum exacting (and in part depend-
ing on) our active, creative, and impassioned allegiance to it. The
Editor's habits of thinking are deep in just the grooves of use-and-
wont that Teufelsdröckh and Carlyle mean to scour out.

Such a project, and the place of metaphor in it, are all but
spelled out by Teufelsdröckh as follows:

> Language is called the Garment of Thought; however, it
> should rather be, Language is the Flesh-Garment, the Body,
> of Thought. I said that imagination wove this Flesh-
> Garment; and does not she? Metaphors are her stuff: exam-
> ine Language; what, if you except some few primitive ele-
> ments (of natural sound), what is it all but Metaphors,
> recognised as such or no longer recognised; still fluid and
> florid, or now solid-grown and colourless? . . . An unmeta-
> phorical style you shall in vain seek for: is not your very
> *Attention* a *Stretching-to?* (73)

"Than which paragraph on Metaphors," The Editor exclaims,
"did the reader ever chance to see a more surprisingly metaphorical?" (74). Indeed: This extravagantly "metaphorical paragraph
on metaphors" argues that Teufelsdröckh's rhetorical and figurative strategies are not fortuitous but programmatic, because
metaphor, as the "stuff" of "imagination" and the essential con-
stituent of "Language," is here revealed as the real matrix of Teufelsdröckh's concerns, simultaneously his subject and his

method, his medium and his message. The terms of the passage make what Teufelsdröckh has to say about "Thought" convertible with what he has to say about "Language"; what licenses this freedom is precisely the dialectical strategies allowed by metaphor in general and by the ambiguity of the clothing metaphor in particular. For example, "Language is called the Garment of Thought: however, it should rather be, Language is the Flesh-Garment, the Body, of Thought" – the tone of which suggests the making of fine distinctions, when actually the clothing-versus-body terms of the metaphor are being conflated, via the middle term, "Flesh-Garment," into a compound clothing-cum-body. (Also spectrally present here is the other term polar to "body," namely "soul," which Teufelsdröckh has just reminded us is "said to be *clothed* with a *body*" [my emphasis].)

But more important than interpreting the metaphor is the observation that this "metaphorical paragraph on metaphors" makes its point both by precept and by example, both by what it *says* and what it *does*. It is an ancient commonplace of rhetoricians that metaphor provides an ornamental clothing for thought; Teufelsdröckh's claim is grander, that metaphor is no mere "adventitious wrappage" of thought, but also its body and even its soul; it does not merely adorn, it *constitutes* thought. Metaphor is both the ur-"stuff" and the end product of imagination's weaving – and more, it is also the weaver, the activity of weaving, and the eventual wearer of the finished "Flesh-Garment": "What is it all but Metaphor?" Teufelsdröckh's arch-metaphor, the clothing metaphor, for all the varied and playfully contradictory meanings with which Teufelsdröckh invests it, is first and last a metaphor for metaphor itself.

This suggests that we approach a Teufelsdröckhian sense of things less by interpreting his (or any) metaphors than by observing how they behave. That they *do* "behave," that (unlike "facts") they change and transform, lending themselves to shifting possibilities of meaning, suggests their value for a freedom-loving intelligence as an alternative to the cause-and-effect belief system according to which all is determined by physical laws that are by definition unchanging and in relation to which will and mind had best acquiesce in the stoic manner of billiard balls in collision. And of course Teufelsdröckh means us to understand that the billiard-table universe of Enlightenment physics, that "naturally" self-regulating and constant *céleste mécanique,* is itself only a metaphor, and its adherents "dotards" (as in "Custom doth make dotards of us all" [259]) to the extent that they have forgotten this and allowed habitual recourse to their metaphor to make it among them a metaphor "no longer recognised as such," that is, a metaphor taken (mis-taken) literally. How we become victims of our own metaphors Teufelsdröckh explains in the chapter of Book 3 called "Symbols," which resumes (and, as we shall see, revises) what Book 1 has to say about "Metaphor":

> Fantastic tricks enough man has played, in his time; has fancied himself to be most things . . . but to fancy himself a dead Iron-Balance for weighing Pains and Pleasures on, was reserved for this latter era. . . . Alas, poor devil! spectres are appointed to haunt him: one age he is hag-ridden, bewitched; the next, priest-ridden, befooled; in all ages, bedevilled. And now the Genius of Mechanism smothers him worse than any Nightmare did; till the soul is nigh choked out of him, and only a kind of Digestive, Mechanic life remains. In Earth and in Heaven he can see nothing but Mechanism; has fear for nothing else, hope in nothing else: the world would indeed grind him to pieces; but cannot he fathom the Doctrine of Motives, and cunningly compute these, and mechanise them to grind another way? (220–1)

We become what we behold, especially when we have forgotten that what we behold – whether metaphor or custom – is an invention of our own imagining.

As we have seen, Teufelsdröckh identifies custom – one of the most persistent of the clothing metaphor's meanings – as the nemesis of "wonder" and "worship"; and what "Custom" shares with "Metaphor" is a fatal susceptibility to a kind of literalization, a naïve mistaking of a fictive human invention for a "natural" and immutable feature of the human condition. A custom "no longer recognised as such" is a custom beyond question, and hence beyond human power to be "altered and made to serve better" or "mechanised to grind another way":

> Custom . . . doth make dotards of us all. . . . Custom is the greatest of Weavers; and weaves air-raiment for all the Spir-

its of the Universe; whereby indeed these dwell with us visibly . . . but their spiritual nature becomes, to the most, forever hidden. (259)

"Custom" here assumes, in relation to social institutions and traditions, a role very like that of "Metaphor" in relation to language and thought: It is the "weaver" (note the recurrence of that metaphor) whose thoroughly fictive action, when "no longer recognised as such," compels literal belief in a fashion to rob us of imagination's "thaumaturgic" prerogatives – an outcome Teufelsdröckh protests, and aims to correct, by the mere bringing of insight, by enforcing recognition of fictions *as* fictions (metaphors, customs, "old clothes") that are "no longer recognised as such":

> Philosophy complains that Custom has hoodwinked us . . . that we do everything by Custom, even Believe by it; that our very Axioms, let us boast of Free-thinking as we may, are oftenest simply such beliefs as we have never heard questioned. Nay, what is Philosophy throughout but a continual battle against Custom; an ever-renewed effort to *transcend* the sphere of blind Custom, and so become Transcendental? (259)

Clearly, this "ever-renewed effort" of "Philosophy" to "*transcend* the sphere of blind Custom, and so become Transcendental" is identifiable with the Teufelsdröckhian project of "seeing through," of mobilizing a consciousness of "the grand thaumaturgic art of Thought" (118) in behalf of a general palingenetic "re-tailoring" of the collective imagination.

The thaumaturgic *art* of thought, then, is, like the "proper art of reading," a kind of thaumaturgic *work* – but very different from the "Work" of Carlyle's later doctrine. Here the project of "seeing through," of reordering the utilitarian calculus of motives so that they "grind another way," is a work of deliberate and self-conscious mind, of intelligence conceived as shrewd, deliberate, analytic, even, in a certain sense, opportunistic and self-interested. Such a project implies a view of the mind and its powers radically at odds with the "anti-self-consciousness theory" we usually associate with Carlyle and diametrically opposed to the precept Carlyle formulated in "Characteristics" within months of finishing *Sartor* that "the sign of health is Unconsciousness" (*Works,* 28:4). In "Characteristics," self-consciousness appears as an inescapable evil, whereas in *Sartor,* Teufelsdröckh's exemplary self-consciousness figures as a means for self-knowledge and self-empowering, conceived as ends worthy and notable in themselves. In "Characteristics," famously, "the healthy know not of their health, but only the sick" (*Works,* 28:1); *Sartor* affirms the converse – that unconsciousness of one's condition is virtual death – in all those "Descendentalist" scenes of hangings, wars, pomps of state, in which human beings are reduced to mere "clothes-screens," and their affairs to "the Somnambulism of uneasy Sleepers." In "Characteristics," "the beginning of Inquiry is Disease," and as in *Genesis,* "the Tree of Knowledge springs from a root of evil" (*Works,* 28:2); *Sartor,* on the contrary, has no more fundamental aim than to incite and provoke "Inquiry" and proposes that a deliberate mindfulness is the way of access to "Fantasy" and "Imagination," the "organ[s] . . . of the God-like" within. The implied invitation here, to become as gods, indicates the audacity of Teufelsdröckh's enterprise and his disregard of injunctions prevailing since Eden that would circumscribe the prerogatives of intellect and imagination.

Teufelsdröckh would surely agree with the later Carlyle that "work" is the single most comprehensive term for the imperatives and possibilities of the human condition, but there is a world of difference between the later Carlyle's dutiful affair of "Silence" and "Obedience" and the revelatory "self-activity" that is Teufelsdröckh's conception of "work":

A certain inarticulate Self-consciousness dwells dimly in us; which only our Works can render articulate and decisively discernible. Our Works are the mirror wherein the spirit first sees its natural lineaments. (162)

Here work is a mirror to the soul, a medium for self-knowledge, not, as in the later Carlyle, an anodyne against it. (Compare Max Weber's characterization of the place of "good works" in the predestinarian psychology of Calvinism: Good works are "the technical means, not of purchasing salvation, but of getting rid of the fear of damnation.")[11]

Esoteric Comedies

Ironically, the nearest thing in *Sartor* to the later Carlyle's doctrine of "Work" as narcotic rather than thaumaturgic is The Editor's (of course) comic misapprehension of the Teufelsdröckhian sense of work. The Editor regularly produces, as an image of his own "work" of ordering Teufelsdröckh's chaos, an allusion from *Paradise Lost* whose implications could hardly be more malapropos:

> Over such a universal medley of high and low, of hot, cold, moist and dry is [The Editor] here struggling . . . to build a Bridge for British travellers. Never perhaps since our first Bridge-builders, Sin and Death, built that stupendous Arch from Hell-gate to the Earth, did any Pontifex, or Pontiff, undertake such a task as the present Editor. (79–80)

This "pontificating" labor (The Editor seems as oblivious to the inappropriateness of these Romish associations as to that of the Miltonic ones) aims, ironically, at just the sort of domestication of the strange and the wondrous that it is precisely Teufelsdröckh's "thaumaturgic" ambition to undo. But The Editor is so fond of his Miltonic figure of speech that he recurs to it no fewer than four more times (205, 208, 225, 268) in the remainder of *Sartor Resartus*.

Book 1's climactic assertion that in the realm of mind "all is Metaphor" (rather than "Fact"), and the cognate implication that in the affairs of societies, all (politics, institutions, morals) is "Custom" (and hence referable to culture rather than nature), sustain the Teufelsdröckhian apocalypse at its most radical, protesting, like Emerson, the condition in which "Things are in the saddle, / And ride mankind" or, like Marx, the condition in which "everything is an authority."[12] Under the thrall of materialism and positivism, duped by paradigms (or metaphors) "no longer recognised as such," but mistaken for literal truth, "we have argued away all force from ourselves" (*Works,* 27:79); and it is this sorry impotence Carlyle-Teufelsdröckh means to redeem by the revelation of the "grand thaumaturgic art of Thought":

> Our Life is compassed round with Necessity; yet is the meaning of Life itself no other than Freedom, than Voluntary Force. (183)

70

Carlyle's Sartor Resartus

The WORD is well-said to be omnipotent in this world;
man, thereby divine, can create as by a *Fiat.* (199)

Culture versus Nature, "Metaphor" versus "Symbol"

Given this radical assertion of the sovereignty of mind and imagination over material and historical circumstance, how does Carlyle become a byword for reaction, pessimism, and political
despair? First, and most simply, Carlyle could not follow Teufelsdröckh so far as to dissolve the explanatory category of
"nature" entirely into "culture." Carlyle seems committed to the
proposition that language and thought are "all metaphor," that
the order of signifiers is constituted by the human mind, but
balks at an idealism sufficiently thoroughgoing to ascribe the
order of the signified likewise entirely to the constituting collective imagination. Just a year before starting to write the piece
"On Clothes," which would become *Sartor Resartus,* Carlyle
wrote in his notebook:

> All language but that concerning *sensual* objects is or has
> been figurative. Prodigious influence of metaphors! Never
> saw into it till lately. A truly useful and philosophical work
> would be a good *Essay on Metaphors.* Someday I will write
> one! (*TNB,* 141–2)

"On Clothes," which survives as Book 1 of *Sartor,* is, in a sense,
the *Essay on Metaphors* Carlyle projects here. But on the very
next page of his notebook, Carlyle jots down a quotation from
Hooker that revealingly invokes "nature": "'The mixture of
those things by speech which by nature are divided is the mother
of all error'" (*TNB,* 143). Here "nature" functions to limit and
check the "mixture" of diverse things allowed to "speech" (language). While "mixture" suggests such joining of disjunct things
(e.g., seraphs and fiends) as The Editor condemns in Teufelsdröckh, it also suggests metaphor itself, which affirms, sometimes
with apocalyptic force, likeness in unlike things. We may speculate, for example, that Hooker would endorse the "mixture" of
"my love" with "a red red rose" but not, perhaps, of "the evening
laid out against the sky" with "a patient etherized upon a table."
In making such discriminations, Hooker would be appealing to

71

"nature." Carlyle, with his fantastic Teufelsdröckhian wit, seems in his "Descendentalist" moods admirably equipped to appreciate the uses of self-consciously "un-natural" metaphors – but when he aspires to the "Transcendental," he seeks to redeem the estrangement from "nature" that his apocalypse of metaphor requires and incites: hence the doctrine elaborated in *Sartor*'s Book 3, of "Symbols," which might seem a reprise of Book 1's "Metaphor" but actually revises and compromises it, assimilating it not to an idealism whose terms and figures ("Metaphors") are compliant to human will and are thus alterable in history, but to a "Supernaturalism" that shall be, precisely, "Natural" and whose "Symbols" are not assignable by the "thaumaturgic art of Thought" but are bound unalterably by "Organic Filaments" to their "natural" referents.

Book 1's doctrine of "Metaphors" affirmed the sovereignty of mind as a function of mind's emancipation, even alienation, from a literal-minded thralldom to fictions that the mind has forgotten were its own creations to begin with, fictions "no longer recognised as such." In contrast to this "seeing through," Book 3, written at a different time and (as we shall see) out of very different ambitions, addresses the human hunger for absolute belief in objects that shall solicit and inspire utter obedience. We are "encompassed with Symbols," writes Teufelsdröckh in Book 3, and he observes, in the now familiar phrase, that these symbols are either "recognised as such or not recognised" (220) – but here the hitherto crucial distinction seems to make no difference:

> It is in and through *Symbols* that man, consciously or unconsciously, lives, works, and has his being; those ages are accounted the noblest which can the best recognise symbolical worth, and prize it the highest. For is not a Symbol ever, to him who has eyes for it, some dimmer or clearer revelation of the God-like? (222)

In Book 1, everything depended upon the recognition or nonrecognition of metaphors and customs "as such": Recognition was freedom and transcendental; nonrecognition was thralldom and virtual death. But here? Here, "consciously or unconsciously," we have differences not of kind but only of degree: Ages are more or less noble; the revelation of the symbol is clearer or dimmer.

Here to "recognise symbolical worth and prize it the highest" is to "see through" not to an ultimate contingent fictiveness, but to an ultimate immutable truth. To "recognise" a symbol in this way is to identify it with its "truth" (rather than to detach it from a former "truth," now discernible as an outworn meaning) and hence to license just the sort of assent that it was the work of Book 1's revelation concerning "Metaphors" to undo. The "Symbol" binds itself and the beholder to its "natural" and "true" meaning; the "Metaphor" affirms the fictiveness in the beholder's eye of its relation to a culturally constituted referent. In Book 3, the symbolical character of the "Symbol" is less important than what the "Symbol" means, whereas in Book 1, it is precisely the recognition that the "Metaphor" is a "Metaphor," the recognition of metaphor "as such," that emancipates the perceiving subject from all given meanings and affirms its sovereignty over the meaning-making activity.

"Metaphor" is radical in its insistence that meanings are always provisional, and in the license it affords to the invention of new ones; "Symbol" more cautiously conserves old meanings and calls them truths. "Metaphor" implicitly assigns all questions of belief, motive, historical and social change to culture rather than nature, insisting that both the impositions of the old (custom, mistakenly lent the sanctions of nature) and of the new (the mechanistic metaphors of materialist science, mistaken for literal truths, or facts) are given by culture; "Symbol," by contrast, grounds the historical process in an eternal and immutable nature. "Metaphor" implies that every historical situation is new, whereas "Symbol" pictures every historical situation as referable to an eternal standard and all of history as a mere oscillation between a proper and ideal "naturalness" and variously corrupted departures from it. The affirmation that "all [is] but Metaphors, recognised as such, or no longer recognised" (73) licences a thorough revision of our human world and (the same thing) our imagination of it; "Symbol" reverts to nature as a standard and a source of legitimacy and "truth." The inventions of "Metaphor" are vehicles for new discovery and thus agents of change in history; in a "Symbol," by contrast, "the commonest Truth stands out to us proclaimed with quite new emphasis" (219) – which is to say that "Symbols" merely locate truths already existent, though perhaps hidden or obscured beneath a film of habit and custom. "Metaphor" implies that new clothes make a new man; "Symbol" implies that new clothes merely lend a pristine appearance to the same essentially unchanged old Adam.

Finally, "Metaphor" and "Symbol" imply radically opposed epistemologies: on the one hand, a thoroughgoing idealism that locates the causes of all historical and social change in the processes of history and culture themselves; on the other, a sublimated (even "supernatural") naturalism that grounds the human (historical and cultural) condition in nature. Hence the limitations and compromises of Carlyle's radicalism and the characteristically Carlylean irony that the decisive check on Carlyle's radicalism is also its enabling premise, namely his philosophical idealism. The difficulty with even so penetrating an effort to excavate a thoroughly radical Carlyle as Philip Rosenberg's in *The Seventh Hero* is that insofar as Carlyle approaches the radical tradition in assigning all explanatory power to culture rather than to nature, he diverges from it in doing so on idealist rather than materialist grounds, and so remains a radical more of Hegel's kind than Marx's. Not that Carlyle ever read Hegel: His infatuation with German philosophy spent itself with Kant, and thus he never had the benefit of Hegel's powerful construction of the antimaterialist thesis (the one Marx stood on its head) that material conditions follow consciousness.[13] But of course whatever a reading of Hegel might have done for Carlyle, it could not have made him proof against the reading of the daily newspaper, wherein each morning he saw, with ironic and grimly self-lacerating satisfaction, fresh evidence that if material conditions follow consciousness, they do so chiefly for the worse and almost never for the better – whence the increasing intemperance and exasperation of his output, even as his applause and celebrity grew: He had made himself the prophet of a "Transcendental" future, but had to address a cultural situation growing (to his eye) more "Descendental" by the day. Hence the further irony that it is precisely as Carlyle's thinking approaches materialism, and his language appropriates its rhetoric of "Fact," that his expression and mood turn most reactionary. Raymond Williams eloquently recognizes that the pathos of the late Carlyle is "that a genuine insight, a genuine vision, should be dragged down by the very situation, the very structure of relationships, to which it was opposed, until a civilizing insight became in its operation barbarous."[14] Indeed: Carlyle's compulsive struggle against materialism amounts in the end to virtual, if unacknowledged, capitulation to it.

Transcendental Idealism, "Descendental" Solipsism

But perhaps even that way of putting it overstates Carlyle's idealism. In fundamental ways, Carlyle distrusts his own ingenious transcendentalizing and cannot bring himself to believe altogether (to believe at all, in some moods) in his Teufelsdröckhian affirmations of the "thaumaturgic art of Thought." Carlyle's idealist "Transcendentalism," his commitment to the notion that mind constitutes, rather than merely perceives, reality, is always qualified by the persistence within him of an earthy and shrewd Scottish-peasant self, impatient of all pretense, folderol, and "transcendental moonshine." This is the Carlyle who, even as a young man, could pronounce his idol Goethe "the greatest genius that has lived for a century, and the greatest ass that has lived for three" (*Letters,* 2:437),[15] or scoffingly dismiss Coleridge, "the Kantean metaphysician and quondam Lake poet," as "unprofitable, even tedious . . . a man of great and useless genius" (*Letters,* 3:90–1). Here Carlyle on Goethe sounds (again) very much like The Editor on Teufelsdröckh – and prefigures the defeat of his wild, democratic Teufelsdröckh self by that quasi-Burkean conservative, The Editor in himself, the downright and commonsensical Carlyle driven at last in desperation to appropriate the materialist rhetoric of "Fact" to his antimaterialist purposes, until at last his obsessive combat with materialism seems motivated less by a conviction of its falsity than by an anxious apprehension of its truth.[16]

Carlyle's temperamental susceptibility to such ironic apprehensions is as often abetted as palliated by the intellectualizations (his philosophical idealism) meant to rationalize and sustain his "thaumaturgic art of Thought":

So that this so solid-seeming World, after all, were but an air-image, our ME the only reality: and Nature, with its thousandfold production and destruction, but the reflex of our own inward Force, the "phantasy of our Dream." (55)

75

This Teufelsdröckhian utterance seems just the sort of "Transcendental" affirmation The Editor is always hungering for: an uplifting, magniloquent declaration of the sovereignty of "our ME," "our inward Force," over the merely material "so seeming-solid World," and so on – in short, an enabling premise from which to deduce the entire liberating and triumphant "thaumaturgic art of Thought." But in context it is no such thing, for Teufelsdröckh produces it in the course of explaining the depression and despair from which his spiritual quest had departed – and to which, throughout his life, Carlyle was chronically subject – in which all human endeavor seems empty and meaningless, a kind of collective sleepwalk:

> What [is it all] but the Somnambulism of uneasy Sleepers? This Dreaming, this Somnambulism is what we on Earth call Life; wherein the most indeed undoubtedly wander, as if they knew right hand from left; yet they only are wise who know that they know nothing. (54)

In "The Everlasting No," Teufelsdröckh describes the mind-created world of his youthful despair in a fashion to remind us that the "thaumaturgic art of Thought" may create a "Descendental" universe of death and dreck as well as a "Transcendental" world of "Wonder and Worship":

> To me the Universe was all void of Life, of Purpose, of Volition, even of Hostility: it was one huge, dead, immeasureable Steam-engine, rolling on, in its dead indifference, to grind me limb from limb. O, the vast gloomy, solitary Golgotha, and Mill of Death! (165)

Idealism "Descendentalised," in short, is alienation of the worst and most desperate kind: solipsism. The ironic liability of Carlyle's idealism is that its demonstration that the mind-forged manacles enchaining us are phantasmal enjoins the corollary that our liberating Daedalus wings of imagination are likewise unreal. What makes the difference, in short, between "The Everlasting No" and "The Everlasting Yea," between despair and faith, between death-in-life and life itself, is nothing more firm than a state of mind.

It is no accident that the most important and long standing of Carlyle's personal "Heroes" should be the prophet of this perception, and of its terror: Luther, psychologist of a redemptive, salvationist "faith" that "works" (or "Work") cannot compel. If Carlyle's "Transcendental" hopes can be called Lutheran, in that they look for profound and redemptive change, his ineradicably "Descendental" sense of ironic futility registers the steady-state predestinarian Calvinism whose temperamental anxieties – of fatedness, of *non*change – Carlyle's hopeful "thaumaturgic art of Thought" could only intermittently assuage.[17] Yet Carlyle's hopes of change, of "conversion" (to use Carlyle's Lutheran word), assume more-than-Lutheran burdens, for whereas Luther regards "conversion" as an affair of individual souls, Carlyle's ambition is to extend the possibility of such change to collectives, to nations and societies. Carlyle is nowhere so "puritanical" in the seventeenth-century sense as in his congenital and imperative assumption that individual salvations model political ones. His assimilation of Lutheran soteriological hopes to the insights of Enlightenment sociology aims to fit the observed facts of historical change, but founders on the unrecognised irreconcilability of the former's catastrophe model of qualitative change with the latter's uniformitarian model of merely quantitative change.

Carlyle's conflation of the categories of culture and nature damages his thaumaturgic program. "Natural Supernaturalism," his grand vista of humanity and nature bound together by "Organic Filaments," is finally only a transcendentalized version of Enlightenment naturalism and thus rather a sublimation of the mechanistic, cause-and-effect world view than a refutation of it. Notwithstanding all talk of the transcendental, the consequence is a naïve immanentism, whence the extravagance of Carlyle's late pessimism and the inevitable disappointment of his too-grand political hopes. When the world – history, politics, "everything that is the case" – commences, as it will, to look grim rather than lovely, the consequences can only be desperate: Such has been the fate of every theodicy since Job that insists too much on the intervention of the divine in human affairs.

Carlyle is insufficiently rigorous a thinker to have articulated all this to himself; the opposed possibilities communicate their tensions to his writing only the more profoundly because the contradictions are so largely unacknowledged, "not recognised as such." It is important to remember (what some critics forget) that Carlyle is a *writer,* not a *thinker;* he tests ideas not analytically in thought, but by their power to summon *in the writing,* on the blank page before him, his own excited assent and an "inspiration" very like, in its effects, the "belief" he so often wants to compel upon his reader. To Carlyle, dispassionate reflection and cool analytic inquiry look like mere logic chopping, dilettante toying with ideas, and (worse) Whiggish *via media*-ism. In a letter to Mill (October 28, 1833, just as *Sartor* was commencing publication in *Fraser's*), Carlyle expresses his contempt of the middle of the road and his preference for the boundaries, where extremes meet:

> The true Atheist in these days is the Whig: he worships nothing but Respectability . . . The Tory is an Idolator; the Radical a wild heathen Iconoclast: yet neither of them strictly are "without God in the world": the one has an *infinite* hope, the other an infinite remembrance. (*Letters,* 7:23)

Here Carlyle revealingly distinguishes the conflicted elements of his own character, the "Radical Iconoclast" represented by Teufelsdröckh in his "Descendental" moods, and the faith-hungry "Tory," prophet of "sincere idolatry" (as Carlyle would call it in *Heroes*), audible in Teufelsdröckh's "Transcendental" rhapsodies – and perhaps more so (and more tellingly) in The Editor's eager applause of them. What the "Radical Iconoclast" of *Sartor*'s Book 1 and the "Tory Idolator" of Book 3 share is a talent and a need for afflatus, and under its spell, whether of "Descendental" wit or of "Transcendental" rapture, Carlyle is lost to the intellectual contradictions whose toll on his emotional and spiritual life would eventually be so great. To trace the surrender of the "infinite hope" of the Radical idol breaker to the "infinite remembrance" of the Tory idol monger is to trace the defeat of Carlyle's youthful hopes of personal and political change before the despairing resignation, the obsessive self-distrust, and the angry (yet also guilty) *contemptus mundi* of his maturity, in which "infinite remembrance" is haunted by the "tradition of all the dead generations [that] weighs like a nightmare on the brain of the living."[18]

Carlyle's Sartor Resartus

The License of "Nonsense," the Burden of *"Literature"*

Still, how did the one sort of afflatus, the "Descendental" wit of the "Radical Iconoclast," come to give way so totally, between Books 1 and 3 of *Sartor Resartus,* to the other, the transcendentalizing of the "Tory Idolator"? Or to put it another way, how are these two conflicting elements, usually compounded so inextricably, so thoroughly (and so uniquely) precipitated out from each other in *Sartor Resartus?* One explanation is that Carlyle's ambitions changed as he was writing: His initial idea was to write something lighthearted and humorous ("I am going to write – Nonsense" [*TNB*, 176]) for *Fraser's;* he wrote and put in the mail fifty pages and, while waiting for the verdict, continued writing. Before long, he was thinking of the piece as two articles rather than one, then as a book rather than magazine writing at all. When *Fraser's* delayed decision, Carlyle wrote to his brother (January 21, 1831) instructing him to withdraw the manuscript and announcing plans for lengthening the work:

> I can devise some more Biography for Teufelsdreck [*sic:* the revision to "Teufelsdröckh" came later]; give a second deeper part, in the same vein, leading thro' Religion and the nature of Society and Lord knows what. (*Letters*, 5:215)

Eventually, through a sequence of ironies that greatly galled Carlyle, the "book" thus lengthened and de-*Fraser*-ized wound up being serialized in *Fraser's* after all. But the project outlined above suggests that (roughly speaking) the present Book 1 is the initial fifty-page manuscript sent to *Fraser's,* that additions afterward encompassed some of the present Book 2 (which narrates Teufelsdröckh's "Biography"), and the as yet unwritten "deeper part . . . leading thro' Religion and the nature of Society" would become the present Book 3.

Clearly, the book evolved from an initial *Fraser*-ian "Nonsense" to a "deeper," more earnest effort toward "prophecy," to use the word by which Carlyle, in his letters and notebooks, refers to his grandest literary ambitions. If Book 1 was launched under a quasi-Swiftian aegis, Book 3 seems to be sponsored rather by Goethe. In Book 1, Teufelsdröckh is a satirist and critic of culture, debunking and demythologizing it; in Book 3, he is its sanctifier and celebrant, a prophet, even a priest, of culture's resa-cralization. "Seeing through" culture in Book 1 left the world "Naked," denuded of all "adventitious wrappages"; the project of Book 3, by contrast, is to reclothe and retailor the world thus denuded in new finery. (Incidentally, the book's present title, which announces the "re-clothing" theme, was virtually the manuscript's last touch, coming fully two years after the writing had been completed; Carlyle settled on the title after *Fraser's* had agreed to publish the manuscript in mid-1833.)

But this change of program, from "Descendental" wit to "Transcendental" rhapsode, was no mere quick-change of liter-ary roles, a versatile writer's facile shift from one sort of literary performance to another. It was rather a process that began for Carlyle as an escape from the heavy burdens of literary ambition with which he had encumbered himself, but inexorably became a vehicle for realizing just those ambitions. It began as a relief from a sort of literary identity crisis, but became an exercise of confronting and negotiating that crisis. The crisis had been of long standing when Carlyle first set to work, in autumn 1830, on what would become *Sartor Resartus;* as his *Two Note Books* show, throughout late 1829 and 1830 Carlyle was acutely depressed about his work, his prospects, his inability to locate his proper subject, to get started. He was experiencing writer's block, excoriating himself as a "Vain Pretender" to literary promise, and profoundly anxious over the (perhaps irredeemable) waste of his talent in hack work and book reviewing.

In September 1830, he records the arrival of the first copies of *Fraser's* he has yet seen and his reaction to them:

Last night came a whole bundle of Fraser Magazines . . . on the whole such a hurlyburly of rhodomontade, punch, loy-alty, and Saturnalian Toryism as eye hath not seen. This out-Blackwoods Blackwood. Nevertheless the thing has its meaning: a kind of wild popular Lower-Comedy . . . a cer-tain quickness, fluency of banter, not excluding sharp insight, and Merry-Andrew Drollery, and even Humour, are available here; however the grand requisite seems to be Impudence, and a fearless committing of yourself to talk in your Drink. – *Literature* has *nothing* to do with this. (*TNB*, 170)

Later that month: "I am going to write – Nonsense. It is on 'Clothes.' Heaven be my comforter!" (*TNB*, 172). By October 28 (only seven weeks after the first sight of *Fraser's*), the piece seems finished: "Have written a strange piece 'On Clothes': know not what will become of it" (*TNB*, 177). Shortly thereafter it is in the mail to *Fraser's*.

What my version of this oft-told story means to emphasize is that *Sartor Resartus* was initially conceived as a bit of "wild popular Lower-Comedy" and that what was liberating about this for Carlyle was just its eschewal of any claim to high seriousness: *"Literature"* – the emphasis is Carlyle's – "has *nothing* to do with this." Carlyle liked the piece he was writing and kept having new ideas for it. No more writer's block: For once in a very long while he had a project on which he could not *stop* writing. But he did not regard the thing as a consequential undertaking; indeed, at the turn of the year, surveying the old year's accomplishment, he does not mention "Clothes" at all and summarily pronounces 1830 "one of the most worthless years I have spent in a long time" (*TNB*, 181). Not until the early months of 1831 does Carlyle begin to think of "Clothes" as potentially approaching art, *"Literature,"* and "Prophecy" – approaching something, that is, that might answer to his ambitions.

Self, *"Selbst-tödtung,"* and Literary Ambition

In this conflict of great ambition with enormous inhibition, we confront the most conflicted issue in Carlyle, the issue of "self." Anxiety about self and self-consciousness runs throughout Carlyle's writings; and there can be no doubt that something in him profoundly distrusted the powerful impulse of self-assertion that made him write. At age nineteen, Carlyle could confess a hankering for "literary fame" (*Letters*, 1:20–1);[19] yet in London in January 1832, with magazine articles behind him but *Sartor* as yet unpublished, Carlyle sees his name "in large letters at the Athenaeum Office," and rather than feeling exhilaration at the sight, as most young writers would, Carlyle reports that he "hurried on with downcast eyes, as if I had seen myself in the Pillory" (*TNB*, 232). Carlyle subscribed to a psychology according to which "self" is the matrix of everything manipulative, low, and grasping in the human constitution; ambition is thus necessarily

81

guilty, accomplishment perhaps more so; it is this psychology that underwrites his distrust of self-consciousness and his celebration of unconsciousness as the condition devoutly (however impossibly) to be wished for.

And so Carlyle's ineradicable sense of "self" as the ur-source of all moral trouble incites a severe and often crippling tension between his powerful ambition and his guilty, reflexive, Calvinist self-distrust. I have written at length above about the intellectual inconsistencies and contradictions that riddle Carlyle's utterance, but they only express the nervous tic of what Freud prompts me to call Carlyle's "moral masochism";[20] it is Carlyle's congenital disposition to self-distrust, rather than lapses of analytic power, that ensure that his grandest visions are always parodied in the most dogged fashion by his grimmest ones. His work of "Prophecy" is always haunted by the worry that it betrays (perhaps damnable) vanity and presumption, and his distrust of satire and wit is likewise the more acute precisely because his own powers in that direction are so formidable: because satire and prophecy alike presume to judge – which, as Jesus warns in the Sermon on the Mount ("Judge not that ye be not judged"), is to presume a great deal. Those who judge invite special judgment upon themselves.

Yet as we have seen, the Teufelsdröckh of Book 2 is a brash, witty, ironic, and exuberantly assertive "self," in style and demeanor far more a creature of the George IV era than a harbinger of that Victorianism that would increasingly value earnestness and sincerity and elevate self-distrust into an obligatory moral decorum. Carlyle himself is, famously, one of the great troublers of the Victorian awareness of "self" and so, arguably, is the Teufelsdröckh of Books 2 and 3 of *Sartor*. The centerpiece of "The Everlasting Yea," the chapter in Book 2 that narrates Teufelsdröckh's conversion from doubt and despair to faith and confidence, is *"Selbst-tödtung,"* or "Annihilation of Self." Given the constancy of Carlyle's anxieties about "self," how can we account for Teufelsdröckh himself, that self-conscious and haughty ironist whose advent apparently made the composition of *Sartor* possible at all for Carlyle?

The first answer is the easiest one: the wit, irony, and self-consciousness belong to Teufelsdröckh, not to Carlyle. As every writer knows, to speak through personae can be liberating.[21] Car-

Carlyle's Sartor Resartus

lyle deploys masks elsewhere – Gottfried Sauertieg, Smelfungus Redivivus, and Teufelsdröckh himself all appear in writing that predates *Sartor,* but without generating effects at all comparable to *Sartor*'s; they appear as no more than the trifling jests of an authorial first person they never eclipse or usurp. In *Sartor,* by contrast, Carlyle never speaks *in propria persona;* all voices in the text are assigned to characters whose flagrant fictiveness licenses displays of extremity and extravagance that Carlyle would never allow himself. The personae of *Sartor* afford full scope to Carlyle's powers of wit and irony precisely by obviating the need, even the possibility, of first-person utterance.

The personae of *Sartor Resartus* enact a dispersal of Carlyle's first-person self that amounts to a kind of literary equivalent of that *Selbst-tödtung,* or "Annihilation of Self," that Teufelsdröckh so self-assertively celebrates. It is ironic and paradoxical – in very much the Teufelsdröckhian manner – that Carlyle's first and most original work should parody the forms of the book review, the introduction, the translation, the selected edition, since these were just the sorts of hack work, falling far short of the estate of genuine "authorship," that Carlyle feared were destroying his talent. And yet in all their protean instability, Diogenes Teufelsdröckh and The Editor assume, between them, the entire inventory of literary roles, often conflicting ones, that Carlyle had ever contemplated for himself: satirist and panegyrist, oracle and interpreter, prophet and persifleur, philosopher and propagandist, wise man and clown, rhapsode and critic, hero and hero worshipper, innovator and conserver, social commentator, historian, biographer, autobiographer, fictionist.

If speaking through personae was liberating to a writer so "self"-obsessed, so was the convention that magazine writing was published anonymously. Carlyle began writing his "Thoughts on Clothes" at a time when he was lacerating himself for not having written or even started a book-length project – "something of my own" (*Letters,* 5:164), as he plaintively puts it in a letter to his brother. Carlyle was initially emboldened by the prospect of anonymous publication, but as his ambitions for his manuscript became grander, he became less content with the usual arrangements whereby the authorship of anonymously printed articles remained common knowledge in and around Fleet Street. Carlyle wanted more anonymity than that. A passion for secrecy begins to appear in his letters from Craigenputtock to his brother in London, directing the effort to get the manuscript published. Carlyle wants as few people as possible to know that he is the author; at one point he anxiously reckons that no fewer than *five* people in London know that "Clothes" is his, and he worries about their trustworthiness with this momentous intelligence. The reason for this secretiveness? "I fear perfect *anonymity* is now out of the question; however swear everyone to secrecy, for I mean to speak fearlessly if at all" (*Letters,* 5:215–6). Carlyle evidently feels that if he is to speak what is within him, he needs freedom from the constraints and inhibitions the overseeing eye of public attention would arouse. (Was it the indecency of his satire that worried him? It seems significant that throughout the protracted period of writing the book and trying to find a publisher, Carlyle's letters to his mother consistently evade her inquiries as to the book's title and theme; likewise his letters to another important superego figure, Goethe. To his intimates, by contrast, his brothers Jack and Alick and above all to Jane, the manuscript is jokingly called "Dreck." Attenuating the indecency of "Teufelsdreck" may have partly motivated the revision to "Teufelsdröckh"; it seems telling that in the summer of 1833, fully two years after finishing the book, when he had at last found a publisher and was facing the prospect of soon seeing in print the manuscript he had for three years been calling *Thoughts on Clothes; or Life & Opinions of Herr D. Teufelsdreck* [alias Teufelsdröckh] *D.U.J.,* Carlyle began casting around for another title, finally alighting on *Sartor Resartus,* which discreetly removes the professor's provocative name.)

Style

The aspect of his own talent that Carlyle seems most certain of, the solidest validation he has of his own genius, is his style.[22] Throughout his early career Carlyle is acutely aware of forging a style at once distinctive, individual, and appropriate for the "sincere" expression of the prophecy he hopes to utter. At its most confident, Carlyle's writing behaves in something like a modernist way, as if "style" itself has a substantive importance in expression, so that to say something, even an old thing, in a new way, is virtually to say a new thing. (Carlyle's "Descendental" corollary of this exalted view of style is that canting and dull expression can make worthy truths seem false.) At other times, Carlyle disdains or distrusts style as a mere instrument or trick, detachable from content, often a distraction and sometimes actually a deceit. The two positions, style as constitutive versus style as ornamental, correspond, again, to everything implied in the distinction between "Metaphor" and "Symbol": Either new clothes make a new man, or they do not.

The issue of style, then, touches in the most intimate way upon Carlyle's profoundest hopes and fears regarding the genius, originality, and sincerity of his own literary talent. As with his Teufelsdröckhian wit and Sansculottic politics, and for the same reasons, Carlyle risks in *Sartor Resartus* a stylistic audacity that goes far beyond his earlier writing; but unlike Teufelsdröckhian philosophical and political radicalism, "Carlylese" does *not* recede in work following *Sartor Resartus.* Through whatever other vacillations Carlyle passes, his style remains distinctive, and provocative. From the time when his style first began to become truly his own, Carlyle firmly resisted all criticism of it, even when the charges against it – egotistical affectation, self-regard, showoffishness – were of just the sort to chafe his Calvinist self-distrust most harshly. An illustrative case is the contretemps ensuing when Francis Jeffrey, editor of the prestigious *Edinburgh Review,* took a blue pencil to Carlyle's "Burns" manuscript, upbraiding Carlyle's *"jargon"* and his "use of words at the mere mention of which everybody at once recognises the writer, and smiles at the recollection" – insinuating that Carlyle exhibits an unseemly impatience with the anonymity of magazine publication. "I am afraid that you are a greater admirer of yourself than becomes a philosopher," Jeffrey intones:

> I am firmly persuaded the great source of your extravagance, and of all that makes your writings intolerable to many, and ridiculous to not a few, is not so much any real peculiarity of opinions as an unlucky ambition to appear more original than you are, or the humbler and still more delusive hope of converting our English intellects to the creed of Germany.[23]

These charges touch mockingly, and on the bull's-eye, some of Carlyle's dearest ambitions, even as they echo, almost verbatim, passages in the "Burns" essay itself in which Carlyle warns that a writer's lapses often combine with "a love of distinction, [and] a wish to be original" to produce "Affectation, the bane of literature" (*Works,* 26:268).[24] Jeffrey takes for granted that style and content are distinct; although he argues that Carlyle should adopt a simpler style by deprecating the originality of Carlyle's ideas, it is clear enough that even if Carlyle had a "real peculiarity of opinions" to offer, Jeffrey would want it presented in the *Edinburgh*'s blander house style.

Carlyle, however, is not to be daunted by talk of being "intolerable to many, and ridiculous to not a few." He refuses to bend the knee either to the reading public or to so influential a figure as Jeffrey himself. He threatened to withdraw the essay, threatened never to publish in the *Edinburgh* again, and when the proofs of "Burns" arrived, restored almost all of what Jeffrey had cut. Faced with risking affectation and egotism or letting others dictate his style, Carlyle unhesitatingly elected to persist in his folly – a testimony to the importance of style for him and the great degree to which he took style as implicated in character, character's "Flesh-Garment," rather than its mere "adventitious wrappage."

"The Authentic Lineaments of Fact and the Forged Ones of Fiction"

I have tried in the preceding pages to sketch Carlyle's esoteric comedy at its most radical and subversive and to indicate the forces within Carlyle that opposed and finally defeated it. Carlyle's protodeconstructionist faith (or conceit? – which is perhaps the whole problem) that imagination is sovereign because "all is Metaphor" is first compromised by an ideology of "Symbol" legitimated by a transcendentalized "Nature," then gradually eroded by a lifetime of disgruntlement. My presentation has rooted these latter developments in impulses of Carlyle's – his doomed "immanentism" and his fatal aspiration to preachify – that emerge in Books 2 and 3 of *Sartor,* when, after an initial liberation in "Nonsense" and "wild, popular Lower-Comedy," his heavier and more guilt-laden aspirations to *"Literature"* and

86

Carlyle's Sartor Resartus

"Prophecy" reasserted themselves. The argument has necessarily seemed to favor the "Descendental" humor of *Sartor*'s Book 1 as against the "Transcendental" rhapsodies of Books 2 and 3. Yet esoteric comedy persists in Books 2 and 3, in ways I want to take up now. My reading of *Sartor Resartus* dropped the thread at the close of Book 1, where Teufelsdröckh unveils his apocalypse of "Metaphors." I wanted to demonstrate in The Editor's transactions with Teufelsdröckh a volatile and elaborately ironic comedy, comparable in complexity and moral purpose to Swift's. The comedy of The Editor's systematic mistaking of Teufelsdröckh's wit and irony continues through the rest of *Sartor Resartus*, and I want to sketch its course briefly here, before drawing conclusions.

Book 2 of *Sartor* consists of fragments of an autobiographical narrative assembled by The Editor from Teufelsdröckh's "Biographical Documents." Here, The Editor often functions as a directly Carlylean mouthpiece, offering a counterpoint of encouraging words to the tale of woe and dejection that is Teufelsdröckh's early life. But Book 2 enacts the same comedy as Book 1, the comedy of a misguided quest (The Editor's) that must fail before it can yield illumination. Book 1 conducted The Editor in all his literal-mindedness to the climactic revelation that "all is Metaphor" and that "the beginning of all wisdom" consists in the recognition of metaphor "as such" and of figurative imagination as the condition and constitutive agent of all thought, language, and perception. Just at this dizzying moment, the long-awaited "Biographical Documents" arrive, thanks to an officious intermediary known as Hofrath Heuschrecke, whose accompanying letter advises The Editor how these strange materials should be read. The Editor is almost too grateful for the excuse to distract himself from Teufelsdröckh's infinite regress of metaphor by plunging into what he confidently expects to be a cache of "factual" Teufelsdröckhiana.

Alas, he finds instead only loose, unsorted scribblings apparently never intended for publication, distributed among six paper bags each marked with a sign of the zodiac, suggesting – what? That half the story remains untold? (Teufelsdröckh is thirty-five, *nel mezzo del cammin,* exactly halfway to his three score and ten.) That knowledge is always an affair we "half-perceive and half-create" rather than a passive reception of data? But questions like these do not occur to The Editor, who finds himself, again, comically entoiled in materials whose difficulty and disorganization stymie his will to order and disappoint his expectation that in the tangible "facts" of Teufelsdröckh's life the phantasmal heart of Teufelsdröckh's mystery will present itself for the plucking.

But just as Book 1 ends by affirming the metaphoricalness of everything, Book 2 at last brings The Editor to some recognition that the heavily romanticized, quasi-allegorical narrative he has been tracing is in some uncertain (but large) degree fictional and that he must be vigilant lest he continue to mistake "as literally authentic what was but hieroglyphically so" (202–3). That is to say (ironically) that at the end of Book 2, The Editor is just figuring out for himself exactly what the Hofrath Heuschrecke tried to tell him at the beginning, that a biography must be "philosophico-poetically written, and philosophico-poetically read" and will yield "truth" only if "Fancy" supplement the "authentic lineaments of Fact" with the "forged ones of Fiction" (75). "Facts," says Teufelsdröckh in a passage The Editor cites at the close of Book 2, "are engraved Hierograms, for which fewest have the key":

> What are your historical Facts; still more your biographical?
> Wilt thou know a Man, above all a Mankind, by stringing-together beadrolls of what thou namest Facts? (203)

The revelation is cognate with the principle that "all is Metaphor": literal-mindedness (mistaking "as literally authentic what was but hieroglyphically so") is letter, law, and death, whereas self-conscious imagination, the "thaumaturgic art of Thought" via "Metaphor [or hieroglyph, or fiction] recognized as such" is spirit, liberty, life.

This liberating apprehension makes "Belief" compliant to desire: Since belief is construed or "constructed" from mere "Fact" by that God-like organ, the Imagination, belief is a "fiction," a fiction truer than any dead-letter "Fact" by reason of the mind's participation in it. "Fact" is no refutation of the mind's sovereign fictions; the fiction that it is, is simply a fiction "not recognised as such." So if the inexorable march of intellectual progress has unmade traditional beliefs, it is yet in the power of the "fictile" and "fingent" mind to make belief anew. These notions about "Fiction" and "Fact" are enacted in the rhetoric of *Sartor* itself, as many critics have recognized.[25] At first glance, *Sartor* looks like a work of "non-fiction," a long book review-essay; very quickly the active reader should see that it is a parody; but then the reader should see that it is not *merely* a parody either, but something more than a parody without ceasing to be a parody: simultaneously a wisdom book and a parody of a wisdom book, a work of wit and humor whose profoundest points are oftener made in the book's structurings and readings of its own structurings than in its mere expositions. Thus does *Sartor's* ambiguous generic status at "the boundaries of fiction" contrive, with entire deliberateness, to solicit the reader's responses, habits, assumptions, "beliefs" and then require that these be made self-conscious, "seen through," and revised.

Unfortunately, the liberating relation Teufelsdröckh asserts between "Fiction" and "Fact" is subject to the same irony illustrated above in the dialectic whereby Carlyle's "thaumaturgic" idealism degrades into "Descendental" solipsism. To say that "Fact" is constituted by "Spirit" sounds the same as, but is fatally different from, saying (what the later Carlyle says, or shouts, with increasing exasperation) that "Spirit is a *Fact!*" The one formulation thumbs its nose at Thomas Gradgrind, and triumphs; the other consents to speak Gradgrind's language and is thus (as no philosopher of "language" should have known better than Carlyle) already defeated. John Rosenberg finds Carlyle's defection (or deconversion) from fiction to fact already implicit in Carlyle's decision, after 1830, to pursue researches in history, to write *The French Revolution* rather than another *Sartor Resartus.*[26] Though Rosenberg's point converges with mine, I would argue that the motive of *The French Revolution* was rather precisely to demonstrate that even the most obdurate and tyrannous "Facts" of history itself are epiphenomena of human fictions, whether or not "recognised as such" – and most obdurate and coercive precisely where least "recognised as such."

The French Revolution demonstrates the "Descendental" terror of an insight whose power to liberate is what chiefly concerns Teufelsdröckh. But even in *Sartor,* the Teufelsdröckhian "Gospel of Freedom," of the "fictile" and "fingent" powers of the Imagination, all that sublime transcendentalism, is elucidated for us

chiefly in esoteric comedy, in The Editor's ironic and predictable
failure to get it right. In his transactions with the "Biographical
Documents," for example, his whole quest is merely to discover
what he had been *told* at the outset and what he should have just
learned anyhow from Teufelsdröckh's "Metaphorical paragraph
on Metaphor." In Book 2, in short, The Editor learns (sort of) to
"see through" biography much as in Book 1 he learned (almost)
to "see through" clothes, or metaphor. He just begins to perceive
what (again) the active reader will have seen much sooner, that
Teufelsdröckh's "humouristico-satirical tendency" not only challenges lazy or impercipient readers, but actually implicates them
in his satire, making them its objects:

> Could it be expected that . . . Teufelsdröckh would all at
> once frankly unlock his citadel to an English Editor . . . and
> not rather deceptively *in*lock [The] Editor . . . in the laby-
> rinthic tortuosities and covered ways of said citadel (having
> enticed [him] thither), to see, in his half-devilish way, how
> the fool [ ] would look? (202–3)

With these insights shakily in hand, "the somewhat exhausted
and exasperated Editor determines here to shut these Paper-bags
for the present" (204), to turn from Teufelsdröckh's life back to
Teufelsdröckh's book, and thus Book 3 of *Sartor* begins, picking
up again The Editor's reading of *Die Kleider*. As before, The Editor continues to lag comically behind the airy Teufelsdröckh, but
for various reasons he is happier than in Book 1 with what he
reads – Teufelsdröckh is now hitting his "Transcendental" stride
– and interrupts less frequently, especially through chapters
"shadowing forth" Teufelsdröckh's "Transcendental" (rather
than "Descendental") vision of society, religion, politics, and science. These chapters, The Editor is gratified to announce, anticipate another book of Teufelsdröckh's, "already in a state of for-
wardness," *On the Palingenesia, or Newbirth of Society.*

Yet "Transcendentalism" notwithstanding, when wit and
irony enter Teufelsdröckh's discourse, The Editor still gets things
hopelessly, and comically, wrong. In "The Dandiacal Body," for
example, The Editor begins by deducing, on what he takes to be
solid Teufelsdröckhian principles, that the Dandy, because his

"trade, office and existence" are "heroically consecrated" to "the wearing of clothes," must be possessed of all wisdom, a "Poet of Cloth," a "living Martyr to the eternal World of Clothes," in short, the Compleat Teufelsdröckhian Hero. With the avidity of the conscientious disciple, The Editor turns to Teufelsdröckh's account of dandyism in order to check his own naïvely literal-minded deductions against the Master's, and is delighted to find them there confirmed – since, completely missing Teufels-dröckh's irony (except to complain of a "perverse . . . ironic tendency"), he cannot recognize the larger irony of the correspondence between his naïvely literal-minded deductions and Teufelsdröckh's fabulously witty sarcasms.

Teufelsdröckh's report on the English Dandy is an elaborately ironic excursus whose boldest stroke is Teufelsdröckh's parodic assumption of The Editor's usual role, that of a baffled reader of barely intelligible texts, in this case the "Mythic Theogonies" of such "Fashionable Novels" as Bulwer's *Pelham.* From these Teu-felsdröckh affects to deduce, with mock-philological fussiness, that the Dandies are a religious sect, whose "Articles of Faith" he conscientiously transcribes (279). The Editor, missing Teufels-dröckh's irony again, obligingly offers to correct Teufelsdröckh's surprising misapprehension – though it does occur to him at last to wonder if Teufelsdröckh's discourse on Dandies might not contain "something of intended satire: is the Professor and Seer not quite the blinkard he affects to be?" On behalf of an indignant public, The Editor demands finally, "Does your Professor take us for simpletons? His irony has overshot itself; we see through it, and perhaps through him" (287).

Conversion and Acceptance: The Stooge as Hero

"Perhaps," indeed. This wrongheaded kind of "seeing through" continues right into the last chapter of *Sartor Resartus,* where The Editor is still complaining that the "mad humours" of Teu-felsdröckh's "piebald, entangled, hyper-metaphorical style of writing" (293) constitute not only an obstacle to understanding *Die Kleider,* but a menace to clear thought and expression at large. Morse Peckham was the first to suggest, and G. B. Tenny-son has argued the case most exhaustively, that in the course of

91

Sartor Resartus, Teufelsdröckh overcomes The Editor's skepticism, so that The Editor undergoes at last a "conversion" to Teufelsdröckh's gospel.[27] I prefer George Levine's reading, and Hazard Adams's, according to which The Editor's attraction-aversion to Teufelsdröckh is maintained in an unremitting state of tension throughout the book, generating rather an agitated stasis than a drama of change or development.[28] The Editor's cavils and equivocations at *Sartor*'s close are the same ones he was sounding at its opening; we end where we began, in much the same mix of enthusiasm and disapprobation, in a way that implies a world where "conversion" is not much to be looked for.

We end as we began, that is, with The Editor still functioning chiefly as Carlyle's comic stooge, and to hang so much on the possible "conversion" of such a stooge seems comically misguided. Granted, The Editor's disposition toward Teufelsdröckh is central and raises issues that prompt such questions; still, the questions and their answers remain ironic, and comic. To begin with, "conversion" to what? One cannot speak (although The Editor and other critics often do) of Teufelsdröckh's "doctrine," except with some archness – in quotation marks, as it were. The content of Teufelsdröckh's "doctrine" is not separable from its style, as we learn from (precisely) The Editor's unavailing attempts to separate them. The Editor aims to reduce *Die Kleider*'s extravagances to system, its fancies to propositions, its chaos to order, but instead manages only – as he himself exasperatedly reiterates throughout – to replicate the very extravagance and chaos he had proposed to subdue; from the very beginning, the Teufelsdröckhian hurly-burly prevails over The Editor's ("pontifical") will to order.

Nothing works out as The Editor planned, in short; yet this seems not only instructive and emblematic of human affairs generally (at least as Carlyle conceives them), but also at last altogether for the best: After all, we want distinct personalities, not clones; we want Teufelsdröckh's vitality, untidy as it may be, rather than an orderly digest in outline form. The Editor never quite arrives at a distrust of his own impulses to system and order (*that,* perhaps, might be "conversion" worthy of the name), but there is an ironic sense in which the defeat of his announced intentions speaks well for his responsiveness (or susceptibility) to

Teufelsdröckhian energies he cannot master but bravely will not ignore, acknowledging if only by protesting them. If not quite "converted" to Teufelsdröckh's ways of seeing and thinking, The Editor nevertheless exhibits an admirable capacity for being overwhelmed by them, even if he did not mean to be, and does not altogether realize that he has been.

But even though the question whether The Editor is "converted" to Teufelsdröckhianism (to call it *that*) seems misguided, I would preserve it as evidence of something unexpected and curious, and significant: that The Editor, despite all his foolishness, and unlike his literary prototypes (e.g., the teller of Swift's *Tale of a Tub*), inspires at last a degree of affection and even respect in his readers. He becomes a presence of more than merely comic consequence in the book. What he thinks finally matters, somehow; he has persisted in his folly and become, if not wise, nevertheless a presence whose earnestness and single-mindedness – the very liabilities that have made him a comic foil throughout the book – finally appear as a kind of integrity. The frustration of The Editor's transactions with *Die Kleider* evinces the tenacity not only of his resistance to, and resolve to be critical about, Teufelsdröckh – overcoming which would be "conversion" – but also of his effort to follow where Teufelsdröckh leads, in short to be (as had been implicit from the beginning) not only Teufelsdröckh's critic but also his disciple. Even if, after such long-sustained effort, he has proven an inadequate reader of Teufelsdröckh, the very willfulness of the effort has amounted to a kind of accommodation with the Philosopher of Clothes. Perhaps he does not entirely *understand* Teufelsdröckh, but he nevertheless *accepts* Teufelsdröckh and thus appears to be a suitably conflicted exemplar of the hoary Carlylean "Egad!-he'd-better!" principle.

It is perhaps at the urging of such example that the active reader likewise "accepts" The Editor. This sort of impasse tempered with acceptance – The Editor vis-à-vis Teufelsdröckh, the reader vis-à-vis The Editor – is of the essence of *Sartor Resartus,* an emblem of Carlyle's apprehension that even with the best will in the world, people remain separate and alone, enclosed irredeemably within the non-negotiable "humours" and inescapable contingencies of "Self." "Conversion," at last, is like "understanding" or any other "work" worth undertaking in Carlyle's universe: not so simple or attainable or immediately gratifying as we would like.

But this apprehension, so demoralizing to Carlyle in his later years, is "fronted" in *Sartor Resartus* as intrinsic to a human condition one can only welcome and be grateful for, in which the wish is, if not as good as the deed, yet good enough, and its fated frustration finally a testimony more to the value than to the vanity of human wishes. What The Editor and Teufelsdröckh share is nothing so fragile as a set of opinions or a style of mind; what they share, in defiance and in default of these differences, is good will and a good-faith commitment to the work of understanding, even if that work promises less than the final or total consummations so devoutly to be wished. The irredeemable distance that separates Teufelsdröckh from The Editor, the would-be Hero from his would-be Hero Worshipper, is suggestive of all the conflict, cross-purposes, and waste involved in any effort toward community.

But the effort to bridge this distance equally suggests that equilibrium of criticism and tolerance that is partly the condition, partly the achievement, of liberal culture. The later Carlyle's authoritarian rantings express his despair of that culture's possibilities, but the Carlyle of *Sartor Resartus*, "Radical Iconoclasm" notwithstanding, expects to function as culture critic well within the terms of that liberal compact, and he expects that his criticism will be accepted in the spirit in which it is offered.[29] Among the qualities that impressed him in the first copies of *Fraser's* he saw was the magazine's "loyalty" (*TNB*, 170); and early in *Sartor* (10–11), The Editor hopes for readers who will put aside "party spirit," even as he himself attempts to hold his own Burkean Toryism in abeyance the better to entertain Teufelsdröckh's radical Sansculottism. The author of *Sartor Resartus* speaks as a reformer of culture from within, rather than as an assailant of it from without. He means to address all sides without himself having to take one side or another; he means to be the part that can speak for the whole, not just another "party" voice. Unfortunately, the literary-journalistic arrangements of his day would not allow him (*even* him) so august a role, and he becomes at last a party of one, not reaching out in charity, but striking ever harsher and more punitive postures of alienation, protecting himself and his jealously guarded integrity as much against his disciples (for nothing so galls the master as his own gospel emitted as cant, and in his name) as against the indifferent world at large. The immediate failure of *Sartor Resartus,* which Carlyle had dared hope might "produce some desirable impression on the world" (*Letters,* 5:202), to arouse anything but scorn and abuse seems in some ways a model for the mature Carlyle's discontents. But the esoteric comedy of the book itself, tempering failure to reconcile Teufelsdröckh's visionary wit and The Editor's stubborn common sense with good-humored acceptance of their differences, models the younger Carlyle's hopeful and confident sense not only of his own genius, but of his culture's possibilities.

2

"HIPPOCLIDES DOESN'T CARE"

NEWMAN'S *APOLOGIA PRO VITA SUA*

Another word I don't want to use is "reality." I try to avoid it. . . .
Occasionally, a really profound man – a Cardinal Newman, for
example – can use the word; there isn't any word you can't use if
you have enough body to make something of it.
> – Louis Zukofsky, interview with L. S. Dembo

A proud man is a lovely man.
> – Yeats, "Come Gather Round Me, Parnellites"

I am become a fool in glorying; ye have compelled me.
> – St. Paul, 2 Corinthians 12:11

I HAVE DESCRIBED this project often enough, to enough
people, to know that talk of the *Apologia* as a comedy strikes
many as prima facie implausible. Yet hardly any commentator who has written at any length about Newman fails to mention his irony, though none that I know of considers it to be more
than an incidental feature of a rhetoric with other and more
potent resources and (particularly in the *Apologia*) with purposes
to which irony, wit, and humor would be inappropriate, even
inimical. Nevertheless, I want in this chapter to read the *Apologia*
– and Newman's project generally – by the light of its more ironic
moments. I want to survey the astonishingly wide range of local
comic effects Newman's wit and his relish of parody and caricature secure for the *Apologia*. I hope to show that the *Apologia* is
an astonishing and bristling book – even, at times, a *funny* book
– in ways obscured by the received image of a great literary and
religious classic, redolent of sanctity, confessional anguish, and a
noble prose style. I want to show that for long passages the *Apol-*

ogia can be a heady brew of sarcasm, satire, and finely calculated outrage – all delivered, somehow, with a disarmingly and unassailably persuasive sincerity – upon all the superstitions of a positivist age. I hope to show that paragraph by paragraph, and sentence by sentence, the demands and challenges of Newman's prose offer pleasures of a comic sort that I have not seen described elsewhere. He parodies his enemies' verbal styles, he parodies their parodies of himself, he manipulates tone to shift arguments from figurative to literal bases (or vice versa), he soothes and provokes, confesses and defies, draws us in and pushes us away – all effects that display the very virtuosity and facility for which Newman was supposedly under indictment.

And more, I want to argue that such passages are more than incidental to the whole. Newman has virtually no peer in his power to make a serene and deft display of virtuosity out of the effort to relate parts to wholes, to join things that seem disjunct, to harmonize contradictions and smooth over difficulties – distrust of this virtuosity, indeed, is one of the prime constituents of the public animus Newman is combating in the *Apologia* – and he insists repeatedly that he must be taken whole if he is to be understood at all. And so I hope to relate the sense of irony and intellectual play that so enlivens the *Apologia* page by page to the larger comic sense that is Newman's own peculiar and idiosyncratic version of the more broadly and conventionally Christian sense of the human drama as a comedy of redemption issuing unexpectedly, miraculously, ironically, from a plot whose données – sin and death – would seem to dictate an unhappier outcome.

Caricature and Parody

The *Apologia*'s esoteric comedy begins in caricature, because the controversy that occasioned it was prompted by a caricature of Newman as a type of Romish cynicism. When Charles Kingsley's slur appeared in *Macmillan's Magazine* (January 1864), Newman had been retired from the public scene for many years; but he was still famous, even notorious, throughout England for his formidable polemical talent, his charismatic personal influence over two generations of England's finest young men, and his stunning conversion to Rome nineteen years earlier in 1845. Indeed, Newman's reputation at large was so palpably a feature of the controversy with Kingsley, that the attempt to disarm it preoccupied Newman through the first two of the seven installments in which the *Apologia* was initially written and published. When he came to shape his seven pamphlets into a book after the controversy had cooled, Newman largely cut these first two sections, eliminating rebuttal of several particular points and excising any mention of Kingsley by name. But what he retained of them as a preface for book publication was precisely the effort to deal with the question of his reputation and to disable in advance its effect on the reception of his argument. Newman acknowledges that since his conversion, "a vague impression to my disadvantage has rested on the popular mind" (1)' and goes on to charge his accuser with playing on that impression so as to "poison the wells" (6), to make any answer of Newman's suspect before it is offered. In this way, Newman explains,

> if I am natural, he will tell them "Ars est celare artem": if I am convincing, he will suggest that I am an able logician; if I show warmth, I am acting the indignant innocent; if I am calm, I am thereby detected as a smooth hypocrite; if I clear up difficulties, I am too plausible and perfect to be true. The more triumphant are my statements, the more certain will be my defeat. (7)

Kingsley is exploiting that "vague impression to my disadvantage" whereby a false Newman, a parody or caricature of the "living intelligence, by which I write, and argue, and act" (12) has arisen in the public mind:

> I must show what I am, that it may be seen what I am not, and that the phantom may be extinguished which gibbers instead of me. I wish to be known as a living man, and not as a scarecrow which is dressed up in my clothes. (12)

It is Newman's sense of the play between a scarecrow and a living man, his sense of their similarities as well as of their differences, that generates the many dazzling displays of parody and caricature that so frequently astonish in the *Apologia;* but it also governs Newman's whole conception of the human effort to distinguish true from false. That this effort is necessarily involved in play and irony is the spring of Newman's esoteric comedy, as against Kingsley's sober demand that Newman's truth be single, verifiable, and, once ascertained, stable. The relation of scarecrow to living man is one of resemblance as well as difference, and therefore interrogation of it admits of degree, as against Kingsley's absolute dichotomy between the categories of true and false. That "living intelligence, by which [Newman] writes, and argues, and acts" is vibrant, ever in motion ("writes, argues, acts": verbs rather than nouns, "writings, arguments, actions"), as against the scarecrow of whose effects the raven-eyed Kingsley demands an inventory: two trouser legs filled with straw, one stuffed shirt, two fluttering sleeves, and so forth. "What, then, does Dr. Newman mean?" The answer will be no formula to settle matters once and for all, but rather more of the same: not static precepts and apothegms, but further interpretations, further embodiments of that mystery whose heart no Kingsley will ever pluck.

Newman's comic sense was operative from the very beginning of the controversy, or at least from the moment it became public. Kingsley attacked as if from the position that interpretations are mere sophistries and equivocations that embroider themselves beguilingly over an otherwise single, ascertainable, and verifiable truth. Newman's first public gesture in the controversy, in effect, put Kingsley on notice that his utterances too would be subject to caricature, would be implicated in the subtle coils of interpretation: Newman published the correspondence that had passed between himself and Kingsley in the wake of the offending paragraph in Kingsley's article; this included Kingsley's chilly, pro forma, and manifestly insincere apology, which Newman printed in one column with, *en face,* in another column, his own gloss, offered as an "unjust, but too probable, popular rendering of it." So that when Kingsley's letter says, for example, "It only remains, therefore, for me to express my hearty regret at having so seriously mistaken him, and my hearty pleasure at finding him on the side of truth, in this or any other matter" (349), Newman mournfully asserts that the "popular rendering" of these "hearty" words will be something like this:

> However, while I heartily regret that I have so seriously mistaken the sense which he assures me his words were meant to bear, I cannot but feel a hearty pleasure also, at having brought him, for once in a way, to confess that after all truth is a Christian virtue. (349)

Of course, Kingsley's apology is transparently sarcastic, and so is Newman's pretense that the "unjust, but too probable, popular rendering of it" would be an unfortunate and unintended misconstruction of Kingsley's straightforward and noble intention.

Now it was Kingsley's turn to play the outraged innocent, though not without broad hints to the instructed – "I never said what he makes me say, or anything like it," he writes; "I never was inclined to say it. Had I ever been, I should be still more inclined to say it now" (381). When Kingsley's pamphlet appeared, interested readers awaited Newman's reply. The first of Newman's pamphlets opened brilliantly with high irony: Kingsley had taken as epigraph to his "What, Then, Does Dr. Newman Mean?" a sentence from one of Newman's sermons that reads, "It is not more than a hyperbole to say, that in certain cases, a lie is the nearest approach to the truth" (355). Newman seizes on this immediately:

> And first of all, I beg to compliment him on the motto in his title page; it is felicitous. . . . The words which he has taken from me are so apposite as to be almost prophetical. There cannot be a better illustration than he thereby affords of the aphorism which I intended them to convey. I said that it is not more than a hyperbolical expression to say that in certain cases a lie is the nearest approach to the truth. Mr. Kingsley's pamphlet is emphatically one of such cases as are contemplated in that proposition. I really believe, that his view of me is about as near an approach to the truth about my writings and doings, as he is capable of taking. He has done his worst towards me; but he has also done his best. (386)

Esoteric Comedies

Newman's strategy here is entirely characteristic: to reappropriate and, as it were, redeem some one of his "writings and doings" that has been wrongheadedly taken over and mocked at by his enemies. Newman does not retreat from his sentence, nor does he offer to explain what he meant; no, he remarks with something almost like gloating satisfaction that Kingsley's misuse of his sentence proves the very proposition it offers. Kingsley doing his best can come no nearer the truth than *this,* and Newman clearly feels no need to fear the worst of a man whose best is so feeble. Explanation, Newman implies, would be wasted on an intelligence so limited; as for conciliation, it is undesired, whether possible or no. The phantom Newman that Kingsley has raised up only testifies, we are told, to Kingsley's dullness, his literal-mindedness:

> In a lecture of mine I have illustrated this phenomenon by the supposed instance of a foreigner, who after reading a commentary on the principles of English Law does not get nearer to a real apprehension of them than to be led to accuse Englishmen of considering that the Queen is impeccable and infallible, and that the Parliament is omnipotent. Mr. Kingsley has read me from beginning to end in the fashion in which the hypothetical Russian read Blackstone; not I repeat from malice, but because of his intellectual build. (387)

Despite mention here of what is doubtless Newman's *funniest* piece of satire (the first of his 1851 "Lectures on the Present Position of Catholics in England"), this indictment is not whimsical; it reaches into the deepest areas of controversy between the two men, as Newman makes clear when he goes on to say of Kingsley:

> Had he been a man of large or cautious mind, he would have not taken it for granted that cultivation must lead everyone to see things precisely as he sees them himself. But the narrowminded are the more prejudiced by reason of their narrowness. (387)

102

The subtle game of hoisting Kingsley by his own petard extends, a few pages later, to verbal parody:

> Now I ask, why could not Mr. Kingsley be open? If he intended still to arraign me on the charge of lying, why could he not say so as a man? Why must he insinuate, question, imply, and use sneering and irony, as if longing to touch a forbidden fruit, which still he was afraid would burn his fingers, if he did so? (392)

The vitriol here is of just the sort that Kingsley had discharged by the beakerful in his pamphlet; furthermore, Newman here creates a caricature of Kingsley whose features uncannily resemble those of the deceitful, unmanly, serpent-like "Dr. Newman" that Kingsley himself had been conjuring with.

Newman's keen and playful sense of the ways an idea and its expression can be monkeyed with is especially acute in the *Apologia,* a work necessarily addressed to an audience diversely disposed, but best presumed hostile. In the remark about the scarecrow, Newman might more accurately have said that not one phantom, but several, were gibbering, for the "public mind" was in no sense at one about the phenomenon of Newman. Versions of the subtle doctor were legion: to Dissenters at one extreme, he was a papist bogeyman, a vicar of Antichrist; to ultrarightist Catholics at the other, he was a dangerously overzealous advocate of intellectual freedom, of a "minimistic theology" (W. G. Ward's phrase) dangerously tainted with "Liberalism."[2]

The spectrum of bafflement between these two poles finds almost complete expression in the redundancy, internal inconsistency, and general rhetorical overkill of Kingsley's pamphlet. Professing inability to comprehend Newman's tortured logic, Kingsley improvises insulting, conflicting, and manifestly unserious "explanations" – like this, for example:

> [Newman] has worked his mind, it would seem, into that morbid state, in which nonsense is the only food for which it hungers. Like the sophists of old, he has used reason to destroy reason. I had thought that, like them, he had preserved his own reason, in order to be able to destroy that of

others. But I was unjust to him, as he says. While he tried
to destroy others' reason, he was at least fair enough to
destroy his own. . . . Too many prefer the charge of insincerity to that of insipience – Dr. Newman seems not to be
of that number. (370)

"Insincerity" or "insipience"? The polemical burden of the *Apologia* is especially heavy because what is at stake is not some issue
that Newman can dispassionately consider, but Newman's own
character; and Newman's usual consciousness of audience,
always acute, is further intensified in the *Apologia* because Kingsley had founded his charge of untruthfulness on Newman's
appeal to the doctrine of "Economy," which, simply put, is all
about audience, acknowledging that any explanation or teaching,
indeed any account of anything, must conform itself to the
understandings of its intended recipients.

"Economy"

"Economy" implies that the truth of things is neither single – or
at least not reducible to a single definitive verbal formulation –
nor external to understanding. It should be easy to see how such
notions and their implications would be as inevitable to an agile
and subtle intelligence like Newman's as they would be infuriat-
ing to one so common-sensical (and anxiously so) as Kingsley's.
Newman bases the "Rule of Economy" on "the words of our
Lord, 'Cast not thy pearls before swine'" (241) and traces its origins to the early history of the Church, when believers had to be
circumspect with their persecutors; he also suggests that it is
founded on the analogue of God's gradual disclosure of revelation in history, in which it is seen that God Himself is "discreet"
in presenting His teachings to humankind. In one passage, after
a few hundred words of learned and involved historical argument
– just the sort of thing that Kingsley had been at pains to warn
against – Newman avers in reasonable and common-sense tones
that "Economy" is an inevitable feature of virtually *all* social
intercourse:

> The principle of the Economy is familiarly acted on among
> us every day. When we would persuade others, we do not

begin by treading on their toes. Men would be thought rude who introduced their own religious notions into mixed society, and were devotional in a drawing room. (301)

But this prose quickly hints, by a sudden change of tone, that in some situations, the most efficacious tactic "when we would persuade others" might be precisely to "tread on their toes":

As to the Catholic Religion in England at the present day, this only will I observe, – that the truest expedience is to answer right out, when you are asked; that the wisest economy is to have no management; that the best prudence is not to be a coward; that the most damaging folly is to be found out shuffling; and that the first of virtues is to "tell truth and shame the devil."(301)

The defiance audible in this proud and, it would seem, self-consciously "English" plain spokenness suggests that the Rule of Economy's "cautious dispensation of the truth" is continuous with answering a fool according to his folly and letting those who have ears but hear not rage with the heathen.

On no issue is the impasse between Kingsley and Newman so absolute as that of miracles. The pamphlets exchanged between the two men skirmish furiously over that vexed and vexing terrain, and it is amusing to observe the rhetorical resources Newman finds to his purpose. Miracles are met with skepticism? Then Newman will don the mask of the cool empiricist in countering that skepticism. Consider the way he meets the skeptic's tactic of dispersing miracle by posing instead of divine agency some purely naturalistic explanation, to show that the alleged miracle is well within the realm of the naturally possible. For purposes of discussion, Newman cites an episode from the fifth century, in which Christian martyrs, their tongues cut out on the orders of a persecuting tyrant, were "miraculously" able to speak as before. True enough, Newman acknowledges, modern investigation shows that "the tongue is not necessary for articulate speech" (269), and he cites the (quite grisly) reports of contemporary travelers in the Middle East, where such mutilations were still practiced. Still, he regards as dubious the claim that such information discredits the miraculous character of the case of the fifth-century African confessors, and in saying so his tone and language resemble that of the cool inquirer who mock graciously declines to be imposed upon by specious appearances:

> I should not be honest, if I professed to be simply con-
> verted, by these testimonies, to the belief that there was
> nothing miraculous in the case of the African confessors. It
> is quite as fair to be skeptical on one side of the question as
> on the other; and if Gibbon is considered worthy of praise
> for his stubborn incredulity in receiving the evidence for
> this miracle, I do not see why I am to be blamed, if I wish
> to be quite sure of the full appositeness of the recent evi-
> dence to its disadvantage. Questions of fact cannot be dis-
> proved by analogies or presumptions. (270)

The substance of this argument mocks all Gibbonesque poses of "stubborn incredulity," even as its style deftly parodies the quintessentially Victorian and self-congratulating manner of candid, quasi-confessional skepticism ("I should not be honest, if I professed myself simply converted by these testimonies") sounded just four years before the composition of the *Apologia* in *Essays and Reviews* (1860).[3] Note the use of religious language – "converted," "testimonies" – to characterize what this voice so politely concludes it must reject.

But the skepticism Newman parries here is intellectual, high-brow; the downright common sense of Kingsley is another affair. The miraculous manifestation that had elicited Kingsley's indignation, once the pamphleteering had begun, was the medicinal oils secreted by the sarcophagus of St. Walburga, as retold in the series of *The Lives of the English Saints,* which Newman had edited and to which he had supplied a preface. In his pamphlet, Kingsley quotes Newman's preface at length until: "I can quote no more. I really must recollect that my readers and I are living in the nineteenth century" (368). Beyond registrations of outrage ("stuff and nonsense, more materialist than the dreams of any bone-worshipping Buddhist" [368]), Kingsley eschews comment on these passages; he regards them as self-refuting, patently absurd. The impasse is absolute; in his point-by-point "Answer in Detail to Mr. Kingsley's Charges" – the notorious recension of the thirty-nine *blots* – Newman takes up the matter of miracles with weary distaste: "It is hard on me to have this dull, profitless work, but I have pledged myself; – so now for St. Walburga" (426):

> What is the use of going on with this Writer's criticism upon me, when I am confined to the dull monotony of exposing and oversetting him again and again, with a persistence, which many will think merciless, and few will have the interest to read? Yet I am obliged to do so, lest I should seem to be evading difficulties. (429)

"Profitless work" indeed; Kingsley, the tone of this is saying, is a man beyond instruction; a man impervious to common sense; no need even to argue; one can only repeat what one has already said many times before – repeat, in fact, the very passages Kingsley cites – repeat with no confidence that the repetition will do any good; the long-suffering Newman can only go through it all for form's sake, "lest I should seem to be evading difficulties." The argument as Newman lays it out is eminently common-sensical. Whether ultra-Catholic or Bible Protestant, if one is a Christian, one must accept the miracles recounted in Scripture; and on the face of it, the proposition that miracles were possible at a time in the remote past but at no time since makes less sense than the proposition that miracles can occur at any time. Therefore, there is no reason to reject out of hand accounts of miracles in recent ages: When surprising events are attributed to miraculous agency, there is no reason they should not be:

> Well, this is precisely what I have said, which this writer considers so irrational. I have said, as he quotes me, p. 368, "In this day, and under our present circumstances, we can only reply, that there is no reason why they should not be." Surely this is good logic, *provided* that miracles *do* occur in all ages; and so again is it logical to say that, "There is nothing, *prima facie,* in the miraculous accounts in question, to repel a *properly taught* or religiously disposed mind." What is the matter with this statement? My assailant does not pretend to say what the matter is, and he cannot; but he expresses a rude, unmeaning astonishment. (430)

"Good logic," *"prima facie"*: The argument makes perfect sense, given its premises; and to reject those is to reject Christianity. (This is the sort of rigor that underlines Newman's remark [179] that there is no halfway house between atheism and Rome.) If Kingsley is too stupid to perceive or too cowardly to face this contradiction, these are luxuries Newman would like to deny him; henceforward, let him be impaled on the horns of his dilemma, unable either to evade or to admit the hypocrisy of his "rude, unmeaning astonishment."

Newman's argument proceeds – too lengthily to quote here – as if common sense and self-evident facts were all on his side, and again, as before, he disdains to do much more than merely repeat, with a great show of patience, the very arguments Kingsley had pounced on as "stuff and nonsense . . . outrages upon common sense." All proceeds with exaggerated weariness, long suffering, and forbearance; the tone is such as to suggest that this "profitless work" is as boring, as little promising of surprise or excitement, to the reader as to the writer; all is foreknown; we are being conducted, Newman and we readers, relentlessly, and purposelessly, to a foregone conclusion. But the conclusion, when we do at last reach it, is as surprising, as unexpected, as unaccommodating as it possibly could be; the careful, plodding, and lengthy show of common sense is, at a stroke, entirely exploded, and we are left, without explanation, back at the most uncompromising impasse possible:

What was the harm of all of this? but my Critic has muddled it all together. . . . One of his remarks is, "What has become of the holy oil for the last 240 years, Dr. Newman does not say," p. 369. Of course I did not, because I did not know; I gave the evidence as I found it; he assumes that I had a point to prove, and then asks why I did not make the evidence larger than it was. I put this down as Blot *twenty-five.*

I can tell him more about it now; the oil still flows; I have had some of it in my possession; it is medicinal; some think it so by a natural quality, others by a divine gift. Perhaps it is on the confines of both. (429)

Newman's Apologia Pro Vita Sua

All talk of "good logic" or "*prima facie* cases" vaporizes as we are imperiously informed that Newman has – but will not disclose – personal experience of these oils whose miraculous powers we have been asked to entertain merely hypothetically for many pages now. We had been indulging them as legend, condescending to them as folktales – charming, simple, and (why not?) innocent. All such literary sentimentality has been solicited only to be dismissed, with Newman's announcement of the literal truth of what is claimed for Walburga's oils.

Provocation and Accommodation

Newman is, of course, entirely conscious of how his words will be received, though this consciousness has as much of recklessness in it as of calculation. I take them as exemplary of one of Newman's most extreme and unaccommodating strategies in the *Apologia;* here the effort is not to mitigate an appearance of deviousness or subtlety but rather so to indulge (and even exaggerate) it as to intimidate or awe susceptible readers while defiantly foreclosing any possibility of accommodation with the hostile and prejudiced. Such passages seem calculated to induce apoplexy in Kingsley, who, in his pamphlet, had blustered,

> If he will indulge in subtle paradoxes, in rhetorical exaggerations, if, whenever he touches on the question of truth and honesty, he will take a perverse pleasure in saying something shocking to plain English notions, he must take the consequences of his own eccentricities. (372)

In various places in the *Apologia,* Newman takes care to do all of the above, "shocking plain English notions" sometimes in a tone to suggest that in being eccentric, he is merely exercising a prerogative traditional to his countrymen and his nation, sometimes with a bristlingly combative ferocity that seems English in Dr. Johnson's way more than Queen Victoria's.

This might be the place to remark that Newman's "Englishness"[4] is a sort of leitmotif throughout the book: insisting that he is both a Catholic and an Englishman, Newman can make of this exceptional circumstance both an appeal to and a critique of national feeling:

> Still more confident am I of . . . eventual acquittal, seeing that my judges are my own countrymen. I think, indeed, Englishmen the most suspicious and touchy of mankind; I think them unreasonble, and unjust in their seasons of excitement; but I had rather be an Englishman (as in fact I am) than belong to any other race under heaven. They are generous, as they are hasty and burly; and their repentance for their injustice is greater than their sin. (8)

We will see this "Englishness" again and again; it recurs throughout the *Apologia,* a persistent theme, here making a sympathetic appeal, there lending to the assertion of some "difficult" Catholic position a John Bullish ferocity, elsewhere again opening an aperture on satire and parody. Nowhere does Newman's parodic finesse more winningly mingle satire of and affection for English foibles than in a lengthy passage given in the eighth installment of the *Apologia*'s serial publication, the "Answer in Detail to Mr. Kingsley's Charges" that Newman omitted from the text of the book as too polemical and ad hominem. In dispute is a passage of one of Newman's lectures, and here again, as in the "lie-the-nearest-approach-to-the-truth" exchange cited above, Newman's "answer in detail" consists chiefly of a more extensive quotation from the same lecture, implying again that Kingsley has simply missed a point that is clear as it stands and that he deserves no new accommodation, no new explanation, but simply a verbatim reiteration of the original statement, which Kingsley will be privileged to overhear (should he please to trouble himself) as a patient Newman addresses it, so to speak, past him, to the reader Kingsley has hitherto misinformed. Kingsley had charged that in the lecture in question, Newman had approved the grossest sorts of idolatry – veneration of relics, worship of the pope and other mere mortals, credulity regarding miracles, insufficiency of critical skepticism when dealing with legends of saints, and so forth. But what the passage goes on to do, in Newman's more extensive quotation, is to assimilate such Catholic practices with English habits of reverence for national heroes like King Alfred, the variously dubious legends concerning him, and the few relics

("There is in the museum at Oxford, a jewel or trinket said to be Alfred's" [434]) that it delights the English to suppose belonged to him. The Tower of London, Newman reminds us, contains in its display cases many an item of doubtful authenticity. As for reverencing mere mortals, what of the English people's adoration of Victoria, their queen?

> There is our Queen again, who is so truly and justly popular; she roves about in the midst of tradition; she scatters myths and legends from her as she goes along; she is a being of poetry, and you might fairly be sceptical whether she had any personal existence. She is always at some beautiful, noble, bounteous work or other, if you trust the papers. She is doing alms-deeds in the Highlands; she meets beggars in her rides at Windsor; she writes verses in albums, or draws sketches, or is mistaken for the housekeeper by some blind old woman, or she runs up a hill as if she were a child. (434)

This is a heady brew: It hints at a quite savagely dry and pointed satire of the silly old queen and the national press that professes to dote on her because its simple-minded readers do.

But that surly possibility is checked by Newman's recognition – a concession made to the reader, in exchange for concessions that Newman will demand in return – that the English public's investment in the queen, and in all the sentimental associations of national glory she symbolizes, is large and important. The very incongruity of legend-laden royalty ("she roves about in the midst of tradition and romance") with the demands of feature journalism ("if you trust the papers") implies an embarrassed if sympathetic condescension to the mortal female who must play her solemn role ("you might fairly be sceptical whether she had any personal existence") through all the comic misadventures even royal flesh must be heir to ("mistaken for the housekeeper by some blind old woman"), now, in the dawn of the age of the telegraph, the human-interest story, and a mass readership, routinely published morning and evening to the world at large. But of course there is affection, too, for the woman Victoria with her triumphantly common touch ("runs up a hill as she were a child"); for the sentimental and simple public that battens on such reports; even for the press itself, whose tobacco-sotted and

111

alcoholic hacks do contrive, however cynically and self-servingly, to uphold the gallant and gentlemanly usages of deference and chivalry to that mother, widow, and national symbol, the very archetype for the English of the fairer sex.

The blind old woman by whom Victoria is mistaken for the housekeeper and the beggars who lie in wait for her on the riding paths at Windsor are representatives of an extensive public that reveres the queen with a touching simplicity and earnestness of mind. But Newman's prose here addresses a more sophisticated reader who might acknowledge in private what it would be bad taste and worse manners to declare in public: that the queen is an anachronism and an absurdity. Lytton Strachey must wait, but Newman's reader here should sense the tone of affectionate amusement and share the unacknowledged and embarrassed condescension, for Newman is addressing an elite readership with a psychic investment in the queen no smaller than the newspaper public's – indeed, given the class issues at stake, their investment is arguably much greater – but whose attitude toward her must be more problematic. Theirs are the ten thousand swords that must be ready to leap from their scabbards and so forth. And yet this prose comes close to conjuring with the educated and witty reader's furtive desire to violate the taboo against mentioning that the empress has no clothes. And so Newman goes on, in what sounds like an elaborate show of protesting too much, to assure us that his own ironical sword will unsheathe itself for the queen's honor as quickly as anyone's.

> Who finds fault with these things? he would be a cynic, he would be white-livered, and would have gall for blood, who was not struck with this graceful, touching evidence of the love her subjects bear her. Who could have the head, even if he had the heart, who could be so cross and peevish, who could be so solemn and perverse, as to say that some of these stories *may* be simple lies, and all of them might have stronger evidence than they carry with them? (434)

And here comes the demand for "concession in return" anticipated above:

> Do you think she is displeased with them? Why then should He, the great Father, who once walked the earth, look

112

sternly on the unavoidable mistakes of His own subjects
and children in their devotion to Him and His? (434–5)

The gravity of this conclusion utterly transfigures all the preceding humor, parody, and finely calculated ambiguity; suddenly
audible is the seriousness of the issues at stake and the depth of
the sympathy and acceptance that effects, so to speak, a communion between the simplicities and vulgarities of popular reverence and all the potentialities of a condescending or satirical
disposition of mind toward them. Newman is again adopting the
strategy so effective in the first of his "Lectures on the Present
Position of Catholics," in which a "hypothetical Russian" reads
Blackstone and "does not get nearer to the real apprehension of
[English law] than to be led to accuse Englishmen of considering
that the Queen is impeccable and infallible, and that the Parlia-
ment is omnipotent" (387). Newman is saying that any complex
of social and historical conventions and pieties can be made to
look ridiculous, can be reduced to a mere caricature or parody of
its true character, by the simple withdrawal from it of the observer's sympathy. As we shall see, he is further suggesting that such
a withdrawal of sympathy also reduces to a shadow of itself the
humanity of those who thus refuse it.

The richness of Newman's self-conscious "Englishness," the
ease with which he can turn a hyper-English pose into a parody
of English foibles, springs from his vibrant and exact awareness
of the prejudices his argument will meet with. Consider the prejudices of the reader inferable, for example, from Matthew
Arnold's essay "The Modern Element in Literature"; it was composed in 1857, just seven years before the *Apologia*. Arnold is at
pains to define the word "modern," although of course he less
defines it than encloses it in a circular meander of suggestion;
here, as so often elsewhere, Arnold apparently allows himself a
degree of imprecision because he feels himself to be expressing
sentiments that so indubitably are – or should be – a matter of
universal agreement. Modernity, says Arnold, is not an affair
exclusively of the recent historical past, not a matter of being in
some proximity to the present; consider two historians, Thucydides and Sir Walter Raleigh. Thucydides, says Arnold, is "modern," because he sticks to "facts"; Sir Walter Raleigh, in sharp
contrast, is clearly a gargoyle because his *History* takes up such

matters as the division of the firmament, the height of paradise, and the constitution of the primum mobile, matters Arnold calls "obsolete and unfamiliar" in a phrase redolent of a tact that fairly cries out to be called "classical."[5] Arnold knows that his hearers will have no truck with such bilge and will probably be provincial enough to say so in about those words. And of course Arnold is entirely right. It is into this intellectual climate that Newman intrudes himself, talking this way:

> It was, I suppose, to the Alexandrian school and to the early Church, that I owe in particular what I definitely held about the Angels. I viewed them, not only as the ministers employed by the Creator in the Jewish and Christian dispensations, but as carrying on, as Scripture also implies, the Economy of the Visible World. I considered them as the real causes of motion, light, and life, and of those elementary principles of the physical universe, which, when offered in their developments to our senses, suggest to us the notion of cause and effect, and of what are called the laws of nature.
> (37)

The unhurried deliberateness of this prose seems to assume that its reader will tranquilly entertain the question of angelic natures and not raise Arnoldian eyebrows or, Johnsonianly, pound tables and kick great stones at the suggestion that angels are the "real causes" of physical phenomena and the true agents of "what are called the laws of nature."

There is a rich irony in this blandly confiding tone, for of course Newman knows that his audience is not much disposed to assess the merits of alternative views of the angels, whether the views come from the writers of the Alexandrian school or some other. One can imagine, though, a reader of good will who will seize on the accommodation implicit in the shift from "what I definitely held" to "I viewed them" and "I considered them": The very coolness of the prose seems to invite at least those in whom "sensibility" predominates over "sense" to suppose that Newman regarded angels as metaphors or figures of speech. And indeed the passage goes on to quote some of the young Newman's breathiest purple in a manner to encourage such an inference:

> This doctrine I have drawn out in my Sermon for Michael-
> mas Day, written in 1831. I say of the Angels, "Every breath
> of air and ray of light and heat, every beautiful prospect, is,
> as it were, the skirts of their garments, the waving of the
> robes of those whose faces see God." Again, I ask what
> would be the thoughts of a man who, "when examining a
> flower, or an herb, or a pebble, or a ray of light, which he
> treats as something so beneath him in the scale of existence,
> suddenly discovered that he was in the presence of some
> powerful being who was hidden behind the visible things he
> was inspecting . . . . nay, whose robe and ornaments those
> objects were, which he was so eager to analyze?" and I
> therefore remark that "we may say with grateful and simple
> hearts with the Three Holy Children," O all ye works of the
> lord, &c., &c., bless ye the Lord, praise him, and magnify
> him forever." (37–8)

Anyone anxious to turn Newman's angels into metaphors will
welcome the suggestions here of "as it were" and the passage
thence to childlike wonder, sermons in stones, books in the running brooks, and good in everything. Is there anything to be
made of the flatly prosaic connecting phrases ("and I therefore
remark") that intermit the high purple or those deflationary etce-
teras ("all ye works of the Lord, &c., &c., bless ye the Lord") that
so impatiently hasten us through the sacred formulas?

Perhaps not. But if saving these appearances – the angelic ones
– seems possible by the invocation of metaphor, Newman
quickly raises the stakes by conjuring with appearances less man-
ageably figurative:

> Also, besides the host of evil spirits, I considered there was
> a middle race, δαιμόνια, neither in heaven, nor in hell; par-
> tially fallen, capricious, wayward, noble or crafty, benevo-
> lent or malicious, as the case might be. These beings gave a
> sort of inspiration or intelligence to races, nations, and
> classes of men. Hence the action of bodies politic and asso-

115

ciations, which is often so different from that of the individuals who compose them. Hence the character and the
instinct of states and governments, of religious communi-
ties and communions. I thought these assemblages had
their life in certain unseen powers. (38)

Newman goes on to consider how such "unseen Powers" might
be "countenanced" by obscure passages in Daniel and Revelation, and transcribes a letter of his written in 1837 in which these
matters are spoken of with an earnestness ("I cannot but think
that there are beings") and an erudition (one breezy parenthesis
encloses "Justin, Athenagoras, Irenaeus, Clement, Tertullian,
Origen, Lactantius, Sulpicius, Ambrose, Nazianzen") that could
only make a mid-Victorian squirm. Then, with no apparent
abatement of earnestness, this discussion of "unseen Powers . . .
who are the animating principles of certain institutions, &c., &c."
takes that perplexed Victorian into its embrace: "Take England
with many high virtues, and yet a low Catholicism. It seems to
me that John Bull is a spirit neither of heaven nor hell" (38).
   In a space of only two pages, the angels and demons of this
account have veered from real entities, literally believed in, to the
furnishings (familiar enough) of a high-flown, artsy, "poetical"
way of talking (indeed, of sermonizing), to satiric barbs darted in
the direction of John Bull's complacencies. A composite forged
of recondite theology, oratorical ornament, and sudden levity
might seem dangerously unstable, especially to John Bull; but
from it, nevertheless, Newman airily launches himself upon a
profession of utter disregard for what John Bull might think: "I
am aware that what I have been saying will, with many men, be
doing credit to my imagination at the expense of my judgement"
– and it is here that he rejoins, "'Hippoclides doesn't care'": the
allusion is to a tale of sublime and energetic insouciance drawn
from Herodotus – about which more later – but we must read to
the end of the passage:

I am not setting myself up as a pattern of good sense or of
anything else: I am but giving a history of my opinions, and
that, with a view of showing that I have come by them
through intelligible processes of thought and honest external means. The doctrine indeed of the Economy has in

some quarters been itself condemned as intrinsically pernicious, – as if leading to lying and equivocation, when
applied, as I have applied it in my remarks upon it in my
History of the Arians, to matters of conduct. My answer to
this imputation I postpone to the concluding pages of my
Volume. (39)

This, of course, has far more the air – parodically so? – of man-
tling itself in an Englishman's right to his "opinions" (even of
"every man in his humour") than of disclosing the "intelligible
processes of thought and honest external means" by which those
opinions were arrived at. We are offered not accommodating
explanation but rather foreclosure of any such expectation. If we
have not understood, "Hippoclides doesn't care." And it is provocative that just here, where explanation and accommodation
are withheld, Newman should mention again that "doctrine of
the Economy" deemed so vexing and unsupportable in "some
quarters." (Is Kingsley diminished or aggrandized in this mock-
respectful phrase?)

If Newman elsewhere parodies the popular notion of himself
as the perfidious Jesuitical logic chopper, here it is the caricatural
image of the benighted and credulous Catholic that he is sending
up; he professes things we cannot believe he believes and then
cryptically mentions "Economy," as if to tease us with the suspicion that he is not telling all. Newman affronts us with a conun-
drum, that is, and gives us to believe that there is an answer for
those who seek it. Indeed, the answer is apparently so potent that
possession of it fortifies Newman against our bad opinion. Newman will not cast his pearls before swine. And just as his impe-
riousness and his indifference to any "pattern of good sense or of
anything else" redeems the view of him, the "version" of him,
the "scarecrow" the public has dressed up in his clothes and pro-
nounced to be a figure of (in Kingsley's language again) "insipience," so this pose equally undercuts its opposite caricature, the
view of Newman as acting out of "insincerity," the casuist whose
sophistries can make black seem white; for here is a voice that is
all too obviously *not* trying to persuade us of anything.

If this imperious display constitutes an exorcism by parody of
the scarecrow of "incipience" Kingsley had dressed in Newman's
clothes, Newman undertakes a few pages later an even more dar-

ingly provocative caricature of the other caricature Kingsley had drawn: that of the wizard of "insincerity," the calculating sophist at the behest of whose enchanter's wand sense and logic and self-evident truth are laid under thrall. Here Newman seems less to admit Kingsley's charge of being a subtle insinuator of Romish doctrines into minds too distracted or unvigilant or simple to detect them than almost to boast of his triumphs in that line and exult over the inattentive or impercipient victims on whom he had practiced his subtle arts:

> I wished men to agree with me, and I walked with them step by step, as far as they would go; this I did sincerely; but if they would stop, I did not much care about it, but walked on, with some satisfaction that I had brought them so far. (51)

If this seems mild enough, what follows begins to sound veritably – that is, parodically – like the brag of the cunning Jesuit, as Newman recalls getting the best of an editor too dull-witted to notice the tendency of things he had agreed to print: "It was a satisfaction to me that the Record had allowed me to say so much in its columns, without remonstrance" (51). Newman goes on to make explicit his consciousness of his intellectual superiority, and to exult in the license and advantage it secured for him as a polemicist:

> I was amused to hear of one of the Bishops, who, on reading an early Tract on the Apostolical Succession, could not make up his mind whether he held the doctrine or not. I was not distressed at the wonder or anger of dull and self-conceited men, at propositions which they did not understand. When a correspondent, in good faith, wrote to a newspaper, to say that "Sacrifice of the Holy Eucharist," spoken of in the Tract, was a false print for "Sacrament," I thought the mistake too pleasant to be corrected before I was asked about it. I was not unwilling to draw an opponent on, step by step, by virtue of his own opinions, to the brink of some intellectual absurdity, and to leave him to get back as he could. (51)

118

Newman's way here of balancing the earnest "good faith" of that correspondent against his own facetiousness in finding the misprint in question "too pleasant to be corrected," at least "before I was asked about it," seems calculated to excite the anger and wonder of the dull and self-conceited against this serpent-like practitioner of the subtle arts of suasion on innocent victims, whether they be harried journalists, otiose bishops, or such scrupulous laymen as write letters to newspapers calling attention to misprints.

> I was not unwilling to play with a man, who asked me impertinent questions. I think I had in my mouth the words of the Wise man, "Answer a fool according to his folly," especially if he was prying or spiteful. I was reckless of the gossip which was circulated about me; and, when I might easily have set it right, did not deign to do so. Also I used irony in conversation, when matter-of-fact men would not see what I meant. (51)

When the *Apologia* began to appear in pamphlet form, the effect on Charles Kingsley was such that his wife put him in bed and took care to intercept all further installments before they fell into his hands. One is relieved not to have to contemplate the effect on poor Kingsley, raging in his bedclothes, of passages like this one. What can have been more maddening to him than to see Newman offering (and the public accepting) as triumphant vindication what Kingsley would have regarded as amounting in substance to a plea of guilty to all charges? Perhaps it was the very baldness of the "confession" that made it seem no confession at all; for even as it reports how subtly and frivolously Newman was (and, by implication, is) ready to play the game of religious debate, the very report is so frank as to seem to declare all: Nothing is concealed. Even when playing to the hilt the role of the sophist and word monger, Newman is so clearly not trying to persuade us of anything.

Provocation and Reserve

All of the "fierceness and sport" narrated in these pages is recalled by Newman in 1864 in connection with a much younger self, the impetuous champion of the Tractarian Movement who had imagined himself upon returning from abroad as another Achilles coming out of his tent: The motto of the *Lyra Apostolica,* composed at that time, was "the words in which Achilles, on returning to battle, says, 'You shall know the difference, now that I am back again'" (42). Newman speaks of the "supreme confidence" he felt in his cause and says that it inspired a "double aspect in my bearing towards others": "My behavior had a mixture in it both of fierceness and of sport; and on this account, I dare say, it gave offense to many; nor am I here defending it"(51). But this nonchalant gesture of "not defending" needs looking at. Its first effect is to make Newman seem ready to acknowledge his own fault, which reflects well on him generally and lends credit to his indignation at other charges. But viewed from a slightly different angle, "not defending" can seem less a concession to critics than a refusal to answer charges. (And note – he is not "*here* defending it" – as if to suggest that he might defend it in another place.) This pose of "not defending" appears regularly throughout the *Apologia* – the airy pronouncement that "Hippoclides doesn't care" is an instance; so is that final assurance without specifics concerning the medicinal properties of St. Walburga's oils – and it signals a curious aloofness at the heart of this exercise in soul baring. "Describing, not defending" becomes a strategy for setting limits to the discussion, the confession, the apologia. The public is put on notice that its warrant extends only into those precincts of Newman's being that Newman himself chooses or agrees to open; the rest is off limits.

At the same time, these closed subjects that Newman places beyond discussion come before us only because he has summoned them. In the present case, of his youthful "fierceness and sport" and his willingness to "play with a man," it is notable that if Newman declines to *defend* these excesses that he has narrated at such length – and so winningly – he also eschews any suggestion that he regrets them. On the contrary, the tone of the recital carries, to my ear at least, an unmistakable sound of pleasure and enjoyment, and suggests not the contrition of chastened retrospect but rather the survival and continuance of the youthful Newman's "exuberant and joyous energy" into the present controversial occasion: George Levine notes that this passage displays "a fierce joy, a real strength, a perhaps arrogant feeling of superiority" and observes that "we feel [these qualities] in the speaker, not merely in the young John Henry Newman being described."⁶ The "antagonist principle of personality" (47) that animated the *Tracts for the Times* is still operative in the text before us. And if much of the youthful Newman's personal style has persisted, it is suggestive that Newman's next point is to reconsider the content that went with that style and to affirm that (with the exception of youthful prejudice against Rome) nothing has changed there either: "What I held in 1816, I held in 1833, and I hold in 1864. Please God, so shall I hold it to the end" (54).

The refusal to defend youthful "fierceness and sport," then, asserted so casually and so tentatively against ironies and sarcasms so potent, appears to be hardly any disclaimer at all; rather its effect is to imply that Newman old still feels the "exuberant and joyous energy" that attended Newman young in the wars of the Oxford movement and that the ironist who writes in 1864 that John Keble's theology "was beautiful and religious, but it did not even profess to be logical" (31) is continuous with the young Turk who in 1833 struck sparks by wondering aloud whether Dr. Arnold was a Christian (42). Accordingly, Newman's coy remarks about youthful readiness "to play with a man," even as they invite misunderstanding from some readers, are *verba sapientibus* to others, advising us that the objects of Newman's play must now be ourselves – if we are the "matter-of-fact" sort who cannot tell when we are being played with. The accents of amused contempt audible in passages like these for the "dull and self-conceited" imply a challenge to the reader, a challenge already implied elsewhere (indeed, implicit in the whole notion of "Economy") when Newman speaks of children not apprehending the perceptions of adults, and prosaic minds likewise insensible to poetry and philosophy. In these passages Newman's youthful "exuberant and joyous energy" is re-called: both remembered and resummoned, called again, to tell us that Newman is still "not unwilling to play" with the suspicious and literal-minded sort of reader who will pounce on these very passages as an unwitting plea of guilty to Kingsley's charges, without seeing that Newman is using irony "when matter-of-fact men would not see what I meant." That they do not see what he means is the whole point.⁷

There are thus at work here quite contrary impulses: on some topics, daring thrusts of provocation and self-exposure; on others, a withdrawal or withholding, a willful refusal to engage, explain, "defend." The boldness of the provocation, given the supposed gravity of the rhetorical situation, seems a "comic" version of that confessional candor that elsewhere speaks so forcefully for Newman's honesty and frankness. Likewise the contrary gesture, the sudden drawing of the curtain, the refusal to say more, to answer the "what then?" that Newman provokes when he suddenly asserts the literalness of angels and demons that his tone had allowed us to suppose were meant figuratively, or when he deftly lays the question of miracles under a pall of evidentiary hairsplitting, then abruptly announces that he can attest to the medicinal values of St. Walburga's oil from personal experience, but hastens on without elaborating: These gestures seem a comic application of that principle of "Reserve" central to the Tractarian Movement in general, and to Newman in particular. "Reserve" is first of all an expression of awe before the sacred, but it also underlies "Economy," insofar as what an audience cannot understand must be "reserved" from it.[8] Typically an "Economical" or "reserved" discourse would discretely keep its own "Economy" and "Reserve" from view, but Newman provocatively makes the condescension implicit in "Reserve" and "Economy" an explicit feature of his esoteric comedy: Thus a device meant to allay difficulties is made to augment them, an audience that expects to receive an appeal finds itself abruptly dismissed, and an exercise that had seemed to promise candor and disclosure suddenly recedes from view, to be discerned at last only through a glass darkly.

I should emphasize that Newman's levity and irony do not undertake to "play" with all readers, but only with those who, like Kingsley ("because of [their] intellectual build" [387]), are unable or unwilling to see the ironies of a rhetorical situation in which Newman has been called upon to make himself and his religion plain and transparent to the simplest understanding. Given that such is an impossible project, especially when, among some readers, slow-mindedness is compounded by animus, Newman can only refuse to cast pearls before swine, a gesture that his irony and "play" effect to carry off as graciously as possible – for what, under the circumstances, were the alternatives? Rather than deal in oblique and glancing sarcasm, Newman might have been direct, but that would have been impossible without being brutal. Or he might have pleaded earnestly that the difficulties of his position were too complicated to explain in the setting of controversy – but that would surely have been called (and justly) evasive. So "play" of this sort responds, in 1864 as in 1833, to a complicated writer–audience relationship. But it also serves Newman old, as it served Newman young, as a way of keeping the hurly-burly of debate from disturbing Newman's relations with (so to speak) his subject matter. This ironic "playing" manner, he explains, "was a sort of habit with me. If I have ever trifled with my subject" – he means he has not – "it was a more serious fault. I have never used arguments which I saw clearly to be unsound" (51).

But more fundamental than all these considerations is what Newman's light and ironic tone suggests about the security and assurance out of which he is writing. The possibility of being misunderstood draws no complaints or protests from him; he takes it as normal and to be expected, and his humor makes clear that it worries him not at all. On this score, too, what was true in 1833 is still true as he writes now in 1864 – so much so that these passages constitute an oblique directive concerning how to read the *Apologia,* a sort of caveat to the effect that the strategies of Newman's youthful polemicizing operate still in the book we are now reading. And Newman considers, too, that he risks little in "playing" with readers this way, for those who appreciate the "play" will perceive that not they, but the "matter-of-fact" and the "dull and self-conceited" are the objects of Newman's satire. Readers capable of appreciating that much are closer than any "matter-of-fact" report could bring them to a worthy sense of "that living intelligence, by which I write, and argue, and act" (12).

Such "play" continues to be the keynote of Newman's self-presentation. Having played the credulous Romish gull, then the subtle Jesuitical deceiver, his next role is that of the mock papist fanatic:

This absolute confidence in my cause, which led me to the negligence or wantonness which I have been instancing, also laid me open, not unfairly, to the opposite charge of fierceness in certain steps which I took, or words which I published. In the Lyra Apostolica, I have said that before learning to love, we must "learn to hate"; though I had explained my words by adding "hatred of sin." In one of my first Sermons I said, "I do not shrink from uttering my firm conviction that it would be a gain to the country were it vastly more superstitious, more bigoted, more gloomy, more fierce in its religion than at present it shows itself to be." (52)

Superstition, gloom, bigotry: One can picture Kingsley writhing – although Newman goes on to offer some qualification – "I added, of course that it would be an absurdity to suppose such tempers of mind desirable in themselves" (52) – but in the very next sentence this gesture toward mildness is turned again in the direction of sarcasm, very dry: "The corrector of the press bore these strong epithets till he got to 'more fierce,' and then he put in the margin a *query*" (52). We pass from here directly to a vision to set spinning the heads of all sensible Englishmen:

> In the very first page of the first Tract, I said of the Bishops that, "black event though it would be for the country, yet we could not wish them a more blessed termination of their course, than the spoiling of their goods and martyr-dom." (52)

Newman next mentions another youthful passage about the proper punishment of heresiarchs, which, he reports, prompted "a Northern dignitary . . . to accuse me of wishing to re-establish the blood and torture of the Inquisition" (53). Newman quotes the passage in question and concedes:

> I cannot deny that this is a very fierce passage; but . . . it is only fair to myself to say that neither at this, nor at any other time of my life, not even when I was fiercest, could I have even cut off a Puritan's ears, and I think the sight of a Spanish *auto-da-fè* would have been the death of me. (53)

Can one doubt the irony here? Particularly rich is that second "even": "not *even* when I was fiercest, could I have *even* cut off a Puritan's ears." Newman is satirizing the grotesque fantasies of cruelty and wickedness popularly attributed to Romish zealots in general and to the bogey of Newman-the-Antichrist in particular.

But this note of satire signals no moral *relachement,* nor does it waive any jot of principle; in what immediately follows it is clear that the humor is continuous with a "fierce" and principled rigor:

> Again, when one of my friends, of liberal and evangelical opinions, wrote to expostulate with me on the course I was taking, I said that we would ride over him and his, as Othniel prevailed over Chushan-rishathaim, King of Mesopotamia. Again, I would have no dealings with my brother, and I put my conduct upon a syllogism. I said, "St. Paul bids us avoid those who cause divisions; you cause divisions: therefore I must avoid you." I dissuaded a lady from attending the marriage of a sister who had seceded from the Anglican Church. (53)

Again, the passage effects a transit from irony (the mock Torquemada too squeamish *even* to cut off a Puritan's ears) through a high oratorical "way of talking" (Othniel and Chushan-rishathaim as cudgels with which to browbeat "one of my friends") to setting filial relations below strict religious principle (dismissing one's brother "upon a syllogism," dissuading an Anglican lady from attending the marriage of her Protestant sister).

In these passages, Newman boldly and grandly caricatures what he takes to be the mean and petty caricature of Catholicism at large among the English public. "Insipience" and "insincerity," the bigotry, gloom, and fierceness of superstition, these are sins the mid-Victorian public would prefer to ascribe to Catholicism alone. But in another passage, Newman provocatively tilts his parody of these allegedly Catholic properties toward precisely the most virulently anti-Catholic segment of the English public: the extremer sects of Dissenting Protestantism. Newman begins by recalling the Protestant prejudices acting on him during his formative years:

> As a boy of fifteen, I had so fully imbibed it ["this pure Protestantism"], that I had actually erased in my *Gradus ad Parnassum,* such titles, under the word 'Papa', as 'Christi Vicarius', 'sacer interpres', and 'sceptra gerens', and substituted epithets so vile that I cannot bring myself to write them down here. (113)

Such are the Protestant bigotries that even a nominally Anglican youth might assimilate in England (Newman had been raised an Evangelical Anglican); one implication of this passage is that the Romish "credulity" so objectionable to the English mind has something in common with hyper-Protestant imagination – later in the passage Newman speaks of his youthful (Protestant) hatred of Rome as an "unreasoning prejudice and suspicion" which, "though my reason was convinced, I did not throw off for some time after" (115) – and this point emerges in connection with themes of Bible interpretation that will make precisely the hyper-Protestant prick up ears:

> ... by 1838 I had got no further than to consider Antichrist, as not the Church of Rome, but the spirit of the old pagan city, the fourth monster of Daniel, which was still alive, and which had corrupted the Church that was planted there. (113–14)

As with the angels and demons passage quoted above, the diction here allows the reader to suppose that Newman regards the Antichrist and the fourth monster of Daniel as metaphors or figures of allegory, variously (i.e., accommodatingly) "interpretable" – an implication that would seem to forbid naïvely literal applications in the manner of the more extreme Dissenting sects. Still, Newman is seeking here to identify these "metaphors" with actualities, not with mere conceits, and in any case the Antichrist and the book of Daniel are props so firmly associated since the seventeenth century with the underground of radical working-class Dissent, that to a Broad or a Low Church reader like Kingsley, Newman's speculations here about their proper interpretation and identification might well sound more like a sudden infusion of Dissenting fundamentalism than Romish sophistry.

We may suppose Newman's gesture here calculated to cut two ways: to discomfit high-rolling Protestants by asserting with them a kinship they will not at all welcome, while also reminding mainstream Anglicans that their progressive and modern society harbors more ignorant, backward, and gloomy superstition than England's tiny Catholic minority can ever be made to answer for. The passage culminates in another of those dazzlingly provocative assertions with which Newman seems almost to taunt his adversaries:

> Soon after this indeed, and before my attention was directed to the Monophysite controversy, I underwent a great change of opinion. I saw that, from the nature of the case, the true Vicar of Christ must ever to the world seem like Antichrist, and be stigmatized as such, because a resemblance must ever exist between an original and a forgery; and thus the fact of such a calumny was almost one of the notes of the Church. (114–15)

It is hard to imagine a more provocative argument to offer Protestants; it is one thing to deny that the pope is Antichrist; it is another to assert that the very "fact of such a calumny" actually constitutes part of the pope's claim to legitimacy as Christ's vicar. The assertion itself is the more provocative for being offered in the blind matter-of-fact tones of a man delivering a Q.E.D.

If the irony here seems augmented precisely by the unemphatic tone, neither the irony nor the tone should encourage doubt of Newman's seriousness on this point. The same point is made twice, with irony and sarcasm that approach sounding shrill, in the *Essay on Development,* where it occasions the only such outbursts in 445 otherwise sober, earnest, and painstaking pages.[9] The circumstances of that work's composition – Newman wrote it during his retreat at Littlemore as an exercise to help focus the effort of working through his spiritual crisis – should discourage any suspicion that the point is made for the sake of the irony. Newman's sense that the point could hardly be made to an English audience *without* irony seems implicit in the publication history of the passage. In the *Apologia*'s original printing, this passage contained another 600 words explaining briefly but earnestly the development of Newman's thought on the matter. Citations from and references to Newman's earlier writings told readers seeking serious discussion of the question where to look for it. In all subsequent printings, these paragraphs were deleted (they are given in Svaglic's edition, pp. 113–15); to read these pages with, and then without, these 600 words is to witness the foreclosure of an important writer-to-reader accommodation.

These several passages effect what I have been calling an "exorcism by parody." Newman had declared in his preface, as we have seen, that his adversaries had raised up a mere caricature of his true character; refuting them would be perforce an exercise in making the true appear and distinguish itself from the false semblance, the caricature, the parody, the "forgery" that, because it is a forgery, must bear a deceptive similarity to its original. Newman explicitly puts the matter, in a passage we have already read, in just these terms:

> I must show what I am, that it may be seen what I am not, and that the phantom may be extinguished which gibbers instead of me. I wish to be known as a living man, and not as a scarecrow which is dressed up in my clothes. (12)

But as he had already pointed out in that same preface, Kingsley had poisoned the wells; the ordinary avenues of argument and defense had been foreclosed in advanced:

> If I am natural, he will tell them "Ars est celare artem"; if I am convincing, he will suggest that I am an able logician; if I show warmth, I am acting the indignant innocent; if I am calm, I am thereby detected as a smooth hypocrite; if I clear up difficulties, I am too plausible and perfect to be true. (7)

Here Newman is in part simply turning Kingsley's trick against him, that is, anticipating his response with irony and sarcasm, just as Kingsley had anticipated Newman's. But he is also, in effect, offering a catalogue of possible arguments and strategies that he will pointedly disdain to employ. Rather than be accused of concealing his art, Newman will brandish it ("I was not unwilling to play with a man"); rather than be accused of logic chopping, Newman will pointedly deny us the flattery of trying to convince us ("I am not setting myself up as a pattern of good sense or of anything else"); rather than show the warmth that might look like innocent indignation, Newman will be coolly, even insouciantly superior ("I liked to make them preach the truth without knowing it"); rather than be "detected as a smooth hypocrite," Newman will oblige by playing that very role – so broadly that it becomes dryly comical ("I used irony in conversation, when matter-of-fact men would not see what I meant"); rather than exhibit an unseemly anxiety about clearing up difficulties, Newman will enlarge and aggravate whatever difficulties you please – the oils of Walburga, for example? Delighted you asked, Mr. Kingsley.

Parody is fundamental to this project because, as this passage's relentless oppositions illustrate, Newman conceives of his task as precisely that of untangling the real Newman from the Kingsleyan caricature. Newman parodies the parody, to great, and more than satiric, effect – but only, of course, for readers capable of telling irony from earnest, parody from original, true from false. The reader is thus challenged to discriminate conflicting "versions" of Newman, and more, is implicated by that challenge in the satire the parody advances. The scarecrow phantoms of Newman have arisen from unthinking prejudice, a susceptibility that inverts some peculiarly English virtues (quick and ready loyalty to custom and established usage, an aptness for vigorous expression) and thus produces a parody of England's more magnanimous and generous character. If Newman's position is to be consistently and maliciously turned into "a phantom . . . which gibbers instead of me . . . a scarecrow dressed up in my clothes" (12), the irony is that Newman's attackers will be transforming themselves into a travesty of their own better, smarter, and more humane selves; it is they who will be gibbering phantoms and raggedy scarecrows. Their lie, again, will only be their nearest approach to Newman's truth. If Newman's parodies of Kingsley's parodies imply, too, a parody of his audience, a parody that satirizes the meaner habits of English thought and feeling, then for the reader who can distinguish truth from travesty such emphasis will imply judgment and critique and perhaps open new access to sympathy, tolerance, and generosity. "I have wished to appeal from Philip drunk to Philip sober," writes Newman. "When shall I pronounce him to be himself again?" (8).

Parody, Economy, Sacrament

Clearly, then, Newman's penchant for parody springs from more than mere delight in seizing local satiric opportunities; it implies the whole project of distinguishing true from false, parody from original, and – in a "Sacramental system" founded on "the doctrine that material phenomena are both the types and instruments of real things unseen" (29) – forgery from "type." As we have seen, "a resemblance must ever exist between an original and a forgery" (115); hence the acrimony between Catholics and Protestants on such questions as whether Rome is a Jerusalem or a Babylon, or the pope a vice-Christ or an Antichrist. Parody, of course, is based on resemblance and can be called a kind of forgery when its parodic character is not explicit, but is calculated, as Newman's self-parodies are, to perpetuate the mistakes of the impercipient and hold them up to the ridicule of those who get the joke. Just as the "Sacramental system" redeems (for Newman) by giving us economies that are never more than incomplete approximations of the truth, so his strategy of parody aims to redeem all those scarecrow phantoms of himself that are circulating about in the public mind: Newman acts every travesty, dons every grotesque mask, that public prejudice and distrust have fabricated and yet contrives to make these shabby caricatures speak forcefully for *him*. If the Kingsleyan parody debases, Newman's parody of the parody redeems; just as the sacrament of the mass – regarded in Newman's way as a type or economy of the Last Supper, rather than in the hyper-Protestant's way as an idolatrous forgery, a superstitious "ceremonial" – transubstantiates the wafer and the wine: conventionalized, stylized, endlessly and even mechanically repeated ritual issuing, somehow, in miracle.

So Newman's strategy of "exorcism by parody" and the complex of ironies by which it operates – that Kingsley's parody degrades but Newman's parody of the parody redeems – bring us to the center of Newman's comic vision. It is ironic and comic in an obvious Christian sense, insofar as redemption, a grand and utterly unmerited outcome, lies at the end of conflict, struggle, and compromise. But is is also comic in an unexpected Romantic way, because it issues from a complex of ideas very similar to one from which Romantic writers, typically steeped in Protestant habits of thought and feeling, wrung very different consequences. In *Sartor Resartus,* especially in its later chapters, Carlyle "shadows forth," as he would say, a "Transcendentalist" vision, shared to greater or lesser degrees by many other writers of the period, according to which all phenomena of the visible world are "Symbols" of an invisible, "Transcendental" truth, of a "Natural Supernaturalism" of correspondences between the finite and the infinite, the temporal and the eternal, the material and the spiritual. This new-fangled oversoul, fashioned of puritan moral absolutism and German idealism, is analogous to an ancient feature of Catholic thought fundamental to Newman's whole habit of mind, namely the complex of ideas he calls "the Sacramental system; that is, the doctrine that material phenomena are both the types and the instruments of real things unseen" (29).

The "Natural Supernaturalism" of the Protestant transcendentalists (Newman might say) amounts to a parody of the Romish "Sacramental system": The resemblances between them are only such as must ever obtain between an original and a forgery. They are as different as tragedy and comedy, for the transcendental divine sought by Carlyle and others remains inevitably at a remove from the intelligence that would be consoled by it. The visible world is called upon to mediate between the solitary soul and the divine, but such mediation is just what a Calvinist temper like Carlyle's most distrusts, with the consequence that the thrust of such transcendental ideas is necessarily *away* from the assurances they were meant to secure. The very need for mediation betokens the soul's distance and alienation from that "Transcendental" overworld that remains at one or more removes from the inquirer searching not for its mere evidences, but for unmediated contact with it.

The paradoxes involved here, if not suffered to remain unexamined, must either rend asunder the baseless fabric of the transcendentalist vision or else lead into some such tangle of contradictions as the doctrine of "sincere idolatry" muddled forth by Carlyle in his *Heroes and Hero-Worship* lectures. By contrast, Newman explicitly dismisses the "suspicion" (charged word) "that one thing and another were equally pleasing to our Maker [i.e., without regard to truth or falsity], where men were sincere" (186) – and of course, as I tried to show in the last chapter, the sorrows of Carlyle have everything to do with his recognition that "sincerity" is not enough. The anxious, "totalizing," reductive Protestant temper, if offered the comfort of the lovely thought that a tree is a "Symbol" of a celestial something that burgeons and fructifies, cannot but reflect fairly soon that a symbol is *only* a symbol after all and so falls short of the consummation so devoutly to be wished. Material and spiritual remain incommensurable categories, beyond the power of any "Organic Filaments" to bind lastingly together. And lest the ironic notion Carlyle in *Sartor* called "Descendentalism" prompt us to consider the failure of his "Natural Supernaturalism" a difficulty merely personal to Carlyle, a *contemptus mundi* attributable to melancholia, spleen, or dyspepsia, the nature worship of Wordsworth and Coleridge, and its fate, should remind us that more than temperament is implicated in the sorrows of Protestantism, for theirs was an idolatry too sincere to do anything at last *but* to disappoint. The same dilemma compels Keats's recognition that "the fancy cannot cheat so well / As she is famed to do" and Shelley's agitation that poetic imagination, poetic image making, can only be an idolatrous "mockery" of those "deep truths" that Demogorgon avows to be "imageless."[10]

In short, the very extremity of transcendental aspirations seems often to entail an ironic, "Descendental" outcome. In Newman's "Sacramental system," the tragic trajectory of aspiration and descent is (comically) turned upside-down – which is to say, right-side-up. The whole structure is not impelled from below, by unstable and imperfect human aspirations *toward* God (or whatever God term), but rather descends and depends *from* Him. It offers not so much mediation as participation; the isolated sensible fact is not a mere emblem or symbol of some grander but utterly remote analogue; it is *part* of that grander analogue, a synecdoche of it. Hence Kingsley's and Newman's cross-purposes over the matter of "Economy": For Kingsley either a given account of something is the truth or it is not, and if not, error at best, doom and woe at worst, ring out for us. But for Newman, the truth is something no one can apprehend more than partially: The miracle (and the comic grace) of it all is that it is a truth so potent that even the tiniest and most partial bits of it can sustain us, provided we do understand, according to our lights, the particular, partial cross section of the whole that is disclosed to us. William Empson memorably sums up the ironic vision of Swift as springing from the view that "everything spiritual and valuable has a gross and revolting parody, very similar to it, with the same name; only unremitting effort can distinguish between them."[11] If I may paraphrase, Newman's comic vision expresses the conviction that even the most gross and corrupt things partake of the divine, if only in the relation of a parody or a forgery to its original; only faith, hope, charity, and as much intelligence as we can muster need attend our apprehension in order to guide us from one to the other.

Newman first encountered the "Sacramental system" in his youthful reading of Bishop Butler's famous and influential *Analogy of Religion, Natural and Revealed, to the Constitution and Course of Nature:*

> The very idea of an analogy between the separate works of God leads to the conclusion that the system which is of less importance is economically or sacramentally connected with the more momentous system. (23)

A few pages later, Newman describes how his youthful readings in Clement and Origen "spoke of the various Economies or Dispensations of the Eternal":

> I understood these passages to mean that the exterior world, physical and historical, was but the manifestation to our senses of realities greater than itself. Nature was a parable: Scripture was an allegory: pagan literature, philosophy, and mythology, properly understood, were but a preparation for the Gospel. (36)

The passage continues with a brief recapitulation of the role of Judaism and paganism (whose "outward framework, which concealed yet suggested the Living Truth, had never been intended to last" [36]) in the unfolding of revelation in history, to the present, when we await "truths still under the veil of the letter, and in their season to be revealed":

> The visible world still remains without its divine interpretation; Holy Church in her sacraments and her hierarchical appointments, will remain, even to the end of the world, after all but a symbol of those heavenly facts which fill

eternity. Her mysteries are but the expressions in human language of truths to which the human mind is unequal. (37)

Significant is the way "Economy" attends these formulations, here where there is no pressure of responding directly to Kingsley's abuse of the word and the idea. As we have seen, where Newman does address Kingsley's misapprehension on that head, "Economy" is given a common-sense justification; here, in the implication that "Economy" and "sacrament" are, if not synonymous words, certainly cognate ideas, we see how "Economy" springs from Newman's whole habit of mind. The word "Economy" had appeared in Newman's youthful essay, "Poetry," as the principle of selection, guided by attention to universals rather than mere particulars, by which Aristotle distinguishes the intellectual activities of "poetry" and "history." "Economy," Newman explains, is of the essence of poetry, because "by confining the attention to one series of events and scene of action, it bounds and finishes off the confused luxuriance of nature"; "with Christians, a poetical view of things is a duty," because with its aid we are able "to colour all things with hues of faith, to see a Divine meaning in every event, and a superhuman tendency."[12] The seeker after religious wisdom must be like a reader of poetry, ready to submit sympathetically to the "Economies" the poet presents: such readiness is an exercise of that "illative sense" Newman took such pains to explain in his *Grammar of Assent.*

In the *Apologia,* of course, the matter is put much less accommodatingly, in remarks that struck many a reader in 1864 as provocatively "shocking to plain English Notions":

Many persons are very sensitive of the difficulties of Religion; I am as sensitive of them as anyone; but I have never been able to see a connexion between apprehending those difficulties, however keenly, and multiplying them to any extent, and on the other hand doubting the doctrines to which they are attached. Ten thousand difficulties do not make one doubt, as I understand the subject. (214)

People say that the doctrine of Transubstantiation is difficult to believe; I did not believe the doctrine till I was a Catholic. I had no difficulty in believing it, as soon as I

believed that the Catholic Roman Church was the oracle of
God, and that she had declared this doctrine to be part of
the original revelation. It is difficult, impossible, to imagine,
I grant – but how is it difficult to believe? (215)

Passages like these cannot but have been unintelligible to Charles
Kingsley. To him, these thoughts would be "unthinkable," literally: that which cannot be thought. Kingsley and Newman, to jar-
gonize in the current fashion, inhabit different *epistemes.* Kingsley charged that "Dr. Newman teaches that truth, for its own
sake, is no virtue." For Newman, "truth" involves, emanates
from, the Christian's duty to see the world sacramentally. For
Kingsley, "truth" must conform at all points with physical or historical fact, as established by scientific and critical evidentiary
tests. Of such natural or historical facts – facts seem not to exist
in any other categories – our knowledge can only be more or less
accurate or complete, and our report more or less candid or
forthcoming.

For Kingsley, in short, truth is an affair of proof, experiment,
and demonstration, in which the mind is properly passive and
impartial, whereas for Newman, it involves faith and witness:
not passive conditions, but self-conscious and deliberate intellectual and spiritual activities. For Kingsley, "truth for its own
sake" involves getting the facts right; for Newman understanding
is always for the sake of something more important than mere
accuracy in ascertaining data. But as Newman points out, the
positivist profession of disinterested search for facts for their own
sake is self-deluding: All inquiry serves purposes, whether consciously or not; even for the disinterested scientific inquirer natural facts must be interpreted differently according to the purposes at hand:

Scripture says that the sun moves, and that the earth is sta-
tionary; and science that the earth moves, and the sun is
comparatively at rest. How can we determine which of
these statements is the very truth, till we know what motion
is? If our idea of motion be but an accident of our present
senses neither proposition is true, and both are true; neither
true philosophically, both true for certain purposes in the
system in which they are respectively found. (378)

Although Newman is looking backward toward Berkeley rather
than forward to Einstein and Bohr, his argument here seems
familiar enough today; but its power to shock a century ago is
audible in Kingsley's citation of it:

> I beg all who are interested in this question . . . to judge for
> themselves whether I exaggerate when I say that [the ser-
> mon containing the passage above] tries to undermine the
> grounds of all rational belief for the purpose of substituting
> blind superstition. (378)

Kingsley discerned in the passage above a "seemingly sceptic
method" – he is only the first in a long line of commentators who
cannot decide whether Newman's faith springs from credulity or
from skepticism and resolve their dilemma by accusing him of
both.[13] To exploit the paradox of a "seemingly sceptic method"
deployed in the service of what to the Victorian public seemed
willful credulity is, as we have seen, a deliberate and entirely self-
conscious strategy of Newman's esoteric comedy, and Kingsley
is taking Newman's bait when he charges that the purpose of
Newman's "seemingly sceptic method" is "to tell us that we can
know nothing certainly, and therefore must take blindly what
'The Church' shall choose to teach us" (378). Newman's point is
that whatever we think we "know certainly" we know only in
relation to some purpose. The professedly disinterested scientific
inquirer purposes to banish from his canons of explanation certain "subjective" concerns deemed irrelevant distractions. Such
professedly disinterested pursuit of "truth for its own sake"
actually represents an "Economy" of tremendous proportions,
whose ability to curb human beings from the exercise of their
humanity grows the more dangerous the more it ceases to be a
deliberate and self-conscious intellectual procedure and becomes
an automatic mental reflex. When the quite specialized purpose
that it initially served is forgotten, what remains is a denatured,
dehumanized, desacralized habit of mind. When positivist
canons come to govern the ways in which we try to think about
belief and knowledge, as conditions of mental acquiescence, mere
effects of facts whose accuracy someone can verify by experiment, then the mind can only imagine itself, and thence become,
passive before experience. And so the empiricist project of mas-

tering nature by obeying her, according to a scientific method whose chief boast is that it places all wits on a level, is at the furthest possible remove from Newman's sacramental or economical sense of the world as a thesaurus of emblems, outward and visible signs of a redemption we gain by learning to interpret them, not under the dead letter of positivism, but in the living spirit of the human enterprise as Newman characterizes it in his *Grammar of Assent:*

> ... though man cannot change what he is born with, he is a being of progress with relation to his perfection and characteristic good. Other beings are complete from their first existence ... but man begins with nothing realized ... and he has to make capital for himself by the exercise of those faculties which are his natural inheritance. Thus he gradually advances to the fulness of his original destiny. Nor is this progress mechanical, nor is it of necessity; it is committed to the personal efforts of each individual of the species; each of us has the prerogative of completing his inchoate and rudimental nature, and of developing his own perfection out of the living elements with which his mind began to be. It is his gift to be the creator of his own sufficiency; and to be emphatically self-made. This is the law of his being, which he cannot escape; and whatever is involved in that law he is bound, or rather he is carried on, to fulfil. (*Grammar,* 265)

For Newman, not external fact, but this inward process of self-making is what matters; scientific method may be valid for investigating the "less momentous system" of physical nature, even if it does so by adopting the "Economy" of regarding physical nature as a radically desacralized confluence of atoms moving in obedience to merely physical forces that are uniform and precisely calculable, but without moral import or consequence. But in religious inquiry, "intead of devising, what cannot be, some sufficient science of reasoning, which may compel certitude in concrete conclusions," what is needed is

> to confess that there is no ultimate test of truth besides the testimony borne to truth by the mind itself, and that this

phenomenon, perplexing as we may find it, is a normal and inevitable characteristic of the mental constitution of a being like man on a stage such as the world. (*Grammar,* 266)

In short, "It is the mind which reasons, and that controls its own reasonings, not any technical apparatus of words and propositions" (*Grammar,* 268).

In passages like these from the *Grammar of Assent* Newman is doing his best to make explicit and plausible, by explaining patiently the logic and psychology of it, a set of assumptions that in the *Apologia* he often prefers to leave "comically" abrupt, baffling, unforthcoming.[14] The *Apologia*'s refusal to kowtow is motivated in large part, as we have seen, by the circumstances of the controversy with Kingsley; but beyond the pique of its polemical occasion, it has its springs in Newman's more fundamental and constant sense of the rhetorical action proper to the limits and possibilities of "a being like man on a stage such as the world." The contrast between the *Apologia*'s provocations of posture and gesture and the *Grammar*'s patient generosity of explanation suggests the varieties of "interpretation" itself: There is explication, as of a commentary on a text; and there is the sort of "interpretation" suggested by Newman's theatrical metaphor ("a stage such as the world"), the interpretation of an actor playing a role, or a musician rendering a score, or a dancer performing a piece of choreography. This sort of interpretation offers neither argument nor elucidation; it does not substitute an abstraction for the mystery that instanced it; it retains implicit in itself all that had been implicit before; it makes its object available not to ratiocination but to experience.

"Interpretation," then, can be enacted as a species of performance, and this brings us close to an aspect of Newman's performance in the *Apologia,* an instrument of "interpretation" whose power has always been acknowledged, namely Newman's style. Newman has always been recognized as a self-conscious stylist, and I have argued here for a range of effects that can only have been very self-conscious indeed, of a complexity and subtlety perhaps possible only to a stylist who confessed to a "habit, from a boy, to *compose.* I wrote in style as another might write in verse, or sing instead of speaking, or dance instead of walking."[15] Newman writes in his "Literature" lecture (in *The Idea of a University*) that the *style* of a composition should not merely ornament its content, but embody, incarnate, or (as we would say) constitute it, and the style of the *Apologia* works in precisely this way to disclose not an exposition of Newman's ideas but an enactment of his personality.[16]

Not exposition but enactment, not ratiocination but experience: These are distinctions fundamental to Newman's sense of the difference between Protestantism and Catholicism. Newman would have savored Yeats's remark, that in the one church there is a pulpit but no altar, in the other an altar but no pulpit. The pulpit is a forum for verbal explanation, argument, and analysis; at the altar, by contrast, mysteries are not explained but enacted – and experienced. Newman's progress from pulpit to altar was motivated by his preference for sacrament over preachifying. (*Sacramentum*, by the way, enters the vocabulary of Latin Christianity as the authorized translation of the Greek *mysterion*.) Early in his Anglican career, Newman had urged that genuine conversions cannot be affected by preaching, however enthusiastic; the potential convert should be, deserves to be, brought to belief and maintained in it, as Newman was urging his correspondents in March 1835, by the awesome experience of the sacraments, thus being exposed to "the more sacred truths" not by way of verbal indoctrination but "by rites and ceremonies":

> In this way Christians receive the Gospel literally on their knees, and in a manner altogether different from that critical and argumentative spirit which sitting and listening engender.

Robin Selby, who located and quotes these hitherto unpublished letters, comments that

> Newman wished to bring forward the Services and Catechizing back to their rightful places, which had been usurped by preaching. Where a doctrine had been delivered over the pulpit in words which were but a feeble representation of the reality, in future Newman wanted the congregation to find the real thing in the Sacraments.

The sacraments themselves, says Newman, are and must be "the means of persuasion. They are the embodied forms of the Spirit of Christ."[17] Selby's language here, contrasting the "feeble representations" proffered by verbal preachment with that "real thing" of which the sacraments are "embodied forms," accords with themes we have been exploring, of parody, forgery, type, and their relations to their "originals," as well as the contrast between an interpretation that expounds and one that enacts or between style-as-ornament and style-as-incarnation.

At the same time, it is the *persuasive* force of the "embodied forms" that Newman is recommending here, a power that operates not merely in default of any gestures toward "explanation," but on the contrary, by arousing, rather than pacifying, the communicant's sense of awe, mystery, and surprise. In relation to that project, "the world" figures not as the positivist machine, mastery of which amounts to becoming a cog in it, but rather a thesaurus of emblems, infinitely interpretable. Infinite interpretation is comic, too, because it acknowledges the futility of the mind's wish for closures and finalities of meaning, even as, properly instructed, it orients itself always toward the one great and infinite truth. It is the Protestant mind that experiences a "metaphysical pathos" before phenomena that defeat the project of definitive interpretation. Robin Selby brilliantly connects Newman's doctrine of reasoning from probabilities with his interest in calculus, that system of reckoning by approximations to a limit never reached.[18] For Newman, religious certainty, religious truth, are limits we approach through signs, through sacraments, through "Economies," whose agency guides us ever in the right direction even as its mediation keeps the goal ever in infinite regress. The "infinite play of interpretation" can conduct us to affirmations other than the Neitzschean.[19]

I made much in my introduction of "fictionalism," the notion that all human "constructions" are constituted by the human mind and thus are "fictions," as a feature bridging esoteric comedy and the masterworks of modernism. This risks seeming to say that Newman did not believe in his religion, but I do not mean that at all. His faith in God is unshakable; that is no "fiction" for him. But Newman holds that all talking and thinking about religion is something different from faith; it is an "Economy," an interpretation, a version, an approximation – it is "about" the truth, an index of the truth, but not the truth. And this condition of things is in the nature not of "truth," but of "human language":

> Moral Truth . . . cannot be adequately explained and defended in words at all. Its views and human language are incommensurable. For after all, what *is* language but an artificial system adapted for particular purposes, which have been determined by our wants?[20]

Everything we say about God and about religion, any "interpretation" we offer, is a "type" of the truth, and thus (in a sense) a parody or forgery of it, not the thing itself but as close as we can come, the best we can do, and yet nevertheless (ironically, comically, miraculously) redemptive for all that. For Newman, "the world" is mere material for that infinite, ingenious, and (at its most fully human) sacramental play of imagination and intellect that redeems the positivist "universe of death"; the world as the empiricist sees it – chooses to see it – is for Newman a mere spectral realm of law without spirit and has, humanly speaking, no existence worth being concerned with.

In the opening pages of the *Apologia,* Newman acknowledges a lifelong "mistrust of the reality of material phenomena" (18) and connects it with the Protestant ambience in which be grew up. It had, he writes, the effect of "isolating me from the objects which surrounded me" and "making me rest in the thought of two and two only absolute and luminously self-evident beings, myself and my Creator" (18). Newman's "mistrust of the reality of material phenomena," of "the world," was corollary to this intensely apprehended reality of god. That this idealism underlines his sacramental habits of mind he acknowledges a few pages later:

> The very idea of an analogy between the separate works of God leads to the conclusion that the system which is of less importance is economically or sacramentally connected with the more momentous system, and of this conclusion the theory, to which I was inclined as a boy, viz. the unreality of material phenomena, is an ultimate resolution. (23)

And again, speaking of "what may be called, in a large sense of the word, the Sacramental system," Newman acknowledges "the connexion of this philosophy of religion with what is sometimes called 'Berkeleyism'" (29).

Blanco White, reviewing Newman's youthful essay of 1828, "Poetry, with Reference to Aristotle's Poetics," shrewdly observed that Newman was a Platonist, not an Aristotelian. He anticipated the complaints of twentieth-century Catholic intellectuals, who, overwhelmingly "realist" and Thomist in their thinking, quite rightly perceive as residually Protestant and irredeemably "modernistic" the idealist cast of Newman's thinking. They distrust Newman's grounding of faith on so personal and psychological (even Lutheran) a foundation as "conscience"[21] – to them it seems perilously close to "private judgement" – and they perceive in Newman's idealist Sacramentalism the dangerous suggestion that it is the believer's mind, not God's creating power, that sacramentalizes the world.[22] One may deplore their rejection of Newman's theology, but at least they are rejecting it for what it is. The same cannot be said for the judgment of Wilberforce, transmitted via Leslie Stephen to the "humane" tradition of literary criticism, that it was a fundamental skepticism that impelled Newman to Rome in search of external, institutional, and historical validations for a fragile and willful faith; much less the surly Kingsleyan types who regard Newman as a coward before experience, moving through a desperate sequence of ostrich-like postures of retreat from the world. Newman's Catholicism was no retreat from the world; on the contrary, his service to it brought Newman into the world, into confrontation and, indeed, combat with it. Hardly an affair of anxious faith seeking an objective correlative in an ancient, historical, and (self-proclaimed) "universalist" worldly institution, Newman's public career was more like an unmerited and gratuitous offer of grace to the external world from that charmed circle of "two and two only," in an effort to enlarge that circle till it should enclose and thus redeem the whole intractable and resisting world.

The Limits of Comedy, the Comedy of Limits

The will empowered in a world infinitely compliant to its sacramentalizing purposes: This is the realm of the illative sense and of those assents that Newman calls, in the *Grammar of Assent,* "notional." It is the realm of intellectual power and confidence, the realm where the self is free to subordinate all enterprises to that of self-making. It is, needless to say, the theater of Newman's "comic" transactions with the world, extending from the sublime of sacramental imagination to the ridiculous game in which Newman makes mock of "plain English notions" and "ignorant common sense" by talking as if dogmas unthinkable to most of his audience are the obvious conclusions to be drawn from phenomenal appearances, "antecedent probabilities," "*prima facie* cases," and the like.

But of course faith is not so easy a project as that; nor, in Newman's view, should it be. The objections of a Kingsley can be easily disposed of – so Newman's genial sarcasm has been telling us throughout – but Newman does not wish us to suppose that faith is as simple an affair as winning a debate or wishing "the Arabian Tales were true." The achievement of a too facile faith is worth little to Newman; indeed, it is just his complaint with the soothing assurances of "Liberalism," latitudinarianism, and "private judgement" that they make the demands of faith all too easy to negotiate. And so he acknowledges in the last chapter of the *Apologia* that although in moods of intellectual confidence and power (the mood of most of the *Apologia*), the world can be invested with sacramental character, there are also moments when such élan wilts before the recognition in appearances of the world's grimmer and more disheartening faces. At such junctures, the arena of Newman's "comic" imagination contracts drastically to the extensionless point of that "thought" of two beings only, a refuge from which the world is necessarily excluded: has, indeed, excluded itself. In such moods the transactions of the mind with the world turn from comedy to something approaching despair – though despair, be it noted, not of God, but of the world. Against the sacramental view of the world as a plentitude of Godly presence, the desperate recognition of a radical alienation of the earthly order from God enters Newman's agon of faith:

> Starting then with the being of a God, (which, as I have said,
> is as certain to me as the certainty of my own existence,
> though when I try to put the grounds of that certainty into

logical shape I find a difficulty in doing so in mood and figure to my satisfaction,) I look out of myself into the world of men, and there I see a sight which fills me with unspeakable distress. The world seems simply to give the lie to that great truth, of which my whole being is so full; and the effect upon me is, in consequence, as a matter of necessity, as confusing as if it denied that I am in existence myself. If I looked into a mirror, and did not see my face, I should have the sort of feeling which actually comes upon me, when I look into this busy living world, and see no reflexion of its Creator. This is, to me, one of those great difficulties of this absolute primary truth, to which I referred just now [i.e., in the remark that "ten thousand difficulties do not make one doubt"]. Were it not for this voice, speaking so clearly in my conscience and my heart, I should be an atheist, or a pantheist, or a polytheist when I looked into the world. I am speaking for myself only; and am far from denying the real force of the arguments in proof of a God, drawn from the general facts of human society and the course of history, but these do not take away the winter of my desolation, or make the buds unfold and the leaves grow within me, and my moral being rejoice. The sight of the world is nothing else than the prophet's scroll, full of "lamentations, and mourning, and woe." (216–17)

This seems to be a contrary to fact statement, an effort to imagine the world "as if" God did not exist. But what the words actually say is quite different: There is no question here of God's existence, but of what Newman elsewhere calls God's apparent "absence (if I may so speak) from His own world" (*Grammar*, 301) – as the shift from the conditional to the declarative mood (signaled by the world "actually") in this sentence reveals:

> If I looked into a mirror, and did not see my face, I should have the sort of feeling which *actually comes upon me, when I look into this busy living world, and see no reflexion of its Creator.* (emphasis added)

Newman is saying here that it is "this voice, speaking so clearly in my conscience and my heart," that projects God outward upon a resistant world whose beauty and design bring proof and conviction of God's existence into the individual conscience. The implicit picture of a world empty of God and resistant to Him comes close to voiding the entire "Sacramental system" by which that circle of two and two only is opened and extended to include the world. Newman is not, however, voiding that system, but acknowledging that it does not justify, but is rather justified by, the primary conviction of God's existence that Newman finds in his conscience. And in the same way, and for the same reasons, "notional assent" depends on "real assent"; when Newman speaks – acknowledging their "real force" – of "arguments that do not warm or enlighten me," he is acknowledging the limits of notional assent, of the illative sense, and of the "comic" sacramentalizing power of the mind over the world. So the picture Newman draws here of a world void of any "reflexion of its Creator" is the measure of the *amor mundi* that informs Newman's sacramentalizing project and of the enormity of that "unspeakable distress" Newman mentions, the ordeal through which Newman undertakes that his "testimony" will be "borne to truth by the mind itself."

This ordeal posed by a world voided of Godly presence threatens almost everything Newman is about – everything, that is, that Newman is about *in the world;* it does not touch that charmed circle of two and two only. But Newman's "apologetic" enterprise is addressed to the world, and Newman acknowledges its vulnerability in, for example, the qualification in that first sentence: Although the being of God is as certain to Newman as the certainty of his own existence, nevertheless, "when I try to put the grounds of that certainty into logical shape I find a difficulty in doing so in mood and figure to my satisfaction." This "difficulty" looms large, inasmuch as Newman's whole project in the *Apologia* is implicated in the suggestion that "logic" and "certainty" (terms that sound abstract and imply the cogencies of irrefutable demonstration) must be expressible in "mood and figure" (devices characterizing the nonrational suasions of such arts as poetry and eloquence) to produce "satisfaction" (a word naming an effect proper more to psychology or esthetics than to logic and suggesting rather the cool, tentative, and above all personal exercise of some such faculty as taste, than either the imperious Q.E.D.s of reason or the raptures of enthusiasm).

And so Newman can proclaim a limit to the satisfaction of "mood and figure" and then go on, in the following two sentences, to elaborate a figure ("If I looked into a mirror and did not see my face ... ") that strikingly registers the mood of "unspeakable distress" he is describing here. The world is a mirror that should reflect God, just as any looking glass reflects your face when you look into it. Observe the irony by which looking "out of myself into the world of men" is likened to looking into a mirror, into oneself. Remark also the assured sense of self and of God that can sustain the submerged syllogism, absence of God equals – or would equal – absence of self.

But even as it posits such limits, this passage enacts the comedy by which limits, in Newman's calculus of convergent probabilities, finally redeem more than they foreclose our approach to what lies beyond them. If a limit is a point of arrest, forbidding access to what lies beyond, it is also and by the same token an index, necessarily advising us in what direction "the beyond" lies. If a limit curtails the search, it also orients the seeker, and thus is a kind of "mediator" between the quester and "the beyond" that is sought. I argued above that Protestant versions of transcendentalism – Shelley's, Carlyle's – distrusting "mediation" and aspiring to "transcend" it in unmediated or "immediate" relation with the divine, aspired to the impossible and thus were doomed to failure and despair. Newman has it both ways: His "two and two only" asserts the "immediacy" or unmediated character of his faith, in a fashion recognizably Protestant,[23] whereas his (very Catholic) faith in mediation – approximations, interpretations, versions, fictions, types, parodies, "Economies," sacraments, which, while not "the truth," are nevertheless sufficient and efficacious mediators between "truth" and the human understanding – asserts a drama (a comedy) of approaching without reaching, ending in the nevertheless happy, and "comic," outcome of salvation.

"Religious Selfishness"

The very incommensurability of "self" and "God" produces despair for the Protestant; faith that the incommensurables are mediated – for, to Newman, that is what Christianity promises –

146

generates Newman's comedy. The abyss between "self" and "God" is for Newman no impasse, for the axes are rather "God"/ "self" on one side of the abyss and "self"/"world" on the other. In the *Apologia,* it is his self that Newman puts forward, exposes, imperils in combat with "the world." "I mean to be simply personal and historical: I am not expounding Catholic doctrine, I am doing no more than explaining myself, and my opinions and actions" (13). That is why the inquirer who asks, "What, then, does Dr. Newman mean?" must be answered not with arguments and propositions and proofs, but with "embodied forms" of that "living intelligence, by which I write, and argue, and act" (12).

The *Apologia*'s power, as every reader has acknowledged since 1864, is that Newman gives us *himself,* not a treatise about his religion. And he gives us himself, as we have seen, in action: making gestures, scenes, moments, rather than arguments, cases, "sense." "If I do not use myself," he explains, "I have no other self to use" (*Grammar,* 264). When he seems to argue, he is often merely parodying the form of an argument; what he is really doing, despite (wryly ironic) talk of "intelligible processes of thought and honest external means," is enacting before scrutinizing and suspicious eyes a grand display of an intelligence magisterially self-assured, self-possessed, confident of its powers and glorying in them. Such displays are themselves "Economies," which "reveal and yet conceal" that living intelligence of Newman's. Newman is making himself an example and a witness of the liberating power of his religion; it is tempting to say that he means to make himself an outward and visible sign of that power that he insists sustains him. He will be a living "type" of the mystery that a submission so total, so far from diminishing his spirit and limiting his mind, is the very action through which all his capacities are given scope and amplitude. Something of the largeness of the issues at stake, and of Newman's audacity in posing them, is audible in his casual quasi-Luciferian remarks that "Catholics can sin with a depth and intensity with which Protestants cannot sin" (438). Likewise, when Newman declares that "in these provinces of inquiry, egotism is true modesty" (*Grammar,* 292); when Newman insists on the prerogative he astonishingly calls "religious selfishness" (198) against the sniffing reproaches of "friends" who felt slighted because at the height of his own spiritual crisis he did not satisfactorily minister to theirs; when Newman declines to make conversion easy, and remarks that "there is something which looks like charity in going out into the highways and hedges, and compelling men to come in; but in this matter some exertion on the part of the persons whom I am to convert is a condition of a true conversion" (*Grammar,* 323); when Newman so serenely indulges in grandly insouciant gestures like these he is displaying a self, *making* a self, exhilaratingly untrammeled by the decorums of diffidence, deference, and modesty that so often made Victorian confidence bland, Victorian tolerance a mask for cowardice, Victorian piety fraudulent, Victorian earnestness insincere – that so often made, in short, Victorian virtues into anxious and spiritless parodies of themselves.

"I used to wish the Arabian Tales were true" (15): How self-pitying these words would sound if they came from J. A. Froude or Arthur Hugh Clough! From Newman, they bear none of the plangent melancholy of bourgeois Byrons whose illusions are gone; they are buoyant, frank, candid, and daringly vulnerable. When Newman presents this childish wish as "having a bearing on my later convictions" (15), he seems to *dare* Kingsley to produce a suitable jibe.[24] But he is also making an oblique appeal to more sympathetic readers who are conscious that some visionary gleam is fled and who long to have their days bound each to each in natural piety, as Newman's are.

In the same way, Newman invites complaints of his "self-righteousness" when he announces that "I have never had any suspicion of my own honesty; and when men say that I was dishonest, I cannot grasp the accusation as a distinct conception, such as it is possible to encounter" (153). Newman knows that he is addressing an audience for whom self-distrust is an obligatory moral style, many of whom will envy more Newman's faith in himself than his faith in God. But he is also addressing readers for whom such assurance, in defiance of its very appearance of presumption, will be powerfully attractive. When Newman sets out to explain his conversion to Catholicism with the remark that "I have done various bold things in my life: this is the boldest: and, were I not sure I should after all succeed in my object, it would be madness to set about it" (91), he knows the words will strike some readers as unseemly, as almost boastful, and will thus challenge them to resist his efforts all the more strongly. But to others, Newman's self-confidence and his utter freedom from the usual Victorian diffidence – no sign here of either its obligatory petty rituals or its massive private torments – will be enviable, and exemplary.

Newman presents himself as an example of faith – faith in self, in intelligence, in God – but he does so as if in entire un-self-consciousness that that is what he is doing. He addresses himself to the problem of doubt, for example, as if it were an inexplicable rarity, reports of which have reached his ears but whose nature seems undeterminable and whose very existence is, well, doubtful. Consider the manner in which Newman takes apart the "celebrated saying" "O God, if there is a God, save my soul, if I have a soul" (30). Newman ingenuously inquires, "But who can really pray to a Being, about whose existence he is seriously in doubt?" The question seems eminently reasonable, so much so that the reader is not likely to notice that it contains within it all the rigor of Newman's remark that there is no halfway house between atheism and Rome.

But of course Newman knows that doubt is everywhere, that he is addressing readers anxious to locate such halfway houses: Indeed, by Newman's time, a token of certain forms of religious "sincerity" was precisely a willingness to confess one's doubt, and to do so had become almost an obligatory gesture, as if to profess unwavering faith would be pretentious and immodest. Yet unwavering faith is precisely what Newman does profess, repeatedly; and he does so with an air of expecting no surprise or challenge about this, as if unwavering faith were the rule rather than the exception he well knows it to be. Such a stance (aside, of course, from expressing perfectly the way Newman thinks things *should* be) will have a complex effect on the doubt-ridden Victorian, troubled by an inability to "really pray" and whose faith is "seriously in doubt." Newman's tone will arouse an intense nostalgia for the days before the new philosophy cast all in doubt. It is unsurprising that so many of Newman's contemporaries, as A. Dwight Culler reports, experienced Newman's rhetoric almost sexually, as a seductive siren song, promising deliverance from doubt and anguish.[25]

Esoteric Comedies

"Exuberant and Joyous Energy"

Of all Newman's strategies of self-assertion, self-making, it is his
levity that is most astonishing and, it may be, most characteristic.
It affronts every expectation a Victorian reader would bring to
the spiritual autobiography of a famous religious controversialist
defending himself from attack. We can imagine a reader like
Dorothea Brooke experiencing considerable perplexity over passages like those we have cited. If Newman is "sincere," why does
he not adopt a more appropriately sanctimonious tone? How can
he trifle over matters so serious? The answer is that Newman is
trifling with his *readers,* not with his *subject matter.* Indeed, the
great discharges of "exuberant and joyous energy" (49) so frequent in the *Apologia* are possible precisely because, for Newman, "divine things" are not at all at issue there. Newman once
described himself as "incapable, as if physically, of enthusiasm,
however guarded":

> I am always languid in the contemplation of divine things,
> like a man walking with his feet bound together. I am held
> as it were by a fetter, by a sort of physical law, so that I
> cannot be forcible in preaching and speaking, nor fervent in
> praying or meditating.[26]

Newman associates this ἀδυναμία (powerlessness) with his youthful dislike of the rituals of Evangelical enthusiasm. But something very like "enthusiasm" is discernible in the *Apologia:* Certainly there is no "fetter" restraining Newman from the exercise
of all his powers of wit and language. He appears before us, at
least partially, in the guise of a holy jester; what the objects of his
jests will make of him, "Hippoclides doesn't care."

It is time to annotate that reference, and I will risk a lengthy
citation – for the pleasure of it – from Herodotus. The story
begins when Clisthenes, a parvenu tyrant anxious to secure his
daughter a husband of wealth and prestige suitable to her station
in life, invites suitors to present themselves at his manor. Among
many others is one named Hippoclides, an Athenian, "eminent
among his countrymen, both for his affluence and his personal
accomplishments."

On their appearance at the day appointed, Clisthenes first inquired of each, his country and his family. He then detained them all for the space of a year, examining their comparative strength, sensibility, learning, and manners: for this purpose, he sometimes conversed with them individually, sometimes collectively. The youngest he often engaged in public exercises; but his great trial of them all, was at public entertainments. As long as they were with him, they were treated with the utmost magnificence and liberality; but he showed a particular preference to the Athenians. Of these, Hippoclides, the son of Tisander, was the first in his regard, both on account of his personal prowess, as well as because his ancestors were related to the Cypselidae of Corinth.

When the day arrived which was to decide the choice of Clisthenes, and the solemnization of the nuptials, a hundred oxen were sacrificed, and the suitors, with all the Sicyonians, invited to the feast. After supper, the suitors engaged in a dispute about music, and in other general subjects. Whilst they were drinking, Hippoclides, who made himself remarkably conspicuous, directed one of the musicians to play a tune called "Emmelia;" his request being obeyed, he began to dance with much satisfaction to himself, though, as it should seem, to the great disgust of Clisthenes, who attentively observed him. After a short pause, Hippoclides commanded a table to be brought; upon this he first of all danced according to the Lacedaemonian, and then in the Athenian manner; at length he stood upon his head, using his feet as if they had been his hands. The two former actions of Hippoclides, Clisthenes observed with great command of temper; he determined not to choose him as his son-in-law; being much offended with his want of delicacy and decorum; but when he saw him dancing with his feet in the air, he could contain himself no longer, but exclaimed, "Son of Tisander, you have danced away your wife." – "Hippoclides cares not," was the abrupt reply. This after wards became a proverb.[27]

It is perhaps unwise to insist that Newman's resort to that proverb was entirely deliberate; still, to read the passage with Newman in mind is to be struck by all sorts of suggestive resonances between Hippoclides's relation to Clisthenes and Newman's with the English public. The suitor who must at the last moment throw away the prize – not the bride really, but her father's approval – because the trial has been dragged out for too long, has been made a pretext, in fact, for the father to indulge himself interminably in the flattering pleasure of being the man upon whom everyone's hopes attend; most of all, that image of the former favorite dancing on his hands on the table, wiggling his legs in the air: all of this resonates with the situation of Newman after nineteen years of nearly total retirement from the world of controversy, wishing only to be left in peace but still a frequent object of newspaper speculation designed to let him know that the terribly high-minded English public still doubts the purity of his motives. ("I was considered insidious, sly, dishonest, if I would not open my heart to the tender mercies of the world" [158], writes Newman, remembering his harrassment by the press during his retreat at Littlemore.)

This allegorizing, if it seems far-fetched, can be reduced to the simple image of Hippoclides, an image of an accomplished man deeming it better for the nonce to persist in folly rather than offer to explain or justify or rationalize. The image expresses Newman's indifference to our understanding him and leaves us to make what we will of this quite astonishing gesture. We might reject it as foolishness, or we might admire its energy and humor and refusal to compromise; in either case, Hippoclides doesn't care. The image is, of course, comical on its face, and it mocks all canons of earnestness and reasonableness that Victorians typically expected to be observed in religious discussion: mocks their pious hopes of reason, sympathy, and tolerance with the impossibility of ever "settling" difficult matters satisfactorily by means of reasonable and patient exchange of views. The gesture announces that at some point accommodation ceases and exchange is no longer possible. Do such impasses occasion despair? Are they instances of a routinely to-be-lamented "failure to communicate?" Not for Hippoclides: He doesn't care. And that he doesn't care, such gestures communicate perfectly.

Such Hippoclidean energy, exuberance, and insouciance are

qualities Newman associated with the highest literary genius:

> ... the elocution of a great intellect is great. His language expresses, not only his great thoughts, but his great self. Certainly he might use fewer words than he uses; but he fertilizes his simplest ideas, and germinates into a multitude of details, and prolongs the march of his sentences, and sweeps round to the full diapason of his harmony ... rejoicing in his own vigour and richness of resource. I say, a narrow critic will call it verbiage, when really it is a sort of fulness of heart, parallel to that which makes the merry boy whistle as he walks, or the strong man, like the smith in the novel, flourish his club when there is no one to fight with.[28]

Wilfred Ward tells an attractive story of Newman as an old and frail man, years after the *Apologia,* still drawing the attention of ambitious debaters seeking the promotion of truth (and their own reputations) in public combat with the venerable Romish veteran:

> When Canon McNeile, the Liverpool anti-Popery speaker, challenged him to a public dispute, Newman replied that he was no public speaker but that he was quite ready for an encounter if Mr. McNeile would open the meeting by making a speech, and he himself might respond with a tune on the violin. The public would then be able to judge which was the better man.[29]

3

"BECAUSE THERE IS SAFETY IN DERISION"

YEATS'S *A VISION*
❧❀❧

... he was always alert, dramatic, and amazingly brilliant. When he told a funny story, he had a trick of looking suddenly at the ceiling, rolling his eyes with little snorts of laughter, and spreading out his beautiful hands as if he were juggling invisible balls. He was a really lovely man to watch. Every pose was right.

– Frank O'Connor, "Yeats's Phantasmagoria"

Every writer should say to himself every morning "Who am I that I should not seem a fool?"

– Yeats, letter to Edith Shackleton Heald

"WE BEGIN TO LIVE when we have conceived life as tragedy" (*A*, 128),[1] wrote Yeats in a grand and oft-quoted phrase. He was writing at age fifty-six about himself at twenty-odd; he was rebuking, if obliquely, the callow youth who had supposed that the chore of living was best entrusted to the servants. Yeats had worked long and hard – well into his thirties – at playing the arty young dreamer; his abandonment of that effort dates from the years just after the turn of the century, when the antiquarian pleasures of Irish folklore, the imaginative license of occult "research," and the luxury of immersions unchecked by anything so mundane as scholarship in Blake and other "mystic" poets evaporated before incitements at once more provocative of passion and less compliant to desire. Irish politics, the Abbey Theatre, the personal struggle against timidity and for self-possession in the hurly-burly of public affairs – all that his mind summed up in his frustrated passion for Maud Gonne – these were the commitments and trials in facing which Yeats was "beginning to live" with something like the

155

tragic hero's awareness of risk, of going forth to a fate he could neither control nor foresee, neither avoid nor help but insist, for honor's sake, that he had chosen. Here are the springs of that impulsiveness, recklessness, even folly Yeats would celebrate in Crazy Jane and the Wild Old Wicked Man of the late poems, that cry of the frenzied mind from within the aged body:

> . . . Never had I more
> Excited, passionate, fantastical
> Imagination, nor an ear and eye
> That more expected the impossible.
>
> (*V,* 409)

But that hunger for the impossible and the wonderful, that reckless choice of a life "tested by passion" (*A,* 128) that Yeats's readers have agreed in calling "heroic," if it invited and sustained an experience of life Yeats welcomed as "tragic," was intermitted often enough by a complementary "comic" motive: the impulse for order, calm, serenity, the wisdom that gazes in detachment upon the world, knowing and foreknowing all, never flabbergasted, never at a loss, never taken by surprise. The mind embattled and in turmoil rises above its struggles; its victories come without effort; all obstacles are imperiously dismissed with a wave of the hand and a magniloquent jest – as in Frank O'Connor's image of Yeats derailing common-sense objections to his fairy talk with a shrug, saying, "That was before the peacock had screamed."[2]

Once during his sojourn at Oxford – at the time when he and his wife were deep into the sessions of automatic writing and "sleeps" that would issue five years later in *A Vision* – Yeats delivered himself of an aphorism: "In farce, the soul is struggling against a ridiculous object: in comedy, with a removable object: in tragedy, with an irremovable object."[3] This formulation is as unstable as any in Yeats, since even the grandest of his tragic "objects" – hopeless love, old age, death itself – can appear to him in various "moods" as now ridiculous, now removable, now irremovable. Yeats's esoteric comedy involves an effort that I will call "the *Vision* project" – a disagreeable phrase, but necessary, for by it I designate not only the two texts Yeats published under the title *A Vision* and such obviously related texts as *Per Amica Silentia Lunae* and poems like "The Double Vision of Michael Robartes," but a distinct and large area of Yeats's interest and activity, preoccupying him throughout his life and registering an effort to systematize and fortify that "mood" in which an idealism fashioned of occultism, Romanticism, and Bishop Berkeley swallows whole, and without strain, all that intractable world whose intransigences Yeats celebrates and protests elsewhere in his work. The *Vision* project, and the pose of esoteric comedian sustaining and sustained by it, exhibit a presumption Yeats was as quick to acknowledge as to enjoy (the 1925 *Vision* was subtitled, in part, "An Explanation of Life") – even as its solicitations absorbed and awed him, until the passion and desire that motivated it, protracted over such long periods of time and through so many labyrinths of error and uncertainty, at last appeared to him yet another embodiment, tenacious and willful, of that "antithetical" impulse he regarded as heroic.

The tragic–comic distinction is, of course, a simplification that will need complicating in the following pages.[4] Yeats's ironic mind was quick to see how the quest for certainty and perfection could be thwarted by the advent of the unforeseen; but he was equally quick to recognize that the heroically reckless desire for the miraculous generally disperses in the apprehension that "life [is] a perpetual preparation for something that never happens" (*Memoirs,* 230). On the one hand disappointment, resignation, the gradual "withering into the truth," the attenuated "desolation of reality"; on the other the catastrophic, all-at-a-blow reversal, after which "all's changed, changed utterly." Both of these sequences are ironic, and both can elicit heroism from the antithetical spirit that meets them. Either can appear as tragedy or as comedy, as dramas of either endurance or humiliation. For Yeats tragedy and comedy have the same shape; it is the beholding eye, altering, that alters all. Hence the paradox Yeats labored and insisted on, and collapsed into the phrase "tragic joy." And hence also its corollary, that for Yeats, rage and despair often provoke the bitter laughter of a kind of "comic pain": a sort of battered kettle at the heel.

But that is earthy comedy, even as that tragedy is earthy: By contrast, Yeats's esoteric comedy is otherworldly, an all-disposing, all-embracing posture unconstrained by the entrapments of active life and so occupying a realm of freedom untrammeled by paradox. It is as close to something pure as the mature Yeats, distrustful of purity, every came; and as close to abstraction as Yeats, all his life possessed by a "hatred of abstraction," ever came. And it is an epitome of that acute self-consciousness that Yeats exhibited all his life. Yeats's esoteric comedy conducts itself in very shrewd (and very "antithetical") relation to an audience preoccupied with taking Victorian seriousness off and putting modern seriousness on. When Auden tells Yeats in his elegy to the older poet, "You were silly like us," he seems generous and confiding, but he is being self-aggrandizing: Yeats *was* silly, but silly in a grand, a magnificent style: not at all silly like *them*.

Funny Stories about Yeats

Anyone who has read around at all in the literary memoirs of Yeats's era will remember plenty of funny stories about Yeats. Robert Graves never missed a chance to remember "a dialogue reported to me by an undergraduate visitant to No. 4 Broad Street, which had seemed a *non-sequitur:*

> UNDERGRADUATE: Have you written any poems recently, sir?
>
> YEATS: No, my wife has been feeling poorly and disinclined."[5]

Graves's strictures on Yeats are funny, and unjust as only the strictures of a competitor can be. (The author of *The White Goddess* is arguably the only twentieth-century writer who could plausibly call Yeats silly "like me.")

But Graves is almost alone, astonishingly, in being so acidly sarcastic; given the incitements Yeats's occultist poses must have offered, what is surprising is the genial acquiescence they usually met with. Even such wits as made rather a specialty of mockery seem not to have known what to make of Yeats's absurdities, beyond the amiable observation that they were absurd. "It seems to me," writes Stephen Spender, "that there was certainly something in Yeats which called out to be mocked at"; and he goes on to record a report of Virginia Woolf's of an encounter with the poet:

> ... when he had finished talking of *The Waves* he went on to speak of the carved wooden head of a baby on a pillar at the foot of a staircase, which Yeats said had spouted Greek to him. She went home impressed and elated and amused and mocking.[6]

But in this account amusement and elation are surely more salient features than mockery; there is even, it may be, a sort of awe. Nor does mockery animate Woolf's own report, in a letter, of another such encounter:

> ... on one side of the fire sat the poet Yeats on the other the poet de la Mare – and what were they doing when I came in? Tossing between them higher and higher a dream of Napoleon with ruby eyes. And over my head it went. ... I mean I know nothing of the spiritual significance of ruby eyes, or a book with concentric rings of purple and orange. But Yeats said, as it might be a man identifying a rather rare grass, that is the third state of the soul in contemplation (or words to that effect – it will not surprise you if I get them wrong). And then? Did I like Milton? Yes. And then – De la Mare does not like Milton. And then – dreams and dreams, and then stories of Irish life in brogue; and then the soul's attitude to art.[7]

Mockery hovers here but seems reluctant to put on a shape, opting rather simply to report Yeats's words (even "if I get them wrong") and let their self-evident absurdity speak for itself. Louis MacNeice, in his posthumously published autobiography, presents a vignette of Yeatsian eccentricity, all the more piquant for the presence in it of E. R. Dodds, the author of that luminous indictment of superstition and credulity *The Greeks and the Irrational*. Remarking that Yeats's manner, even in small talk, was "hierophantic," MacNeice tells us:

> He talked a great deal about the spirits to whom his wife, being a medium, had introduced him. "Have you ever seen

them?" Dodds asked. (Dodds could never keep back such questions.) Yeats was a little piqued. No, he said grudgingly, he had never seen them... but – with a flash of triumph– he had often *smelt* them. (As he saw us out at the gate he was urging Dodds to remember that Julius Caesar was killed at a full moon.)

There is no end to such stories. John Eglinton remembers Yeats casually referring in conversation to that great Irishman William Blake. Beverley Nichols recalls Yeats at the height of the Irish troubles mournfully lamenting that "if the English could only learn to believe in fairies, there wouldn't ever have been an Irish problem." L. A. G. Strong remembers Yeats at Oxford gratified that he had been able to save a doubting young Anglican's faith by reading with him "through all the forty-nine articles." (Yeats lifted this joke from Oscar Wilde, who also liked to advert to "the Twenty Commandments.")[8]

The Abbey Theatre, of course, was the arena for some of Yeats's most wonderful displays; there his authority as one of the theater's founders and directors gave license almost without limit to his obstinacy, his perfectionism, and his refusal to make the usual kinds of sense. P. J. Kelly recalls an occasion when, having already intolerably protracted a rehearsal with his dissatisfactions, Yeats broke the camel's back when he disclosed to his exasperated players, by way of explanation and guidance, his desire that "the first act must be horizontal, the second act perpendicular, and the third act circular." On another occasion it was "Dossie," the stage electrician who was being put through such paces; Gabriel Fallon narrates:

Abbey Theatre lighting in those days was of the most primitive kind. While Yeats paced the stalls, "Dossie" was engaged in putting one coloured gelatine slide after another into a kind of biscuit tin "flood" off stage. Nothing seemed to satisfy the poet. A thoroughly fed-up "Dossie" decided it was time for a smoke. Having lighted his cigarette, he accidentally flicked his still-lighted match into the box of gelatine slides. The whole thing flared up into a five foot blaze. As "Dossie" rushed for the nearest fire extinguisher, he heard Yeats shout from the stalls: "That's it, Dossie, that's the colour I want!"

If it is tempting to suppose that such stories are too good to be true, others are just too bizarre to be anything *but* true, like this one, recounted by Hugh Kingsmill:

> On another occasion a story I told brought out a certain humour which I had not suspected Yeats of possessing. "That is bizarre," he said. "I like what is bizarre in life. A short while ago I was asked by John Harris to give a lecture in Cambridge. The father of John Harris is a surgeon in Harley Street, and when I went into a barber's shop the barber was speaking of the father of John Harris, who, he said, was in reality the only surgeon in London, the others being merely his agents. A patient, the barber said, would call upon these men, who would be reputed to be skilful in some branches of surgery, and an operation would be arranged. But when that patient was under chloroform, the father of John Harris would come up through a trap door, perform the operation, and vanish before the patient was again conscious." Yeats laughed, there was a cunning gleam in his eye, and he looked very Irish.[9]

The sheer weirdness of this story helps us see a deliberateness in all of Yeats's eccentricities. Yeats wishes to cultivate a style, a manner, a persona that overwhelms the usual habits of response governing how we make sense of such phenomena as he. That eccentricity needs a defense, of course, Yeats always knew; he learned early to endure sarcasm, trekking through crowded railway terminals with Maud Gonne, carrying her numerous caged birds –

> Either alone would have arrested attention; together with cloaks and bird-cages, amid the fuss and paraphernalia of a railway station, they set the platform astare. Once he had to carry a full-grown Donegal hawk to her compartment.[10]

– or wearing his floppy tie, recognized and honored in Dublin as attire proper to a poet, through the more circumspectly appareled literary salons of London, where, as "Austin Clarke" remembers in W. R. Rodgers's wonderful "Dublin Portrait," "poets no longer wore any specific sign or symbol of their art. They were all dressed in hard stiff white collars, like business men."[11]

Memoirists tell their funny stories about Yeats with a roll of the eyeballs, yet all remain as harmless, finally, as a cartoon by the Incomparable Max. The very extremity of Yeats's foolish poses, rather than making him vulnerable to mockery, instead so dumbfounds his would-be mockers as to sap all their powers of sarcasm. The very astonishment his absurdity arouses bends them to his will; they become mere conduits, mere media, for the propagation of an image that remains in his control rather than theirs. I do not wish to overstate, and picture Yeats as some wizard of guile and manipulation, taking in hand the strings of every puppet that bobs onto his stage; but some such effect is palpably there, and there partly just *because* so many of the people reporting such stories (like so many of Yeats's readers) sensibly but wrongly assume that such bizarre displays are *not* deliberate, but rather spontaneous and unconscious manifestations of a personality so enrapt in its own world as to be utterly oblivious of any impression it might be making in this one.

The *Vision* Project

In all of these anecdotes Yeats appears as a sort of "humour character," but this was a highly self-conscious role and involved motives of mastery and mask that are central to all his enterprise – as we can see by considering one funny story about Yeats that wounded him deeply, in the aftermath of which the motives of the *Vision* project seem to have crystallized for him. George Moore's sketch, "Yeats, Lady Gregory, and Synge," appeared in two installments in the *English Review* (January and February 1914) and again – slightly revised under threat of legal action from Lady Gregory – as Chapter 7 of *Vale*. In it Moore announces publicly, while professing to scold those who whispered it privately, that Yeats was ashamed of his family's social standing; presents as a frequent matter for speculation in Dublin the interesting question whether Yeats and Maud Gonne ever "gratified" their "passion"; reports as from the poet's own lips that the answer was no, Yeats explaining that as a young man he had made himself content with the "spirit of sense"; represents himself as having replied to this disclosure, "Yes, I understand, the common mistake of a boy"; then makes mock of lamenting the death of Yeats's inspiration and the effective end of his literary career, prematurely passed "because it had arisen out of an ungratified desire."[12]

This was the article in the wake of which Yeats wrote that all his priceless things had been made "a post the passing dogs defile" ("While I, from that reed throated whisperer" [l. 14, *V*, 321]). The poem in which those words appear, printed as a coda to *Responsibilities,* speaks of forgiveness; but, in fact, Moore's attack was one insult Yeats found impossible ever to forgive. Vulgar, deceitful, and malicious, its effect on Yeats was profound, profound enough, perhaps, to have played a role in prompting him to another change of mask. For the first thing to notice about Moore's attack is that its target is not the esthetic and mystic Yeats, but the tough-minded public man that Yeats had striven to become in the preceding decade. During his decade of political involvement promoting a national literary movement for Ireland and directing the Abbey Theatre, Yeats had shed his ninetyish poses of detachment from the world, and downplayed – not just for public consumption – his interest in spiritualism and the occult. He wished to appear not as an otherworldly dreamer, but as an active public man, dealing shrewdly and effectively with the irksome and mundane realities confronted by "ordinary men."

Whether or not Moore's attack can be credited with launching a new phase – the Great War and Yeats's disappointment in the Irish literary movement were part of it also[13] – it certainly coincides with one: a period of reflection and consolidation in which Yeats pressed the antitheses of active and contemplative, esthete and nationalist, occultist and controversialist to yield new syntheses concerning self and antiself and the project of compelling their tensions and interplay into a "unity of being." Yeats is withdrawing from his "public man" role and investing his energies again, after a lapse of several years in that complex of esoterica and spiritualism I am calling the *Vision* project.

The change is signaled by "Ego Dominus Tuus," completed in October 1915, a poem that in many ways seems to be a response to Moore's challenge: One of the topoi that *Hic* and *Ille* revolve is whether great art comes from fulfilled or unfulfilled passion. (Moore's coarsest sarcasm, "the common mistake of a boy," is one Yeats administers to himself repeatedly in his later poems.) "Ego Dominus Tuus," in any case, initiates a labor of questioning that Yeats himself regarded, for a time at least, as having matured and been brought to term with the publication in 1925 of a systematic exposition of an esoterica of his own. "I can now, if I have the energy, find the simplicity I have sought in vain," he wrote, as he put the manuscript of *A Vision* in shape for the printer. "I need no longer write poems like 'The Phases of the Moon' nor 'Ego Dominus Tuus'" (*AV-A,* xii).

Well might Yeats declare himself free, in 1925, of the need to write such poems as "Ego Dominus Tuus" and "The Phases of the Moon," but they were necessary poems when written. Both effect a reprise of themes and interests that had occupied Yeats as a young man of the nineties, when he was editing Blake, sitting at the feet of Madame Blavatsky, and creating friction among his fellow students of the occult with his odd and contrary insistence that their experiments – for example, raising the ghost of a deceased flower – be conducted with more regard for scientific method.[14] Yeats's *Vision* project poems do not, of course, resemble his nineties verse, but they pointedly eschew the "public" tone, accessible however high, that he had spent the preceding decade mastering. Gnomic, complicated, mysterious in their air of displaying things through a glass darkly, of intimating doctrines that only a very few readers will be capable or worthy of receiving, they may reasonably be regarded as the sort of poem that the young Yeats had one day hoped to write, and so to arise from an ambition long put by.

The young Yeats, seeking mystic knowledge, had spent years turning the pages of queer old books – Blake, Swedenborg, Boehme – books that promise wisdom even as they withhold it, that compliantly invite interpretation, but – such is the inscrutable irony of "text" – finally authorize none. The temptation to elicit, even to extort, gratifyingly orderly meanings out of such texts is one that Yeats experienced fully and rather indulged than resisted. (In a preface to a translation of *Axel,* Yeats remembers how, as he worked through the original in his poor French, the play "seemed all the more profound because I was never quite certain that I had read a page correctly.")[15] The ambiguity of ora-

cular texts and the uses of ambiguity for any pose laying claim to
special wisdom were not lost on Yeats. Indeed, we find him very
early on, and with great deliberateness, polishing small masterpieces of enigma and illusion. A poem like "Who Goes with Fergus?" begs every question patient analysis can ask, including the
one the poem itself asks in its own title. Such calculated ambi-
guities are part and parcel of symbolism. As adumbrated in
France, *symbolisme* meant the promotion of mysterious and elu-
sive effects through the presentation of symbols whose referents
were entirely suppressed; as introduced into England by Yeats's
intimate friend, Arthur Symons, symbolism referred itself to Carlyle's remark, quoted on the second page of *The Symbolist Movement in Literature,* that "in a symbol, there is concealment, yet
revelation."[16]

A gnomic vagueness that can accommodate a great breadth of
interpretive response: To some degree, it is in such vagueness
that the continuing power of the Bible or the Kabala inheres.
While a student of the occult, Yeats came to regard indistinctness
as a virtue, as permitting the stylization, or reduction, of the particular to archetype. In his teens he had spoken, following Pater
and Ruskin, of the desirability of clear, firm outlines in art; but
by the nineties, dimness, vagueness, faintness of outline had sup-
planted that clarity in his esthetic thinking. To both esthete and
occultist, the art of the poker face is essential, and we can picture
the young Yeats acquiring the rudiments in drawing rooms and
at dinner tables, playing the Sensitive Plant to heartier men of
sense, parrying their assaults with cryptic and imposing solemnity. Yeats's folklore researches are relevant here: Imagine Lady
Gregory and Yeats – the callow youth in pince-nez and velvet
cravat who stares nervously from the Coburn photograph –
materializing on some remote Irish coast, making inquiries about
the local faeries, ghosts, leprechauns, what have you? Again,
there is great art involved in uttering the preposterous without
fear of contradiction, and Yeats's mastery only grew with time;
in later years Sir Edmund Gosse and Gilbert Murray were to
demur all but wordlessly on an occasion when Yeats imperiously
confided to them that he had observed an aquaintance of his and
theirs being followed about by a small green elephant.[17]

A willingness to appear silly, coupled with a sense of the ambiguity of experience and of all attempts to achieve a settled under-

Esoteric Comedies

standing of it: such are the underpinnings of that pose of wise fool, jester-cum-sage, esoteric comedian that Yeats continues to strike, ever more flamboyantly, through the later years of his life. Oscar Wilde once explained that a gentleman is one who never offends unintentionally; to paraphrase, Yeats's esoteric comedian is never laughable unintentionally – although of course the intention will be lost on most people. It is a validation of Yeats's instincts that even at his callow dreamiest, he never made himself ridiculous in quite the way that, for example, his friend Arthur Symons did. In a specifically nineties context, Symons's *The Symbolist Movement in Literature* can be of use to us chiefly as a thesaurus of the unintentionally ludicrous. On every page we find Symons whispering in reverential tones and *au très grand sérieux* such things as this, about the sublime author of *Axel:* "He lived his faith, enduring what others called reality with contempt, whenever, for a moment, he became conscious of it."[18] That a milieu existed, indeed, *thrived* on such twaddle underlines for us the ready availability of the handles of parody to writers like Joyce, Eliot, and Wyndham Lewis; it also goes far to explain the intemperances of Ezra Pound.

But Yeats had partaken of that milieu, and he was intensely loyal to friends ("old friends the most"). By the time Joyce spoofed Yeats in *Ulysses* ("Couldn't you do the Yeats touch?" inquires Buck Mulligan of Stephen: "'The most beautiful book that has come out of our country in my time. One thinks of Homer'"),[19] Yeats had evolved his own way of exploiting the literary situation, by fabricating texts that gently satirize the nineties sensibility even as they gratify it. He does this as early as 1897 in a slim volume called *Rosa Alchemica.* In that book we hear a perfectly plausible young esthete expressing himself in the breathy confessional Paterian style then familiar; and this speaker is not readily distinguishable from the book's little-known author William Butler Yeats, an obscure young dandy, poet, occultist, and (ahem) Irishman.

We may speculate that in London in 1897 the impact of *Rosa Alchemica* varied widely from reader to reader. At exactly what point would a given reader decide that this text was fiction? To *épater le bourgeois* was ever one of the esthete's keenest (though grossest) pleasures; it is not impossible to imagine a reader proud

166

of his healthy skepticism, and with a rational explanation for everything, reading all three stories (perhaps at the behest of his fiancée) and supposing them to be a lightheaded sensitive's cracked-brained account of his more hallucinated meanderings around London.

Robartes, Aherne, and the Fictions of *A Vision* (1925)

But if such a reader would have to be a dunce, the error – taking a fiction literally – is one that the latter-day careers of *Rosa Alchemica*'s two principal "characters" seem calculated to trick much wittier readers into. "Michael Robartes" and "John Aherne" (a.k.a. "Owen Aherne") are phantasmal self-projections that flicker in and out of Yeats's early poetry and fiction. During his Abbey Theatre, "public man" decade, Yeats sent this odd couple on holiday: They appear in no more of his new work, and where possible, in the poems preeminently, Yeats revised so as to eliminate them from new editions (e.g., "Michael Robartes Bids His Beloved Be at Peace" becomes "He Bids His Beloved Be at Peace"). But from 1918 on Robartes and Aherne begin to reappear in Yeats's writing; and especially in the annotation that Yeats began to furnish to his volumes of poetry, the two wraiths from *The Secret Rose* take on a spuriously convincing life. In a September 1918 preface to the second edition of *The Wild Swans at Coole,* for instance, Yeats mentions that he has added "a number of new poems":

> Michael Robartes and John Aherne, whose names occur in one or the other of these, are characters in some stories I wrote years ago, who have once again become part of the phantasmagoria through which I can alone express my convictions about the world.

Then comes a playful touch:

> I have the fancy that I read the name John Aherne among those of men prosecuted for making a disturbance at the first production of "The Play Boy," which may account for his animosity to myself. (*V,* 852)

But this confiding gesture turns unaccommodating a couple of years later, when Yeats composes a preface for the volume of poems called *Michael Robartes and the Dancer;* here Yeats attributes some of the esoterica of his "system" to "Michael Robartes' exposition of the *Speculum Angelorum et Hominum* of Geraldus" and describes his own hand in the work as mere "arranging and editing." He goes on to add that

> I have given no account of Robartes himself, nor of his discovery of the explanation of Geraldus' diagrams and pictures in the traditional knowledge of a certain obscure Arab tribe, for I hope that my selection from the great mass of his letters and table talk, which I owe to his friend, John Aherne, may be published before, or at any rate, but soon after this little book. (*V,* 853)

Thus the preface, and thus likewise the notes at the end of the book; reminders that Robartes and Aherne are fictional characters are dispensed with, and the two begin to emerge as Yeats's actual fellow students of the occult. Their letters from points east are quoted and sometimes adduced as "sources" for poems; their disputes over doctrinal minutiae are reported; the vicissitudes of their relations with each other and with Yeats himself are recounted. Within the domain of print, that is, they commence to commute freely between realms frankly fictional and realms speciously documentary.

In the 1933 *Collected Poems,* Yeats cut most of these notes. In particular, a note of 850 words on "The Second Coming" and another of more than 1,000 on "An Image from a Past Life" disappeared without a trace, evidently because the hints they offered concerning the esoteric "system" seemed to the poet premature. But Yeats's cavalier way with the ambiguous status of Robartes and Aherne remains the salient feature of the note that survived into the 1933 *Collected Poems* (and the subsequent reading editions of 1956 and 1983).

> Years ago I wrote three stories in which occur the names of Michael Robartes and Owen Aherne. I now consider that I used the actual names of two friends, and that one of these friends, Michael Robartes, has but lately returned from

Mesopotamia, where he has partly found and partly thought out much philosophy.

"I now consider": The insouciance is grand.[20]

This playful teasing continues in the first version of *A Vision*, published in 1926 (but dated 1925). In his dedication of the volume to Moina Mathers, Yeats speaks of "the documents on which this book is founded" (*AV-A*, xi); and both the introduction and one of the principal chapters ("The Dance of the Four Royal Persons") are attributed to Owen Aherne. Both Yeats and Aherne refer often to Michael Robartes as their principal informant on the arcane matters the book treats of; both also register dissents at key places from Robartes's conclusions and, of course, from each other's. Owen Aherne's introduction presents itself as a personal reminiscence, recounting how, after a separation of many years, he and Robartes met by chance in the National Gallery in 1917, began talking, and brought up the name of Yeats. "Where is Yeats?" asks Robartes. "I want his address. I am lost in this town and I don't know where to find anybody or anything." Aherne explains,

I felt a slight chill, for we had both quarreled with Mr. Yeats on what I considered good grounds. Mr. Yeats had given the name of Michael Robartes and that of Owen Aherne to fictitious characters, and made those characters live through events that were a travesty of real events. (*AV-A*, xvi)

But reservations notwithstanding, they go off in search of Yeats, and Robartes explains that in the years since "the village riot which Yeats exaggerated in 'Rosa Alchemica,'" events had turned Robartes from his "favorite studies"; he had renounced occult researches in favor of amorous ones. Robartes relates how in one such course of investigation, with a "fiery handsome girl of the poorer classes," his bed collapsed: One of its legs had been propped up by a stool and by the remains of an old book, missing all its middle pages. The book proves, by the light of day, to be Giraldus's "Speculum Angelorum et Hominorum," the obscure text on which, we are to understand, the disclosures of *A Vision* have been based. Where did it come from?

My beggar maid had found it, she told me, on the top shelf
in a wall cupboard where it had been left by the last tenant,
an unfrocked priest who had joined a troop of gypsies and
disappeared, and she had torn out the middle pages to light
our fire. (*AV-A,* xviii)

Robartes takes up the strange old book and, after "a quarrel with
my beggar maid" and an episode of "wine and gloom," resolves
to be done with sensuality and devote his energies instead to
piercing the secrets of Giraldus's book. His quest leads him
through desert sands, wherein strange diagrams, coinciding with
those in Giraldus's book, have been inscribed by learned old wise
men, members of a "tribe" (or "sect": Yeats, or rather Robartes,
or rather Aherne uses both words) "who are known among the
Arabs for the violent contrasts of character amongst them, for
their licentiousness and their sanctity" (*AV-A,* xix). One old sage,
seeing Robartes's strange book, initiates Robartes into the mysteries of the Judwali arcana, which descends via oral tradition
(for all written records "had been lost or destroyed in desert fighting some generations before his time") from "a certain Kusta Ben
Luka, Christian Philosopher at the Court of Harun Al-Raschid"
(*AV-A,* xix).

Robartes's narrative here terminates, because he and Aherne
have arrived at "the little Bloomsbury court where Mr. Yeats had
his lodging" (*AV-A,* xx); but having arrived there, Robartes now
decides against knocking on Yeats's door. He and Aherne wander
on, and over dinner in a hotel Robartes shows Aherne his "diagrams and notes":

The sheets of paper which were often soiled and torn were
rolled up in a bit of old camel skin and tied in bundles with
bits of cord and old shoe lace. This bundle, he explained,
described the mathematical law of history, that bundle the
adventure of the soul after death, that other the interaction
of the living with the dead and so on. (*AV-A,* xx)

Aherne agrees – because "such things fascinate me" – to collab-
orate with Robartes on arranging these materials for publication
but narrates how after several months, much travel, and the com-

pletion of eighty or ninety pages of manuscript, the collaboration breaks up in a violent quarrel, Robartes charging Aherne with Christianizing the material. Robartes resolves to turn the materials over to Yeats ("You will give them to a man," Aherne objects, "who has thought more of the love of woman than of the love of God" [*AV-A*, xxi]); amid much bickering (to which a footnote signed "W.B.Y." observes that "I think Mr. Aherne has remembered his own part in this conversation more accurately than that of his opponent" [*AV-A*, xxii]), the two repair to Yeats's flat and strike the deal that has produced the book we are now reading: Yeats's exposition of Giraldus's system, with an introduction (the present one) by Owen Aherne. Aherne concludes his narrative by observing that Yeats's exposition – of which the "completed manuscript now lies before me" – has erred too far in the other direction from his own (i.e., has understressed the Christian, or "primary," elements in the system) and pithily observes, by way of further criticism:

> The twelve rotations associated with the lunar and solar months of the Great Year first arose, as Mr. Yeats understands, from the meeting and separation of certain spheres. I consider that the form should be called elliptoid, and that rotation as we know it is not the movement that corresponds most closely with reality.

To ratify this hair-splitting doctrinal objection, Aherne appeals to unimpeachable authority:

> At any rate I can remember Robartes saying in one of his paradoxical figurative moods that he pictured reality as a number of great eggs laid by the Phoenix and that these eggs turn inside out perpetually without breaking the shell.

With these portentous words, delivered in the tones of a crushing refutation, Owen Aherne concludes his admirably candid introduction to "Mr. Yeats's book." He signs off ("O.A., LONDON, *May,* 1925" [*AV-A*, xxiii]), and the reader is now launched on an exposition of the system itself, which commences with that very difficult poem "The Phases of the Moon."

But we have not heard the last of Owen Aherne, for the next section of the text, called "The Dance of the Four Royal Persons," also appears under his name. In his introduction, Aherne had professed to narrate the "real life," behind-the-scenes story of the present book: as it were, the "LONDON, *May,* 1925" story. In "The Dance of the Four Royal Persons," he gives us a fairy tale account (Michael Robartes is cited as the source) of the legendary origins, remote in time and space, of the book's mystic "system":

> A Caliph who reigned after the death of Harun Al-Raschid discovered one of his companions climbing the wall that encircled the garden of his favourite slave, and because he had believed this companion entirely devoted to his interests, gave himself up to astonishment. After much consideration he offered a large sum of money to any man who could explain human nature so completely that he should never be astonished again. (*AV-A,* 9)

To forestall astonishment: That is this "system's" promise – and we do well to recall here that the book we are reading is subtitled "An Explanation of Life." (*A Vision* indulges what, in "Ego Dominus Tuus," *Hic* had reproached *Ille* by calling "the unconquerable delusion," namely that life can be "explained.") The "astonishment" at issue here, too, is of just the passionate and conflicted sort that interests Yeats most, bringing the loyalties of friendship into collision with the incitements of sexual passion. The Caliph wants to be delivered from astonishment, and delivered from it by mere "explanation," externally supplied; he does not wish to escape astonishment by changing his life, renouncing the political, emotional, and sensual attachments that give rise to it. In response to his offer of reward, the wise man Kusta Ben Luka comes forward

> with his book of geometrical figures, but the Caliph, after he had explained them for an hour, banished him from the palace, and declared that all unintelligible visitors were to be put to death. (*AV-A,* 9)

Like everybody else, the Caliph not only wants his explanation, but wants it simple, too. In the wake of Kusta's banishment, four dancers appear at the palace, offering to remove from wisdom its difficulty and "reveal all in a dance" (*AV-A*, 9). But the Caliph is still not amused. "Their dance is dull," he grumbles, "and they dance without accompaniment, and I consider that nobody has been more unintelligible" (*AV-A*, 10). The meaning of the dance, however, proves to reside not in the motions of the dancers but in the marks left by their feet in the sand. Kusta is summoned to explain these, and after several days, the Caliph pronounces himself satisfied: "I now understand human nature," he announces: "I can never be surprised again" (*AV-A*, 10).

Into this confident announcement of a happy ending, Owen Aherne now intrudes, with fussy scholarly sounding objections ("According to the Robartes MSS.," etc.; "I am inclined to see . . . a later embodiment of a story," etc.). It is as if the fairy tale text has collapsed into the learned commentary, and as before in his introduction, Aherne now concludes (*AV-A*, 11) by confessing with scrupulous candor his dissents from Yeats on key points:

> I cannot, however, let this pass without saying that I doubt the authenticity of this story, which Mr Yeats has expanded into the poem "Desert Geometry or The Gift of Harun Al-Raschid," at least in its present form, and that an almost similar adventure is attributed in one of the Robartes documents to a Mahometan grammarian of a much later date. I will, however, discuss all these matters at length in my own book upon the philosophy and its sources.
>
> O.A.
> *May,* 1925.

Apart from some exception-taking notes toward the close of the text, this is Owen Aherne's last contribution to the 1925 *A Vision*. Here the frame ends, more or less, and the picture begins.

Let us review the "comedy" of all this. Throughout all these framing pages, Robartes, Aherne, and Yeats himself have appeared as anything but selfless and serene questers after wisdom: They are sometimes collaborators, sometimes rivals; they are beset at intervals by all the posturing foolishness and egotism

173

of pedantry; they lapse frequently into self-righteous avowals of commitment to *this* mumbo jumbo and unbending condemnation of *that other,* not, in any obvious way, much different. Such a presentation, of course, mocks the very quest that motivates Yeats to write *A Vision,* and ourselves to read it, by presenting it as little different from other human pursuits in which people grow contentious and self-important. (And it is characteristically and curiously Yeatsian, too, that this mockery should also be a kind of praise.)

More significant, though, is that the fictive status of Robartes and Aherne should be undeclared: The evident intention is that any but the thoroughly instructed reader should experience some initial confusion deciding just how to read the pages that frame the great poet's *Vision.* This difficulty serves, most simply, to remind the novice that it is necessary to read with care, and the effort of sorting things out that it exacts replicates, in a small way, the truth-seeking activity that *A Vision* is all about. Art and fictiveness generally are deeply implicated in that activity; not merely because Yeat's "philosophy" will not present itself as detachable from its "art" – there is nothing startling about a truth that offers itself as discoverable only through fiction – but because a salient feature of this fiction's playful teasing about its own fictive status is that it is not one fiction but two, a fiction within a fiction: the fiction of Robartes, Aherne, and Yeats in London in "the present" wrangling over a proposed book, enclosing another fiction of "once upon a time," of Caliphs and Judwalis and dancers in the sands. It is Yeats's neat trick that of these two fictions one should look so much more fictional than the other (thus making the spuriously "true" one seem more genuine), for the one reads like literary gossip, the stuff of book-page chat, the other like something out of the *Arabian Nights.* This and the quasi-documentary presentation of Owen Aherne's introduction encourage the reader to suppose that the task in these pages is to sort out "the fictional" from "the true," when of course it is really to discern that "the true" is fiction, too.

Mrs. Yeats and the "Facts" of *A Vision* (1937)

In the foregoing discussion, it has been useful to propose different categories of reader and of readings: to speak of "the novice" on one hand, "the instructed reader" on the other, of the responses that might attend a first reading versus those the quester-reader might arrive at after some "sorting out." Still, after all the sorting out, the instructed reader is left with a common enough situation: Yeat's clever parodies of fussy doctrinaires and self-important scholars are all a fiction from his own hand; having realized this the reader can accord them the sort of attention conventionally due to any literary fiction. There is, in short, an end to the confusion in the apprehension that all this is an invention contrived by Yeat's imagination. In the years following the 1926 publication of *A Vision,* Yeats revised the book so heavily that it became virtually another and different book. He revised the "system" by the light of further occult researches, of course; but more to our purpose here is his revision of the frame that introduces the revelation. In 1929, Yeats privately printed 425 copies of *A Packet for Ezra Pound,* in which the surprising role of Mrs. Yeats in the gathering of the spirit disclosures is for the first time revealed. Yeats was preparing for a new edition of *A Vision* to be published as part of a *Collected Works* in 1931 or 1932,[21] though in the event the revised *Vision* was not published until 1937 in England, 1938 in the United States. The later text's prefatory matter balances the "factual" *Packet for Ezra Pound* with the fantastic *Stories of Michael Robartes and His Friends,* which Yeats first published (again in a small run, only 450 copies) in 1931.

Taken altogether, this new prefatory matter exhibits many of the same features as that of the earlier text: the leg-pulling playfulness that invites unwary readers to take fictions literally, a farcical fairy tale account of the system's origins counterpointed with another professedly "true" account. What has changed is that Yeats has decisively augmented the reader's perplexity by offering a "true" account that refuses to be categorized as fiction, insists with genial bemusement that it is the literal truth, and reports with open-handed candor a long yarn of mediumship and spirit instructors that no reader in its self-consciously "modern" audience will know how to deal with. T. R. Henn has written that the second version of *A Vision,* with its "true" account of Mrs. Yeats's mediumship, is "toned down" from the first version, "modified so as to admit . . . of a half-serious interpretation";[22] if he means that it retreats in provocativeness from the first version, he is surely wrong. A laboratory case is provided by

Edmund Wilson, who wrote about *A Vision* both before and after the advent of *A Packet for Ezra Pound*. When he first reviewed the 1925 text, he noted "the ambiguity . . . in regard to the author's real beliefs"; he responds to *A Packet for Ezra Pound* in *Axel's Castle* (1931): "As we read all this, we say to ourselves that Yeats, growing old has grown credulous. . . . the psychological situation seems plain."[23]

The contrast between Wilson's measured patience with the "fictional" *Vision* of 1925 and his exasperation with the "factual" account that would preface the 1937 version suggests that the efforts of writers like R. P. Blackmur, Allen Tate, Cleanth Brooks, David Daiches, Austin Warren, and W. H. Auden to come to terms with Yeat's "beliefs" (and of others to dismiss them as amiable eccentricities or patent absurdities) would not have been so strained as they are if only the "fictional" first version of *A Vision* were in question. (Compare I. A. Richards's dismissal of Yeats's occultism in 1926, even in a book [*Science and Poetry*] advancing the doctrine of "pseudo-statement.") It is the claim of literal factualness asserted in *A Packet for Ezra Pound* that caused all the trouble, and in calculating the claim and its effect, Yeats would not have been unmindful of the contemporary "pseudo-statement," "poetry-and-beliefs" debate of Richards, Eliot, and Wyndham Lewis. Yeats's personal investment, I mean his investment of his own person, in his cranky "beliefs," his insistence on identifying himself with his mask, implicitly challenged that severance of poet and persona, and of poetry from what it has to say, that "T. C. Eliot" (as Yeats once called him [*V*, 854]) had urged in revolt against everything Yeats represented.

And ironically, if Yeats's account of the spiritual "Instructors" seems to invite dismissal as amiable nonsense, it nevertheless did secure for his "ideas" a kind of consideration they would never have received if presented merely as allegory. (Compare the polite lip service accorded Eliot's Anglicanism.) As the editors of *The Permanence of Yeats* observe,

> An age of formalist criticism has chosen, surprisingly, to deal with Yeats as a problem in cultural values, and thus to make him the only modern poet whose beliefs have been tested enough for us to be reasonably sure that we are distinguishing the poet from the culture hero.[24]

Yeats's A Vision

Many critics have saved themselves trouble by treating the "system" simply as an imaginative creation, a "text for exposition," and been justified by the results, when, as exposition, their accounts are as fine as Richard Ellmann's, Northrop Frye's, or Helen Vendler's or as provocative as Harold Bloom's.[25] But if in one way such critics honor Yeats's principle that art is all and supreme, in another way they miss Yeat's deliberate effort to turn this proposition from a truism into a problem and a provocation.

Fact and Fiction

It is clear enough why Yeats should want a book growing out of mystery and the incredible to entoil the reader in an impasse not negotiable via the conventions of reading-as-usual. The 1937 prefatory matter to *A Vision* brings to its highest pitch the comedy of arcane quest and discovery that Yeats had been increasingly ready to share with his readers throughout the preceding two decades. Although *A Packet for Ezra Pound* and *Stories of Michael Robartes and His Friends* appeared in advance of the 1937 *Vision,* no commentator apart from Edmund Wilson seems to have laid hands on them; so I will consider them now in the context, or as the context, of the completed 1937 text of *A Vision,* where they and their arrangement and placement play a complicated and complicating part in the effect of the whole.

The amorphousness of such a term as "prefatory matter" seems, initially, apt, for the pages that introduce Yeats's revised account of his esoteric system offer us four very different kinds of writing that have the look of an extremely casual, almost random, assemblage – an effect promoted, for example, by the word "Packet," under which three of the pieces are gathered. The pieces called "Rapallo" and "To Ezra Pound" are of the class of writing we would call ephemeral, or occasional; they have the look of having been included merely as a gesture of friendship, not because of any compelling connection between them and the book's larger subject. The farcical *Stories of Michael Robartes and His Friends* appears at first glance to be a bit of the purest whimsy. The introduction appears to have been written, as it were, on the run, for differently dated sections refer to the main text as now in progress, now complete. Inspecting the typography

177

of the table of contents, we find that these four pieces are sub-sumed under two heads: *A Packet for Ezra Pound* and *Stories of Michael Robartes and His Friends*. These two headings cover two different accounts of how the manuscript of *A Vision* came to exist in the first place, and of these accounts we are to understand that the first is the "true" one, if only because the other is so extravagantly farcical.

The "true" account, in which Mrs. Yeats's mediumship is "revealed," is sandwiched between the two pieces addressed to Pound, a move that serves obliquely but forcefully to thrust what we are reading, spirit communicators and all, into the realm of documentable fact, where fellow poets visit with each other in towns locatable on maps and discuss, with a candor for which the earnest reader is grateful, their very fascinating schemes of Art and Life. The spirit communicators, tucked in between the two addresses to Pound, partake of their ambience of the factual; yet we are getting, no doubt, a very crazy salad with our meat.

It should come as no surprise that the spirit communicators are proffered with plenty of documentary handles. We are given dates ("On the afternoon of October 24, 1917 . . . " [*AV-B*, 82]); we are given places ("We were in a hotel on the edge of Ashdown Forest" [*AV-B*, 9]); we are given all the circumstances attendant upon crucial junctures ("I was on a lecturing tour in America to earn a roof for Thoor Ballylee. . . . We had one of those little sleeping compartments in a train, with two berths, and were somewhere in Southern California" [*AV-B*, 9]). These personal disclosures assure us that we are privileged to be in the poet's fullest confidence. The muted comedy that animates the entire account even promotes this sense of intimacy – spirits cannot transpose themselves, after all, into the realm of restaurants and sleeping cars without occasional misunderstandings:

> After they had entranced my wife suddenly when sitting in a chair, I suggested that she must always be lying down before they put her to sleep. They seemed ignorant of our surroundings, and would have done so at some inconve-nient time or place; once when they had given their signal in a restaurant they explained that because we had spoken of a garden they had thought we were in it. (*AV-B*, 10)

Yeats's A Vision

There is also the age-old question of what to tell the help:

> Servants at the other end of the house were disturbed by a "whistling ghost," and so much so that I had to ask the communicators to choose some other sign. (*AV-B,* 15)

The comedy of this has the look of being unconscious. The reportage hastens on with its burden, passing up occasions for laughter; empirically, crossed connections between the material and the insubstantial realms are simply part of the story to be told, and telling it is the main business of this prose. Indeed, Yeats is at pains to assure us of his scrupulous fidelity to observed phenomena, even the seemingly trivial: "Upon one occasion when my wife smelt hyacinth, a friend smelt eau-de-cologne" (*AV-B,* 15). Noted. And in the interests of truth, even malodorous manifestations must be duly, if gingerly, reported. *Item:* "A smell of cat's excrement announced some being that had to be expelled" (*AV-B,* 16).

The low-key humor of this disarms disbelief, showing us that the poet is just like ourselves, mildly but not seriously disarrayed by what we must agree, after all, is a most *curious* experience. If, however, we entertain the possibility that the offhandedness of this humor is conscious, that it points in an unemphatic way to a strategy of put-on, the comedy suddenly becomes a knowing wink from the author, letting us know that we are in on some kind of joke. Viewed in this way, the unforthcoming poker face pushes the events we are reading about gently but firmly in the direction of the ludicrous and the incredible – toward a comic response, that is, and toward fiction.

Returning to the text with our angle of vision suitably adjusted, we find, in fact, other suggestions that the "reportage," for all its casual appearance, is highly estheticized. We learn, for example, that when the automatic writing first commenced, "The unknown writer took his theme at first from my just published *Per Amica Silentia Lunae*" (*AV-B,* 8) – that is, from one of Yeat's own books. And as the paragraph unfolds, its frame of reference remains firmly fictional. Yeats compares himself not to Paracelsus, but to Browning's Paracelsus and to Goethe's Wilhelm Meister, "his history written by another" (*AV-B,* 9). And when we

Esoteric Comedies

recall that Yeats, a notoriously obsessive reviser, spent years reworking *A Vision,* we are likely to question the introduction's casual pretense of work-in-progress. When Yeats tells us that the original edition contained deceptions, our response is not confidence in his candor, but an increased readiness to look askance at this final version as well, with its confessional air of "now the truth can be told." We note that Yeats makes much of the spirit communicators' delight in duplicity: "Remember," he reports one of them as saying to him, "we will deceive you if we can" (*AV-B,* 13). And touches of playful "textuality" abound: The introduction, for example, sports a joking epigraph about introductions from Swift, whose ironic exploitation of the pseudonym, the nonexistent editor, The Introduction, The Address to the Reader, The Letter from the Author's Cousin, The Printer's Apologie, The Digression, The Footnote, The Marginalium, make him, as Hugh Kenner has pointed out, past master of the comic manipulation of the format of the printed book.[26]

A similar ironic cue is provided by Yeats's elaborately literary gesture in situating Ezra Pound, whose contempt for Yeats's occult interests was loud and of long standing, so honorifically in the opening pages of a volume that promises to "proclaim a new divinity." In one of Yeats's journals, Pound figures as a type of skepticism,[27] so there is a rich comedy in Yeats's presentation of his esoteric epitome to so unreceptive a friend; and Yeats unemphatically acknowledges as much in suggesting that Pound is something like his opposite type, a poet "whose art is the opposite of mine, whose criticism commends what I most condemn" (*AV-B,* 3). (Thirty-odd years later, Pound remembered: "Once out at Rapallo I tried for God's sake to prevent him from printing a thing. I told him it was rubbish. All he did was print it with a preface saying that I *said* it was rubbish.")[28] The estheticized sketch of Rapallo, too, with its allusions to Keats, affronts the emerging "activist" Pound, whose move to Rapallo betokened a rejection of estheticism in favor of economics, politics, and *temporis acti.*

If such hints suggest fiction only ambiguously, they should do no more, for the best tall tales are those we cannot decide whether to believe. But it is expressly into fiction that we are hurled headlong when we turn to the next section of the prefatory matter,

180

Stories of Michael Robartes and His Friends: An Extract from a Record Made by His Pupils. (We note without comment that while "stories" cues us toward fiction, "extract" and "record" wave a blatantly fraudulent rag of documentary in our faces.) Under the aegis of fiction, Yeats grows expansive, holding commerce with his earlier selves, presenting some farcical emblems of *A Vision* itself, and engaging in banter with a few of his fictional characters. He even contrives, like a good press agent, to extract from one of them (*AV-B,* 53–5) an advance review, as it were, of *A Vision,* more sympathetic than any it has received since (or before; its author is John Aherne, now identified as Owen's brother, and one of its obliquely stated purposes is to mitigate the harshness of Owen's introduction to the 1925 text).

The first of the *Stories* is a longish first-person narrative signed "John Duddon" (*AV-B,* 33–53). Its comically vertiginous device is the ancient one of a tale within a tale: Narrators enter, succeed one another, and spin yarns within yarns. The confusion of speaker and story that results immediately overtakes all but the most indefatigable attention to quotation marks and inverted commas; the effect is to blur the outlines of the various antithetical pairs we encounter, permitting antiselves to change places with dizzying facility. First we meet Daniel O'Leary, an excitable sort whom we can immediately identify as a caricature of Yeats in the late 1880s and 1890s. O'Leary is obsessed with his own lack of bravery and self-possession; he also holds Yeatsian ideas about verse drama, and his great moral crisis occurs at a theater where a "realistic" production of *Romeo and Juliet* sends him into fits of anxiety. He finally works up the great courage required to fling his boots at the stage, and naturally his aim is faulty. Fleeing the theater, he bumps into a strange old man who ushers him into a waiting cab, hands him fresh footwear, and remarks tranquilly: "I was told to wait at the corner for a man without boots" (*AV-B,* 34).

Next we hear of the love triangle of Huddon, Duddon, and a young girl who "insists on calling herself Denise de L'Isle Adam" (*AV-B,* 35). Between Duddon and the girl there is true love, sealed by impotence; between Huddon and the girl there is a relation frankly carnal. Duddon, the impotent one, is a penniless artist; Huddon, the virile one, is a wealthy man of the world and

Duddon's (sole) patron. Their bickerings are punctuated at intervals by Denise's inconsequential bids for attention, to which neither pays the slightest heed.

Enter Robartes and Aherne, who tell us the story of the *Speculum Angelorum et Hominum* (The mirror of angels and men): The discovery of this obscure and mutilated old book (most of its pages are, in fact, missing) is an absurd yarn involving "a ballet dancer who had not an idea in her head" (*AV-B,* 37), another, different female, "an ignorant girl of the people" with whom Robartes "cohabited" in rooms "ostentatious in their sordidness" (*AV-B,* 38), and an Arab tribe, the Judwalis, whose ritual dances "leave upon the sand traces full of symbolical meaning" (*AV-B,* 41).

We next hear of John Bond and Mary Bell, whose story involves their deception of Mary's husband, an eccentric who has retired from human endeavor to work for the redemption of birds, which will occur, he believes, when cuckoos, a non-nesting species, build nests. "I decided to devote my life to the cuckoos," the pious old gentleman humbly remarks:

> My great object was of course to persuade them to make nests; but for a long time they were so obstinate, so unteachable, that I almost despaired. But the birth of a son renewed my resolution. (*AV-B,* 48–9)

The son, of course, was begotten on this man's wife by John Bond; but both wife and paramour are determined to sustain the husband's illusions, even to the extent of presenting him, on his deathbed, with a counterfeit cuckoo's nest, conscientiously crafted after the best scientific knowledge (furnished her by Bond) of what a cuckoo's nest would be like if cuckoos built nests.[29]

So then: two adulterers laboring to maintain the illusions of the man they are cuckolding by means of an artifact so crafted as to be indistinguishable from its model in nature, which model, however, does not exist. This farcical bit of nonsense pre´ ʾnts a paradigm sufficiently complex of the relations of art, artist, audience, nature, knowledge, and illusion. We shall return to it, but let us here simply remark the wit of Yeats's so orchestrating his fable that our attention moves from a bogus bird's nest to a mysterious ivory box from which is produced, with appropriate ceremony, "an egg the size of a swan's." It is (as "those of you who are learned in the classics will have recognized") the Third Ledean Egg, and like *A Vision,* it is equipped with a dubious provenance: purchased from an old man in a green turban in Teheran, says Robartes – until Aherne points out that Robartes was never in Teheran, at which Robartes shrugs indifferently and says, "Perhaps Aherne is right" (*AV-B,* 51). Wherever it came from, the egg, ominously, abides. Robartes and Aherne have appointed themselves to supervise its imminent and portentous hatching, and amid much talk of antinomies and antitheses, the two announce their impending departure for the desert, where the egg will be buried and hatched by the sun's warmth, after which divine influxes can be relied upon to ensue. All of which having been said, "Robartes put the egg in its box again, and said good-bye to us one after the other" (*AV-B,* 53).

The comedy of the Huddon–Duddon–Denise triangle establishes an ironic distance between the author of *A Vision* and the star-crossed lover laid waste by Maud Gonne; the O'Leary story does the same to the young "activist" Yeats. The Robartes–Aherne comedy likewise invests Yeats's lifelong interest in the occult with an affectionate facetiousness, even as it insists that their eccentricities and his are to be seen as continuous. The John Bond–Mary Bell story accuses all fictive activity of deceit and illusion, of creating simulacra of nonexistent realities; at the same time there are clear hints that this activity has redemptive possibilities. That implausible cuckoo's nest, whose author insists it is genuine, offered to a dying man desperately in need of it and enabling him to die happy, is a suggestive (and elaborately ludicrous) emblem of *A Vision* itself, offered to a doubt-ridden public in an age of crisis as a "system" for understanding the cycles of history and the individual soul.

It is especially suggestive that Yeats did not suppress his original impulse to provide a farcical account of his system's genesis when making his final revision, but retained it, counterposing it neatly with the new, "genuine" account (and of course seeming to make a clean breast of it by explaining that "I was fool enough to write half a dozen poems that are unintelligible without it" [*AV-B,* 19]: The poems are not named, and I can think of none that fit the description). Between its two editions, *A Vision*'s most

Esoteric Comedies

Portrait of Giraldus from the *Speculum Angelorum et Hominum.*

interesting change is the superimposition of another explanation of where it came from, a particular in which it resembles the universe in which Yeats grew up. Like the book of nature, the text of *A Vision* remains essentially the same; only the question of authorship is substantially complicated, and in a way to trouble conventions of belief.

If *A Vision* has a factual and a fictional origin, it also has a factual and a fictional author. The factual author, of course, is Yeats; his fictional counterpart, compellingly, is presented by means of a visual aid, a woodcut of the author of *Speculum Angelorum et Hominum,* a certain Giraldus, said by one of Yeat's more "literal-minded" fictional characters to bear a strong resemblance to Yeats himself. Than this woodcut there can be no better "objective correlative" of all the elaborate textual put-on in which we have been for so long now entoiled, nor can there be any more decisive validation of the rather tortuous argument I have been trying to advance. This face is the acid test; let the (properly) skeptical reader contemplate for a moment the inscrutable smile and shifty eyes of that supremely crafty visage. His hand is extended toward us, proffering, no doubt, a mystic and revelation-bearing manuscript; his ancient, glittering eyes are gay with the assurance that he knows more than we, and always will. He is laughing at us; and we have not even noticed. Is there any doubt that we have to do here with a shell game magus?[30]

A Vision's double genesis elaborates a paradoxical mirror imaging of fact and fiction central to all of Yeats's thought about the imagination: Note that the farcical account of the system's origin implies, via conventions we take for granted, an empirically tenable origin (namely fiction), whereas the purportedly "true" account asks us to believe literally what most of us (as Yeats well knows) will insist is impossible. We effortlessly swallow the camel of fiction but strain at the gnat of "fact." Such manipulations are discernible beneath Yeat's earliest concern with the "transmutation of life into art," words found on the first page of *Rosa Alchemica.* We have already noted that book's way of keeping its status as "fiction" equivocal; on its opening page we hear of an earlier book, by the same author, also called *Rosa Alchemica,* a move anticipating that which we have just observed in *A Vision:* The actual book in the reader's hand, and its actual author, are each furnished with a fictional avatar.

A like blurring of fact and fiction is enacted comically in the prefatory matter of *A Vision* (and elsewhere) by Yeats's willingness to engage in elaborate exchanges, quarrels, and commiserations with his fictional characters. The careers of Robartes and Aherne illustrate the possibilities. They first appear in *Rosa Alchemica,* where they so discompose our narrator that he precipitously takes flight to his study and his rosary beads. By the time they reappear in the 1937 text of *A Vision,* Yeats stands in a posture of aloof disdain toward them. He communicates with them only through an intermediary, Aherne's brother, John, who reports that Robartes and Aherne are annoyed with Yeats for exposing (and misrepresenting) their activities of thirty years earlier in *Rosa Alchemica.* A salient objection is to the Paterian prose of that volume, and as we have observed, the *Stories of Michael Robartes* makes giddy fun of several Paterian types. It is John Aherne who tells us (remarking coolly that it "interests, but does not astonish" him [*AV-B,* 54]) that Yeats's system duplicates that of Giraldus's *Speculum Angelorum et Hominum* – although neither he nor anyone else has ever seen its missing pages.

Here endeth the prefatory matter. On the next page the exposition of the "system" proper begins with the poem "The Phases
of the Moon," and it is here that the transactions of the fictive
Robartes and Aherne with their actual author attain unprece-
dented comic complexity. The two stand beneath Yeats's tower,
looking up at his lamp-lit window, and mock at the futility of his
enterprise: "He has found, after the manner of his kind, / Mere
images," sneers Robartes, himself one of those images: "And now
he seeks in book or manuscript / What he shall never find." What
Yeats seeks, it is implied, can be found not in book or manuscript
in the high tower, but outside, in nature, in experience, on the
muddy road where Robartes and Aherne are journeying. The
characters claim knowledge that their author can never attain;
they mock his ignorance, but then, when Aherne asks Robartes
to sing that knowledge, he remarks of the song: "Mine author
sung it me"; mysteriously, the text puts these words in quotation
marks. Why? To remind us, perhaps, of the presence of the
author? To remind us that Robartes and Aherne lead an existence
purely textual? To remind us that their quest, their muddy road,
their very persons have been invented by Yeats, and in book or
manuscript? In any case Robartes sings the song, Aherne wishes
he were warm and dry in the tower, and a bat, like the ones
Robartes has mentioned earlier in the poem as emblematic of
Phase 1, of all knowledge at last unified in objective darkness,
rises with a cry, and the light in the tower abruptly goes out. Has
the author pulled rank on the characters by terminating the poem
they inhabit? Or has he been guileful enough to eavesdrop at the
window while Robartes sings his song?[31]

It is worth remarking that the comedy of this poem is generally
lost on readers, who immediately apply themselves to the doctrine of the twenty-eight phases Robartes sings of; in a laconic
note on this and two other poems, Yeats remarks: "To some
extent, I wrote these poems as a test for exposition" (*V*, 821). But
the implications of the poem's comedy are that the system is fictional – it comes out of the mouth of a fictional character – and
that Yeats is in some way master of his fictional characters: In
the poem, he never deigns to confront them, whereas thirty years
earlier, their first appearance in his work, in *Rosa Alchemica*, had
resulted from his seeking them out; having done so, he was

186

entirely overwhelmed by them, as we have seen, so that his encounters with them ended in terror and months of clutching his rosary.

If I were not reluctant to plunge into the stuff of Yeatsian esoterica proper, I might be tempted to suggest a comic reading of the whole of *A Vision*. On the first page in the first paragraph of the first book, for example, we find that dicta from Empedocles are exactly reversed by the learned commentaries of one Burnet, which Yeats adduces as if to clear things up; in the second paragraph, we are referred to an ancient scholiast on Aristotle who goes by the dubious name of Simplicius. (The compleat Yeatsian eager to confirm a "fictional" reading will discover, upon inquiry, that Simplicius and Burnet are "real" enough.)

But what effect does all this have on the system *A Vision* presents? We may savor first the amusement Yeats, an autodidact who failed his entrance exams, derives from holding forth in mock-learned tones (and to a public he fully expected would not listen) on the lifetime imaginative creation that is his esoteric system and enforcing (or disabling) our perplexed assent by insisting that the story of its otherworldly deliverers is *literally* true. That the fiction is unacknowledged would be a joke, in the tradition of Swift's Discourses, Meditations, Proposals, and other assorted tales of a cock and a bull, on an age committed to the fallacy that "myth" means the opposite of "fact." (More particularly, the joke is on literary critics, whose gingerly solicitousness in dealing with "the problem of Yeats's *beliefs*" emerges as more and more distinctly risible.)

I have already asked the reader to consider the art of the tall tale and the complex comedy that results, implicating all overly serious response, from the indignation of the skeptic, who promptly erects a shield of irrelevant rationality, to the eager credulity of the sensitive soul with pretenses to mystic knowledge; the wink is to the hearer who perceives, among other things, the considerable interest of these postures. It is a certain single-mindedness that is being satirized, the obtuseness of being earnest. And yet at the same time, it is another sort of single-mindedness that Yeats is celebrating, and exemplifying. The self-evident (but unacknowledged) ludicrousness of the "system" (a richly comic word, really, for that funhouse of gyres and cones), the protestations of crankiness, absurdity, madness, even hoax that it invites, and that it undoubtedly amused Yeats to anticipate, make of *A Vision* a heroic, gay, quixotic *credo quia impossibile est,* rising ebulliently out of the stony rubbish of the disillusioned postwar wasteland: The very implausibility, that is, lends intensity to the willfulness of Yeats's witness.

It is a faith he is witnessing, although less a faith in the ghosts and Great Wheels than in his own power (and ours) to imagine and make something of them. To say as much only points to what Yeats's poems tell us again and again, that making and remaking the soul is a conscious, deliberate activity, a disciplined recovery of "radical innocence" possible only through volitional imaginative activity, which is to say fictive activity – for the fictions we make transform us. But the regnant materialism of Yeats's age scorned the fictions of imagination in favor of "facts," supposed to be real in some ungainsayable way. In "reality" (a compromised word, which Yeats defiantly liked using) "facts" are only the Gradgrindian mainstay of another fiction, or myth, the myth of science. When we say we are mastering "facts," we are only making matter the measure of our minds, so that "fact" masters us, narrowing the possibilities of human prerogative and imagination. A fiction, like science, that we have forgotten how to disbelieve, has us in its power; that it thus enslaves us by offering mastery over nature is a supreme irony. *A Vision*'s prefatory play indicates the power of fact and fiction to accommodate each other. Each becomes, with a slight rolling of the beholder's eye (such as Giraldus has clearly got the hang of) its antiself. Fact and fiction (since "man made up the whole") exist on a continuum, rather than in an either–or relationship; the two are gyre and cone or the yolk and white of one shell. Yeats invites us to join his enterprise and bring to it our whole minds; we are invited to indulge freely both our belief and our doubt, our urge to revere and our impulse to mock. Yeats has fabricated a text to which any discerning response will be relevant: We need not willingly suspend anything.

All of this in a book of which Yeats once remarked that "the young men I write for may not read my *Vision* – they may care too much for poetry – but they will be pleased that it exists."[32] This, too, seems more than half mockery, for while all of us have read the book, few of us have been happy about what we found there. The relevant gloss is to be found in a poem called "The Apparitions":

> Because there is safety in derision
> I talked about an apparition,
> I took no trouble to convince,
> Or seem plausible to a man of sense,
> Distrustful of that popular eye
> Whether it be bold or sly.
> *Fifteen apparitions have I seen;*
> *The worst a coat upon a coat hanger.*
>
> (*V*, 624)

To write *A Vision,* which no one will read; to take no trouble to convince; to talk nonsense to the man of sense: For poet and man of sense alike, there is safety in derision. Which apparition is worse, Yeats's ghosts and gyres or the mechanistic utilitarian's, in which all mysterious life, including our own, emerges as but a coat draped over a chair, old clothes upon a stick to scare feathers upon a stick still smaller? This poem asserts safety in derision, then turns to mock safety and derision both.

Esoteric Comedy, Tragic Joy

I have been using the term "comedy" (rather loosely) to designate a range of things from outright farce to the most elaborate textual flimflam. But Yeats's *Vision* project is comic in more fundamental ways than these, as we can discover by inquiring into what Kenneth Burke would call its "motives." We can begin by considering the 1925 text of *A Vision* as a companion volume to *The Tower,* published in 1928; both were written during roughly the same period and out of the same experiences: the end of the Great War, the Russian Revolution, the Irish Troubles and Civil War, the founding of the Irish Free State, and (private counterpoint to these public events) Yeats's marriage, the commencement of the spirit dictation disclosed in the 1937 *Vision*'s introduction, the birth of Yeats's two children, his appointment to a seat in the new Irish Senate in 1922, his Nobel Prize in 1923, the printing of *A Vision* in 1926, and the publication of *The Tower,* to enormous acclaim, in 1928. Peace returns to the world and to

Ireland, and Yeats secures the greatest successes yet in a long and distinguished career: Both in private and public realms, the omens are favorable.

The poems in *The Tower* celebrate all this and to that end are arranged for dramatic effect. The volume opens *molto con brio* with "Sailing to Byzantium," in which Yeats solicits the artistic immortality he half knows, half hopes is his, and "The Tower," in which the aging and weakening man bids defiance to the consolations of "philosophy," mocks Plotinus's thought and cries in Plato's teeth:

> Death and life were not
> Till man made up the whole,
> Made lock, stock and barrel
> Out of his bitter soul.
>   (ll. 148–51; *V*, 415)

But although they come first in the table of contents, these two poems are, chronologically, among the latest in the book; they represent not the point of departure, but the culmination of a long sequence that begins in despair and demoralization, in such poems as "Meditations in Time of Civil War" and "Nineteen Hundred and Nineteen" and, most desperately perhaps, in such private poems as "A Prayer for My Son." (Whenever, as in "A Prayer for My Son," Yeats appeals to the Christian myth, it is a sure sign that his morale is at its nadir.)

The Irish Troubles and the other tribulations of the period from 1918 to 1922 seemed to destroy many of Yeats's fondest and most grandiose aspirations. He had committed much to a public pose that public events were now rendering untenable; in retreat – virtually imprisoned – in his lonely tower, he felt he had lost his bearings:

> We are closed in, and the key is turned
> On our uncertainty; somewhere
> A man is killed, or a house burned,
> Yet no clear end to be discerned:
> Come build in the empty house of the stare.

He is shocked and remorseful at the potency of the rages circumstance now induces in him, and in his nation:

We had fed the heart on fantasies,
The heart's grown brutal from the fare;
More substance in our enmities
Than in our love; O honey-bees,
Come build in the empty house of the stare.
("Meditations in Time of Civil War,"
vi, *V*, 425)

He turns his back on all the public hopes that had animated his career through two decades, even reproaches himself for having entertained them:

I turn away and shut the door, and on the stair
Wonder how many times I could have proved my worth
In something that all others understand or share;
But O! ambitious heart, had such a proof drawn forth
A company of friends, a conscience set at ease,
It had but made us pine the more. The abstract joy,
The half-read wisdom of daemonic images,
Suffice the ageing man as once the growing boy.
("Meditations in Time of Civil War," vii, *V*, 427)

The tone of this is audibly the same as that of the first section of "The Tower," though it affirms the opposite, that Yeats *can* make himself be "content with argument and deal / In abstract things" (*V*, 409). But the "ageing man" does not sound "sufficed," any more than the growing boy ever was, by a merely "abstract joy"; the "half-read wisdom of daemonic images" – the reams of cryptic utterance Yeats and his wife were generating in their sessions of automatic writing and which Yeats was trying to edit into some sort of "sacred book" – sounds decidedly more like a chore and sour grapes than a labor of love.[33] His mood is bitter, a compound of tragedy and farce: the soul, struggling with an object – politics – that is irremovable and, it now seems (for "we were crack-pated when we dreamed" [*V*, 431]), ridiculous, contemptibly so, "weasels fighting in a hole" (*V*, 429). Nothing for it but privatism and withdrawal:

He who can read the signs nor sink unmanned
Into the half-deceit of some intoxicant
From shallow wits; who knows no work can stand,
Whether health, wealth or peace of mind were spent

191

On master-work of intellect or hand,
No honour leave its mighty monument,
Has but one comfort left: all triumph would
But break in upon his ghostly solitude.
("Nineteen Hundred and Nineteen,"

i, *V,* 429)

Again, a page later, "triumph can but mar our solitude": He is
urging upon himself the same consolation he had offered years
before "To a Friend Whose Work Has Come to Nothing." But
this "abstract joy" of withdrawal from the outside world sounds
more desperate than joyous, its power to "suffice the ageing man"
feeble, spectral, "abstract" indeed. A truer emblem of Yeats's
mood is the universal mockery proposed in the fifth section of
"Nineteen Hundred and Nineteen" ("Come let us mock at the
great . . . at the wise . . . at the good . . . Mock mockers after
that"), a bitter, convulsive, all-embracing motion of contempt
that quite emphatically includes mockery of self, "for we / But
traffic in mockery" (*V,* 432).

This is Yeatsian despair: Joys grow abstract, as hatred, contempt, and self-mockery grow passionately, even sensuously,
intense and actual. Yeats is experiencing here the reality of a
dilemma he had been able to entertain more intellectually in
1915 in "Ego Dominus Tuus"; that poem had asked how one can
be a great artist, given that the artist's "vision of reality" is overwhelming and disabling:

What portion in the world can the artist have
Who has awakened from the common dream
But dissipation and despair?
(ll. 49–51, *V,* 369)

In the poem's terms, either one is a "man of action," and then
no artist, or one awakens from the "common dream" into a condition of impotence and paralysis. There seems to be no way out,
except for the truly great, like Dante, who "set his chisel to the
hardest stone." The truly great artist overcomes the greatest challenge, triumphs against the most daunting obstacle. In the following years, Yeats tempered this formulation significantly by adding the important qualification that the challenge must be great,
but not quite insuperable: "the greatest obstacle that can be con-

templated without despair" (*A*, 132). It is an idea Yeats returns
to often in the late teens and early twenties; his richest statement
is one of the latest, in which he elaborates the theme that "revelation is from the self, but from [the] age-long memoried self":

> . . . genius is a crisis that joins that buried self for certain
> moments to our trivial daily mind. There are, indeed, per-
> sonifying spirits that we had best call but Gates and Gate-
> keepers, because through their dramatic power they bring
> our souls to crisis, to Mask and Image, caring not a straw
> whether we be Juliet going to her wedding, or Cleopatra to
> her death; for in their eyes nothing has weight but pas-
> sion. . . . They have but one purpose, to bring out their cho-
> sen man to the greatest possible obstacle he can confront
> without despair. They contrived Dante's banishment, and
> snatched away his Beatrice, and thrust Villon into the arms
> of harlots, and sent him to gather cronies at the foot of the
> gallows, that Dante and Villon might through passion
> become conjoint to their buried selves, turn all to Mask and
> Image, and so be phantoms in their own eyes. In great lesser
> writers like Landor and like Keats we are shown that Image
> and Mask as something set apart. . . . but in a few in whom
> we recognise supreme masters of tragedy, the whole contest
> is brought into the circle of their beauty. Such masters –
> Villon and Dante, let us say – would not, when they speak
> through their art, change their luck. (*A*, 182–3)

This passage (written around 1920) is interesting and crucial in a
number of ways. In one sense, it provides an answer to the question *Ille* asks in "Ego Dominus Tuus" – where to find that
"Image" he is seeking? But it is also a revision of "Ego Dominus
Tuus," an interrogation of the same figures – Dante, Keats – in
order to ask the same questions – Where does the greatest art
come from? What is the character of the major artist? – but
answering those questions now in a manner that offers some
accommodation to lesser figures than Dante or Villon: to figures,
that is, more on the scale Yeats (in 1920) dares to conceive as his
own. This accommodation, of course, implies no moderating of
ambition; the grandeur of Dante and Villon, the lesser greatness
of Keats and Landor, still imply a challenge, a "greatest obsta-

cle," that Yeats clearly intends to do his best to meet. As much as it offers the minor writer a place to begin, that is, this passage also charts a direction toward major stature. In the poise and courage of Dante and Villon, Yeats finds images of triumph not only over the greatest obstacle that can be faced without despair, but over all obstacles – preeminent among them, despair itself.

Which is to say that Yeats is working here, in prose roughly contemporaneous with the grand despairing poems looked at above, toward an apprehension nowhere visible in those poems, the apprehension he would later call "tragic joy," that (as he credits Lady Gregory with having remarked [*E & I,* 523]), "Tragedy must be a joy to the man who dies." In "Meditations in Time of Civil War" and "Nineteen Hundred and Nineteen," the ordeals of despair are not a joy to the man undergoing them; the speaker of those poems, clearly, would change his luck if he could. Those poems are catharsis: Despair is purged – cast out, rejected – by being indulged and expressed; the pose of tragic joy requires rather that despair be sublimated, denied, repressed. The catharsis model makes the poet passion's object, its passive sufferer: in Yeats's language, "primary" and "objective." What Yeats wants to be is "antithetical" and "subjective," the maker and disposer of his passions, not casting out but introjecting and integrating all, like Dante and Villon, those "masters of tragedy [in whom] the whole contest is brought into the circle of their beauty" (*A,* 183).

A short digression might be useful here on those two pairs of terms, "primary" and "antithetical," "objective" and "subjective." In Yeats's systematically unsystematic system, these are "technical" terms, but I want here to relate them to a pattern discernible throughout Yeats's career: his need for control over events and over self, constantly put to the test and sometimes defeated. When Yeats has control of things, all's well; when things have control of Yeats, all's bad. In "Nineteen Hundred and Nineteen" and "Meditations in Time of Civil War," Yeats has been gotten the better of by a sequence of events he had sought to guide, direct, influence. In defeat, he feels out of control and at the mercy of events. He is not controlling circumstance; it is controlling him. He is its object. This is what "objective" means: reduction to passivity. The materialist, who would (following Bacon) master Nature by obeying her; the Christian, who would consign all power of will to God; the naturalistic novelist, "helpless before the contents of his own mind" (*E & I,* 405); the spiritual quester who goes astray, gets lost in the phantasmagoria, and mounts *Hodos Chameliontos* (Path of the Chameleon: a passive taking of color from experience, rather than an active imposition of one's own "tincture" upon it); the whole "disillusioned," helpless, postwar world, which, Yeats remarked – at about the time he was writing "The Second Coming" – "itself has come to *Hodos Chameliontos*" (*A,* 251): All of these evince, for Yeats, the "objective" or "primary" condition. What is common to all is a loss of control, an acquiescence to circumstance unstiffened by any heroic resistance. Here is that "passive suffering" that – as Yeats put it in explaining why he had included no Great War poets in his *Oxford Book of Modern Verse* – "is not a theme for poetry."[34]

As an artist, of course, Yeats regards "control" as central to his stitching and unstitching enterprise. He finds utterly uncongenial the notion of the artist as a kind of "medium," whether in the spiritualistic sense that his wife was a medium – he identifies that sort of mediumship with *Hodos Chameliontos* – or in the sense of the scientific metaphor proposed by T. S. Eliot in "Tradition and the Individual Talent," of an inert, nonparticipating catalyst, a sort of materialist's unmoved mover: part of the scene, but not a part of the action. Yeats is ready enough to acknowledge that his matter might come from some medium: "Where got I that truth?" one poem asks, and answers, "Out of a medium's mouth" – though the next line revises the answer by adding, "Out of nothing it came" ("Fragments," ll. 5–7, *V,* 439). But the mere matter thus disclosed requires Yeats's agency to effect its transubstantiation into poetry. An artist-like control over the drama of life makes for both beauty and heroism; what Yeats says of civilization in the "Dove or Swan" section of *A Vision* is also true of persons, or at least of antithetical, heroic figures such as Yeats is trying to become:

A civilisation is a struggle to keep self-control, and in this it is like some great tragic person, some Niobe who must display an almost superhuman will or the cry will not touch our sympathy. The loss of control over thought comes toward the end; first a sinking in upon the moral being, then

the last surrender, the irrational cry, revelation – the scream
of Juno's peacock. (*AV-A*, 180; *AV-B*, 268)

Self-control, self-possession: These are constant themes in all of
Yeats's work. The issue becomes acute when his combat with the
world entoils him too deeply, when he discovers that he has
risked more than he thought, when he learns, in defeat, that he
had cared too much. (Of course, one cannot care too much in
victory; victories secured indifferently are worth little.) Such disappointment in defeat is just his condition in "Nineteen
Hundred and Nineteen" and "Meditations in Time of Civil
War"; devastated by the defeat of his grandest public hopes, he
is full of impotent rage, with no one to vent it on except himself,
as victim of events, of his own "crack-pated" dreams, and of his
present emotion.

Of course, Yeats's attitude toward "passive suffering" is no
deduction from principle: He hates it as one hates an old, impla-
cable, and very personal enemy. He has been reduced to paralysis
too often himself: in love, by Maud Gonne (that is why one
should "Never Give All the Heart"); in spiritualism, by that
bewildering onset of too much mystery called *Hodos Chameliontos;* in his writing, by various projects that refused to jell (in connection with his abandoned novel, *The Speckled Bird,* Yeats calls
such artistic defeat also a sort of *Hodos Chameliontos* [*A,* 250]).
As Richard Ellmann notes,[35] the word "mask" – kernel of some
of the *Vision* project's central themes – is first used prominently
in the ostentatiously "disillusioned" little love poem in which girl
asks boy to unmask and reveal his true self, only to be told that
true selves are beside the point:

> "O no, my dear, let all that be;
> What matter, so there is but fire
> In you, in me?"
> ("The Mask," ll. 13–15, *V,* 263)

As the image of a "mask" suggests, Yeats's recourse in defeat is
retreat and disguise: Get some distance, reestablish inner control,
then advance when ready to close with events again. The "primary" type is so invaded by events as to have internalized them
as part of "character"; the "antithetical" type must open a gap
between external events and inner sources of energy and power,

giving "personality" room to resume its drama of pose and gesture. The "antithetical" moment is most crucial, the crisis most intense, when it is an old self, an old mask, that must be shed, drawn back from, and opposed by a new. "We make out of the quarrel with others, rhetoric, but of the quarrel with ourselves, poetry" (*M*, 331); that is why poems of crisis, where Yeats's mastery is threatened – "Meditations in Time of Civil War" or "Nineteen Hundred and Nineteen" – have the power and intensity they have: because they propose that Yeats must now be "antithetical" to his own past work. By contrast, the poems of "tragic joy," of accomplished mastery in the quarrel with the world, become poetry and escape mere rhetoric because it is Yeats's extraordinary genius to make *all* quarrels a quarrel with self.

This contrast bears on the course of Yeats's career, from the despair expressed in the poems of roughly 1919 to 1922, to the "tragic joy" that in his later years he celebrated and – because "Beauty is an accusation" – struggled to embody. The contrast can be explored by juxtaposing two poems, "All Souls' Night," written at the height of the Irish troubles during Yeats's sojourn at Oxford in 1920, and, from sixteen years later, the great "tragic joy" poem, "Lapis Lazuli," completed during the opening weeks of Franco's revolt against Spain's Popular Front government. Both poems acknowledge the world's alarms, but in very different ways. "All Souls' Night" treats violent strife (in, tellingly, a conditional construction) as a distraction to be overcome by the sheer will of the passionately concentrated mind:

> I need some mind that, if the cannon sound
> From every quarter of the world, can stay
> Wound in mind's pondering
> As mummies in the mummy-cloth are wound;
> Because I have a marvellous thing to say . . .
> (ll. 11–15, *V*, 471)

Here phantasmal things – the visitation of spirits insubstantial as wine breath, the marvellous things Yeats has to say – are to eclipse all the noise and distraction of global conflict; attention is to turn from war, politics, and public events to a private and occult vision of Yeats's personal past and of friends long dead. In "Lapis Lazuli," by contrast, the Yeatsian mask is turned

197

toward, not away from, the strife of the public world; King Billy's bomb balls, the prospect of the town beaten flat, are not banished, but welcomed as a backdrop against which the heroically minded strike their poses and accomplish their terrible, beautiful destinies. The gaiety, the "tragic joy," of heroic acceptance of fate is likened in the poem to the nonchalance of the master artisan, for whom the cracks and discolorations in the piece of lapis lazuli present no obstacle, but are integrated with great show of ease into the design and thus welcomed as opportunities to display artistry.

For us, with Auschwitz and Hiroshima and Tuol Sleng behind us, Yeats's pose in "Lapis Lazuli" can seem heartless; it seemed so to some of his contemporaries – "hysterical women," Yeats called them – who had the Brown Book and the Nuremburg decrees on their minds. However shortsighted historically, though, Yeats was seeking in his pose of "tragic joy" after more heart, not less, as the contrast with "All Souls' Night" helps us to see. The single-mindedness and sheer negation of the effort of concentration registered in that poem come close to making Yeats susceptible to the reproach he had addressed to the sixteen heroes of the Easter Rising:

> Hearts with one purpose alone
> Through summer and winter seem
> Enchanted to a stone
> To trouble the living stream.
> ("Easter 1916," ll. 41–4, *V,* 393)

Yeats is alive to the solicitations that can "make a stone of the heart" ("Easter 1916," l. 58): "a marble or a bronze repose," such as he elsewhere commends ("Among School Children," l. 52, *V,* 445) is a property of images, not of the human heart that makes or is moved by them:

> . . . only an aching heart
> Conceives a changeless work of art.
> ("Meditations in Time of Civil
> War," iii, ll. 13–14, *V,* 421)

Yeats had long protested the power of merely intellectual opinions to impose upon perception and enforce universal judgments according to some abstract scheme. Eva Gore-Booth, Con Markiewicz, and most of all Maud Gonne were for Yeats living instances of the power of political passion to transform beauty into shrillness and stridency. Surrounded everywhere, during the Irish Troubles, by political obsession and acutely susceptible himself, as we have seen, to its solicitations to hatred, his resolution to wrap himself in "mind's pondering / As mummies in the mummy-cloth are wound" seems to offer no more than the exchange of a public and politically inspired stonyheartedness for a private and occult one.

"All Souls' Night" then is a crucial poem. Because it is a poem of triumph compelled out of defeat, it tells us how and at what cost – in privatism, unwonted single-mindedness and willful isolation – Yeats was willing to purchase victory over the greatest obstacle before him, his despair. Facing away from the public and ordinary world, though, it indicates a different course than that leading to "tragic joy"; it points rather to the *Vision* project, over which it presides not only as the initiating and annunciatory text – think of it as the antithetical swan to the primary hysterical Leda of Yeats's political and other despairs – but also as a summarizing gesture, a ritual of closure, because it occupies the last pages of both the 1925 and the 1937 versions of Yeats's "sacred book." In all printings from *The Tower* on (it stands as the last poem in that volume, too) a subtitle pointedly denominates it: "Epilogue to *A Vision*." But "All Souls' Night" is a long way, in all its hieratic grandeur, from that esoteric comedy of willfulness, whimsy, irony, poker faces, and "textual flimflam" that characterizes the *Vision* project. It is as remote from all that as "Nineteen Hundred and Nineteen" is from "tragic joy" – and that distance can remind us that the final ebullience and flamboyance of the *Vision* project had its springs in a much darker mood.

Finding the "Honeycomb"

Yeats's marriage to Georgie Hyde-Lees on October 21, 1917 (with his initial certainty that it had been a terrible mistake and the great happiness it eventually brought him) is a suitable emblem for this progress, this widening of the antithetical gyre, from gloom and defiance to mirth and teasing. The automatic writing itself commenced four days after marriage at least in part as the ruse of a clever bride to distract and interest a deeply depressed bridegroom. (Allowing himself to be so distracted and interested, Yeats provides a most compelling instance of Solomon growing wise in conversation with his queen.) "All Souls' Night," with its myth of advent, initiates the movement away from that mood of static retreat, where the nearest approach to heroism is mere obstinacy, where joy is abstract. In "All Souls' Night" Yeats gets some distance, opens a space between himself and the public world in which to dramatize his defiance and independence, and his mastery of a private and occult world altogether "antithetical" to the one that had defeated him. With the announcement in "All Souls' Night" that inner worlds, too, are susceptible of mastery, the *Vision* project is fairly launched in the direction of its maturity. If, before, Yeats had harangued the provincials from the stage of the Abbey Theatre about art and national consciousness, in "All Souls' Night" he turns his back on the house and resolves to be deaf to the uproar coming over the footlights. Presently, when some calm and quiet return, he will be discovered affecting a complacent air and talking to himself about ghosts, gyres, cones, Arabian travelers, the fantasia of history, the career of the soul after death. Because there is safety in derision, he talks about an apparition; he takes no trouble to convince or seem plausible to a man of sense.

If what had begun in the antithetical bitterness of an abstract joy became in a few years the joyous entertainment of a newly subversive sort of opposition to the world and all its canons of "mechanical" common sense, that is because the whole project had its springs in a motive whose dynamic would allow no other outcome: to defeat despair, discouragement, and, at last, any sort of disappointment or unhappiness.

> To show how violent great hearts can lose
> Their bitterness and find the honeycomb.
> ("The Gift of Harun Al-Raschid," *AV-A*,
> 122; *V*, 463, ll. 47–8)

– that is the whole point of my wisdom, and of my publishing it here, says Kusta Ben Luka himself, in a poem that introduces a section of the 1925 *Vision*. The ascending curve from the despair of the earliest poems in *The Tower* to the "tragic joy" of the *Last Poems* is visible in the course of the *Vision* project, too: the increase in audacity, willfulness, and provocation between the

Yeats's A Vision

1925 and the 1937 texts of *A Vision* and its relation to the themes we have been discussing can be instanced by juxtaposing two passages. In the earliest written section of the 1925 text – a section, Yeats's note tells us (*AV-A*, 117), "finished at Thoor Ballylee, 1922, in a time of Civil War" – Yeats describes his heroic "antithetical" type by recourse to the by now familiar formula (to distinguish it in a text already studded with Yeats's own italics, I capitalize it in the following quotation):

> One can describe the *antithetical* man by comparing him to the *Commedia del Arte* or improvised drama of Italy. The stage manager having chosen his actor, the *Will,* chooses for this actor, that he may display him the better, a scenario, *Body of Fate,* which offers to his Creative Mind THE GREATEST POSSIBLE DIFFICULTY THAT IT CAN FACE WITHOUT DESPAIR, and in which he must play a role and wear a *Mask* as unlike as possible to his natural character (or *Will*) and leaves him to improvise, through *Creative Mind,* the dialogue and the details of the plot. He must discover a being which only exists with extreme effort, when his muscles are as it were all taut and all his energies active, and for that reason the *Mask* is described as "A form created by passion to unite us to ourselves." (*AV-A,* 17–18)

The revised 1937 text deploys the same *commedia del arte* metaphor to the same purpose, but the qualification that had been so crucial is now eliminated:

> When I wish for some general idea which will describe the Great Wheel as an individual life I go to the *Commedia del 'Arte* or improvised drama of Italy. The stage-manager, or *Daimon,* offers his actor an inherited scenario, the *Body of Fate,* and a *Mask* or role as unlike as possible to his natural ego or *Will,* and leaves him to improvise through his *Creative Mind* the dialogue and details of the plot. He must discover or reveal a being which only exists with extreme effort. (*AV-B,* 83–4)

This excision has many implications: It removes a Panglossian suggestion of providential benevolence in the transactions

201

between personalities and their daimons and thus responds, perhaps, to charges frequently brought against Yeats's system that it is deterministic. But more significant, for our purposes, is that the removal of any sense that perils are minutely scaled to our capacities to meet them makes the world seem a riskier place – fate is as likely as not to confront us with obstacles we *cannot* overcome – and thus makes the task of sustaining poise and self-possession that much more arduous and challenging. It thus answers better than the earlier formulation to everyone's apprehension as the twenties and thirties progressed; it better accommodates what Yeats regarded as indispensable to great art, a "vision of evil"; and, of course, its augmented sense of life's dangers entails a corresponding gain in heroic grandeur for those who do not break up their lines to weep, but gaze on all the scene with eyes that are ancient, glittering, and gay. If the deletion of the oft-invoked formula registers a darker "vision of reality," it nevertheless registers a greater confidence of Yeats's part in his own power to master it.

One sign of this increased confidence is Yeats's greater willingness to "go public" with his *Vision* work; first to publish it at all, at last to make it as much as possible a provocation to its audience. Starting around the turn of the century, when he undertook to be a "public man," Yeats ceased to publish much about occult or psychic matters, and (as we have seen) even revised already published work so as to minimize these aspects of it. In the teens, he began writing and thinking along such lines again, but not initially for public consumption. "Ego Dominus Tuus" sat in Yeats's drawer for two years, unpublished, although he showed it to friends. By a coincidence that must have seemed magical, or at least ominous, to Yeats – given the timing and the rush of events, it is doubtful that even Yeats could have contrived things this way – "Ego Dominus Tuus" appeared in print (in *Poetry*) in the very month of his marriage, October 1917, almost as if to solemnize and "publish" (in the same way that a wedding is a making public) a new and deeper commitment to the *Vision* project. In 1919, in *The Wild Swans at Coole*, Yeats went public with more *Vision* poems, although these still comprised, relatively speaking, only a small portion of the book; a reader in 1919 would certainly have noticed them, but the general impression would have been of a collection that continued Yeats's by now familiar "public" manner.[36] The poems, for their part – "Ego Dominus Tuus," "The Phases of the Moon," "The Double Vision of Michael Robartes" – sit blank and unforthcoming among masterpieces so much more accessible, almost as if the masterpieces will protect them from criticism. The public is offered the privilege of a glimpse into some inner sanctum; it is the author of "In Memory of Major Robert Gregory" and "Upon a Dying Lady" who accords this privilege; let the public appreciate or keep silent. The public is being shown what it will not understand, and the "Image" *Ille* seeks in "Ego Dominus Tuus," when he does come to disclose the revelation *Ille* wants, is bidden to

> ... whisper it as though
> He were afraid the birds, who cry aloud
> Their momentary cries before it is dawn,
> Would carry it away to blasphemous man.
> ("Ego Dominus Tuus," ll. 76–9; *V,* 371)

Not until the appearance of the 1925 *Vision* is there any sense that Yeats is doing more than merely letting us overhear an unfamiliar range of his work, but is shaping it with us in mind, calculating to some degree of fineness just what sort and how extensive an affront he wishes to offer "blasphemous men." Even at that, though, the 1925 *Vision* was, strictly speaking, never "published" at all; it was issued by private subscription only in 600 copies from a small and obscure London printing house. *A Packet for Ezra Pound,* in which Mrs. Yeats's surprising part in the *Vision* work is disclosed, was "published" in 1929, but in only 425 copies, from Elizabeth Yeats's Cuala Press; apart from initial reviews (only four of them, according to the Cross and Dunlop *Bibliography of Yeats Criticism 1887–1965*) among commentators writing before the publication of the revised *Vision,* only the scrupulous Edmund Wilson, in *Axel's Castle,* so far as I know, ever wrote about it. The later text, by contrast, was published in both London (1937) and New York (1938) by large trade houses, in runs of 1,500 and 1,200, respectively. (It is arguable that this had more to do with considerations of marketability than with Yeats's wish, but Yeats's stock was in some ways higher in 1926 than in 1937: The 1925 *Vision* could have been boomed as the wisdom, the philosophy, and the latest production of the new

Nobel laureate, indeed, his first substantial publication since winning the prize. It seems likely, then, that the private printing of *A Vision* in 1925 resulted from Yeats's deliberate decision to limit its availability to the public at large.)

"A Sixty Year Old Smiling Public Man"

I have been arguing that the increasing flamboyance, audacity, eccentricity, and provocativeness of the *Vision* project as it proceeds reflects Yeats's increasing confidence in his own powers and the encouragements of his growing stature as a major literary figure. But a motion so contrary and willful cannot but have been "antithetical" in its motivation also. Certification as *éminence grise* brought with it, along with new accesses of lip service, a greater willingness among younger writers to carp and criticize, and of course Yeats's occultism was a particularly inviting object of such attention. What had been indulged when it was merely a matter of a few strange, quasi-didactic poems in otherwise admirable collections of verse became deplorable, regrettable, dismissable when presented as a large and important baggage, insistently declared. Pound and (for a while) Eliot stayed respectful at least in public, but their younger champions took from their experiments in jarringly "un-poetic" metrics, imagery, and subject matter incitements too powerful to resist. I. A. Richards, in *Principles of Literary Criticism* (1925), opened the can of worms by calling attention to "such pathetic spectacles as Mr Yeats trying desperately to believe in fairies" and stirred its contents further the following year in an essay in the *Criterion* that shortly became the climactic chapter of *Science and Poetry:*

> Mr Yeats retires into black velvet curtains and the visions of the Hermetist. . . . Mr Yeats's work from the beginning was a repudiation of the most active contemporary interests. . . . Later . . . he made a more violent repudiation, not merely of current civilisation but of life itself, in favour of a more supernatural world.

Richards was writing before *A Vision* appeared – although in anticipation of its appearance: "Mr Yeats' promised treatise on the states of the soul has not yet appeared," he observes with audible disappointment.[37] His sarcasm set the tone for *A Vision*'s reception (or nonreception) in the coming years. In the most influential quarterlies and journals, Richards's case was stated again and again. The brilliance of *The Tower* (1928) only intensified a general need to disassociate the wonderful poetry from the ridiculous "philosophy." Reviewing *The Tower* in the *New Republic* (October 10, 1928), Theodore Spencer found the poetry flawless – except where words like "pern" and "gyre" brought the "privacies" of *A Vision* to mind. Edmund Wilson reviewed *A Vision* (*New Republic,* January 16, 1929) and expanded his observations, as we have seen, in the very influential *Axel's Castle* (1931), where exasperation and admiration were not mediated in any but the feeblest ways. In 1930, William Empson's *Seven Types of Ambiguity* inspected "Who Goes with Fergus" as an example of the sixth type of ambiguity, the type, Empson explains, that "must say nothing." F. R. Leavis, in *New Bearings in English Poetry* (1932), praised Yeats's achievement but warned that it was a dead end: If Yeats's response to experience were the only one available to poetry, then "poetry would cease to matter. Adult minds could no longer take it seriously."[38] Leavis's supple and large-minded assessment – it is Leavis at his best – argues powerfully against a too hasty dismissal of Yeats but secures its points, notably, by leaving out of the account any consideration of *A Vision* at all.

For all of these critics, Yeats represented an older order ripe for overthrow; the hero of their new order was, of course, T. S. Eliot. In 1934, nine years after *Science and Poetry,* Eliot approvingly quoted Richard's words on Yeats's "repudiation of life itself ... in favour of a supernatural world" in his own "primer of modern heresy," *After Strange Gods.* "It is, I think, only carrying Mr Richards's complaint a little further to add that Mr Yeats's 'supernatural world' was the wrong supernatural world." In succeeding sentences, Eliot commends Yeats for having "at least discarded, for the most part, the trifling and eccentric, the provincial in time and place."[39] It is quintessentially Eliotic jujitsu: Speaking as if Yeats has discarded his esoterica constitutes Eliot's oblique directive that he do so.

It was in the face of such directives, such coercions, such challenges, such well-intentioned advice that Yeats not only decided not to discard his "trifling and eccentric" interests, but on the

contrary committed himself to them more willfully and tena-
ciously than ever – not least by revising *A Vision* so as to set the
problem of literal belief most provocatively in the foreground.
He undertook this revision at a time when Richards's *Science
and Poetry,* published the same year (1926) as the first edition of
A Vision, had made the problem of "poetry and belief" a subject
of intense discussion. It is hard not to feel that Richards's vehe-
mence against Yeats in that book is prompted partly by the
embarrassment that Yeats's occultism presented to Richards's
elegantly reasonable doctrine of "pseudo-statement." (Richards's
later epigones, the New Critics, would draw from his estheticism
the opposite conclusion, that Yeats's "beliefs" were not worth
assessing.) In any case, the poetry-and-belief discussion remained
a central preoccupation in the writings of Eliot ("Dante" [1929]
and *After Strange Gods* [1934]), Wyndham Lewis (*Men Without
Art* [1934]), and others throughout the period between the two
versions of *A Vision,* and Yeats was surely aware of it. (Lewis,
who attacked "pseudoism" in *Men Without Art,* was a special
enthusiasm of Yeats's during this period.)

Yeats evidently thus committed himself to his "trifling and
eccentric" interests – much as he had once committed himself to
Irish nationalism in large part to mortify and thus purge his
timidity – with the express intention of testing his lifelong investment in supernaturalism against an increasingly inhospitable climate of criticism, to see whether he could carry off a resolve to
invite and endure such criticism without defensiveness or bitterness, but on the contrary make the whole performance a happy
display of smiling and whimsical gaiety and good humor. In a
letter (April 25, 1928) to Olivia Shakespear, Yeats wrote that he
was rereading the just published volume *The Tower* and was
"astonished at its bitterness."[40] Bitterness, Yeats knew, poisons
the wells of joy and so must be cast out. Such bitterness had been
vented in his poetry often before; in 1914, in the wake of George
Moore's jeers and slurs on his family and his love, Yeats had
written in a black mood, to protest the "undreamt accidents" of
circumstance:

Those undreamt accidents that have made me
– Seeing that Fame has perished this long while,

Yeats's A Vision

Being but a part of ancient ceremony –
Notorious, till all my priceless things
Are but a post the passing dogs defile.
   ("While I, from that reed throated
      whisperer," ll. 10–14, *V, 321*)

Now, notoriety is just the condition sought for, against which to test and oppose the power of his own "deliberate happiness" – as can be seen by Yeats's resort to the same metaphor of dogs with legs aloft in his "Pages from a Diary Written in Nineteen Hundred and Thirty":

> I too have had such [supernatural] experience and others "spiritualistic" in type which I shall publish when ready – to adapt a metaphor from Erasmus – to make myself a post for dogs and journalists to defile. (*E, 330*)

Here the "priceless things" Yeats is preparing to commit to the attention of "dogs and journalists" are quite obviously the revisions then going forward in the text of *A Vision,* and in particular the disclosure of Mrs. Yeats's automatic writing and the visitations of the spirit instructors – all of which Yeats could expect to be greeted with hoots, all of which he therefore would present precisely to elicit hoots, all of which "I shall publish when ready."

The *Vision* project is "antithetical," in short, in every possible way Yeats can make it so: He contrives always to do just what others wish he would *not* do, and this principle applies not only to his critics, but also to his wife, who wanted her part in the automatic writing kept secret (she exasperatedly called her husband "William Tell"), and even to the spirit communicators themselves, since the first thing Yeats tells us they told him was that they did *not* want Yeats to spend his time assembling a system out of the "scattered sentences" of his wife's automatic writing, but to draw from it instead "metaphors for poetry":

> On the afternoon of October 24, 1917, four days after my marriage, my wife surprised me by attempting automatic writing. What came in disjointed sentences, in almost illegible writing, was so exciting, sometimes so profound, that I

207

persuaded her to give an hour or two day after day to the unknown writer, and after some half dozen such hours offered to spend what remained of life explaining and piecing together those scattered sentences. "No," was the answer, "we have come to give you metaphors for poetry." (*AV-B*, 8)

The first page of *A Vision* tells us, that is, that *A Vision* should never have been written at all, that Yeats should have stayed with poetry[41] – and it tells us this on just the "authority" that Yeats's critics indignantly or derisively dismiss, even though its injunction accords altogether with their own wishes. At its very advent, the revelation announces itself as not to be revealed, much as, at its close, on the book's last page (before the epilogue, "All Souls' Night") Yeats acknowledges that, after all, nothing *is* revealed, that at the end of all that *Vision* work, "nothing comes – though this moment was to reward me for all my toil":

Then I understand. I have already said all that can be said. The particulars are the work of the *thirteenth sphere* or cycle which is in every man and called by every man his freedom. Doubtless, for it can do all things and knows all things, it knows what it will do with its own freedom but it has kept the secret. (*AV-B*, 301–2)

The "unconquerable delusion" is unconquered and unconquerable still – and on reflection it is clear that Yeats would not have wanted it otherwise.

This is, perhaps, Yeats's "comic" way of saying the marvelous tragic thing he has to say on his deathbed, that "man can embody truth but he cannot know it."[42] Throughout, the *Vision* project had advanced, with a show of sublime indifference to the difficulties, as if on the premise that its truths would be such as the initiate might know without having to embody them. It had offered "an explanation of life" (*AV-A*, iii), an explanation so comprehensive that its understanders "should never be astonished again" (*AV-A*, 9). But of course Yeats hungered for astonishment – his excited, passionate, fantastical imagination's pride was that it expected the impossible – and so Yeats's wish to put on the knowledge without the power is necessarily but another phase of his passion for contact with just those powers – especially those powers – he might embody but cannot know.

Determinism and Freedom

The "thirteenth sphere" Yeats adduces in the last, closing section of the revised *Vision* ("The End of the Cycle") had been mentioned, but made little of, in the 1925 text; in the 1937 version, it is the wild card, the joker in the deck, that makes all the seeming stability of the rest of the system contingent and conditional again – or rather, shows it to have been contingent and conditional all along. Richard Ellmann shrewdly notes that by planting here at the end of the wound-up spool the spring that unwinds it all again, Yeats is making yet another boldly "antithetical" gesture:

> Only at this point do we realize that Yeats, after building up a system over three hundred pages, in the last two pages sets up that system's anti-self. All the determinism or quasi-determinism of *A Vision* is abruptly confronted with the Thirteenth Cycle which is able to alter everything, and suddenly free will, liberty, and deity pour back into the universe.[43]

The passage on freedom and secrecy has no analogue in the 1925 text, and Yeats may have inserted it partly to answer the one review of *A Vision* we may be certain he read, by his old friend A. E., who complained that "to follow in the wake of Mr. Yeats's mind is to surrender oneself to the idea of Fate and to part from the idea of Free Will."[44] A. E.'s reservations are couched in the perennial vocabulary, and so is Yeats's "answer" (if that is what it was), the vocabulary of "Fate" and "Freedom." Yeats eschews, consciously I think, the more fashionable vocabulary of the period, which refers not to "Fate" but to "determinism," and to "Freedom" as little as possible, having no handy ideological synonym (which is part of what Yeats would have disliked about "ideologies").

Complaints about the "determinism" of Yeats's "system" are not much heard nowadays, and not, I think, merely because Yeats's canonization has put him beyond reproach: Even Harold

Bloom's multicount indictment of Yeats and of *A Vision* does not revive this particular charge. But the issue of the "determinism" of *A Vision* was central to discussion of Yeats through the early 1950s.[45] I would not beat this dead horse now if it were not so evidently a live horse in Yeats's own lifetime, and especially during the *entre deux guerres,* when Yeats composed, published, revised, and republished his esoteric system in its two versions. The contemporary best sellers of H. G. Wells, Spengler, and Toynbee were all well known to Yeats; their historicisms and many cruder Marxist and nationalist versions were a major vehicle of ideological discourse in a period when any "outline of history" seemed an ideological provocation – which is doubtless why so many poets attempted one: Joyce incorporated Vico in *Finnegans Wake;* Brooks Adams likewise animates Pound's *Cantos;* Zukofsky's *"A"* fuses Marx and Henry Adams. These attempts to grasp history whole, along with such smaller-scale efforts as Eliot's *The Waste Land,* Woolf's *Orlando,* and Graves's *Autobiography of Baal,* sufficiently attest that fantasias of history were very much a "period" phenomenon.[46]

Yeats surely confected his own pageant of history with all of these tendencies in mind, and though his own motive was surely to enlarge freedom, I would not put it past him to have anticipated with some amusement, and even to have invited, the complaint that his system was deterministic. The complainants, professing disbelief, attributed to Yeats a literal belief in his gyres and cones that Yeats disowns repeatedly; but having wrongly attributed it to him, it is themselves whose judgments are henceforth governed, not to say determined, by it. (In a letter, commenting on reviews of *A Vision,* Yeats remarks "the stupidities of men who attribute to me some thought of their own and reply to that thought. They all think I was bound to explain myself to them. It is just that explaining which makes many English books empty.")[47] Professions of critical objectivity begin to look "objective" in Yeats's sense, for complaints about the determinism of the system merely evince a habit of mind which assumes that anything calling itself a system must articulate an analytic and universalizing scheme, rather than assay, as Yeats's does, a dialectical, imagistic, and invincibly idiosyncratic series of "stylistic arrangements of experience comparable to the cubes in the drawing of Wyndham Lewis and to the ovoids in the sculpture of

Brancusi" (*AV-B*, 25). *A Vision* presents no "philosophy," but rather – because "you can refute Hegel but not the Saint or the Song of Sixpence" – a fantasia of images, poses, gestures.

Argument, in any case, is beside the point for Yeats; the "argument" of *A Vision* is a mock argument. In his description of Phase 17, the phase he regarded as his own, Yeats hints that the undertakings of Phase 17 personalities have an integrity rather different than they contrive to have appear:

> As contrasted with Phase 13 and Phase 14, where mental images were separated from one another that they might be subject to knowledge, all now flow, change, flutter, cry out, or mix into something else. . . . The *Will* is falling asunder, but without explosion and noise. The separated fragments seek images rather than ideas, and these the intellect, seated in Phase 13, must synthesise in vain, drawing with its compass point a line that shall but represent the outline of a bursting pod. The being has for its supreme aim, as it had at Phase 16 (and as all subsequent *antithetical* phases shall have) to hide from itself and others this separation and disorder, and it conceals them under the emotional *Image* of Phase 3; as Phase 16 concealed its greater violence under that of Phase 2. When true to phase the intellect must turn all its power to this task. (*AV-A*, 75–6; *AV-B*, 141)

Under the flurry of "technicalities" about this phase and that, Yeats is saying that projects like his own, like this one we are now reading, aim for a look of logical coherence that they do not really have. "Remember, we will deceive you if we can."

But more simply, it is foolish to protest the determinism of a book that so pointedly refuses to solicit our assent, so insistently incites us to argue against it; in that sense, too, it is antithetical, and in the sense also that its historical panorama images just such a "body of fate" as antithetical personalities make it their heroism to oppose. Yeats has created his system not to enslave others, but to elaborate an image of his own freedom. Those who see in *A Vision* instead an unwitting determinism have missed Yeats's comedy of mystery and freedom; all solemn squints and furrowed brows, they refuse to smile even when the punch line is explained to them – though, admittedly, it is explained only cryptically: "it knows what it will do with its own freedom but it has kept the secret." If this declaration at the end of so ambitious an effort toward an "explanation of life" unwinds Yeats's tightly wound spool or sets up his system's antiself, it does so not by opposing to the *Vision* project's esoteric comedy the sort of limitations that enjoin tragedy.[48] Quite the contrary, this aperture opens on a prospect of mystery and freedom without limit, a setting not of returns to the narrow pound, or witherings into the truth, but pregnant instead with the promise of just such consummations – the scream of Juno's peacock, a transit of dolphin-borne spirits, an apocalyptic shudder in the loins – as Yeats's passionate, fantastical, excited imagination so devoutly wished.

Of course, Yeats could not always sustain such grandiose affirmations, as so many of his masks of the thirties attest: The nostalgic spokesman for the "last romantics," whose vision of "Traditional sanctity and loveliness" ("Coole Park and Ballylee, 1931," ll. 41–2, *V*, 491) is being displaced by an ugly "modernist" art that prefers "a man fishing behind a gas works, the vulgarity of a single Dublin day prolonged through 700 pages" (*AV-A*, 211–12); the celebrant of heroism mocked by the recognition that his antiheroic age regards his own heroic poses as of a like foolishness with the calculated folly of his esotericist pose; the old-school Irish nationalist, looking on as Cosgrave's benignly oligarchic Free State gives way to De Valera's priest-ridden Republic, resolving to outrage responsible opinion by writing marching songs for Ireland's protofascist Blue Shirts, then revising the songs and publishing them with a note (*V*, 837) that would outrage the Blue Shirts as well; the mad old sailor ranting "on the boiler" until driven off, then, rowing a boat along shore, "sculling it in whenever he saw a crowd, then, bow to seaward, denouncing the general wickedness, then sculling it out amid a shower of stones" (*E*, 407). Bitterest of all these images – Yeats's Timon – is the "Old Man" who comes onstage to introduce Yeats's deathbed play, *The Death of Cuchulain:* He explains that "I have been selected because I am out of fashion like the antiquated stuff the [play] is made of," derides his audience as "people who are educating themselves out of Book Societies and the like, sciolists all, pickpockets and opinionated bitches," declares that he spits on this and that, and makes his exit shouting, "I spit! I spit! I spit!" (*Plays*, 438–9).

Yeats's A Vision

Tragedy and Comedy

Out of all such quarrels with the world arises a great bitterness, and in battling with that Yeats locates the quarrel with himself that makes for his late poetry of tragic joy. But part of the impressiveness of that tragic and joyous mask is the evident strain displayed and transfigured in it: We are made to recognize the will, the energy, and the art of that difficult pose. When the happy, smiling face of apparently absent-minded, un-self-conscious obliviousness to surrounding common sense evinced by Yeats's esoteric comedy is juxtaposed with Yeats's other masks of the thirties – masks of "lust and rage" on the one hand, of "tragic joy" on the other – its look of solipsistic self-absorption must seem less that of an unguarded, open, and unwittingly foolish face and rather more like yet another cunningly wrought mask, a mask self-conscious and heroically deliberate, a mask purged of any sign of all the bitterness and anger – and all the heroism and triumph, too – ventilated in Yeat's other work. If the art of the tragic mask consists in part of putting the art on display – an image of passion infinitely protracted, "Till meditation master all its parts" ("All Souls' Night," l. 92 *V,* 474) – the art of looking happy consists in part, and more classically, of concealing the art.

Which is to say that in its artificiality, Yeats's comic mask registers his "antithetical" impulses at their purest and most potent, most confident and extreme. The author of *A Vision* is no fool. The *Vision* project has the last laugh on all who regard it as an incautious folly, an ill-considered self-exposure, a display of unwitting credulousness, unwitting naïveté, unwitting absurdity. There is nothing unwitting about it; it incarnates as knowingly as any of Yeats's major works an entirely self-conscious repertoire of gestures and poses. Its seeming un-self-consciousness is perhaps the most esoteric thing about Yeats's esoteric comedy, a comedy of whimsy, irony, calculated preposterousness, poker faces, "textual flim-flam," a comedy that will deceive you if it can, a comedy that plays with the look (and with the real peril) of that solipsism and delusion to which mystic and occult investigations are so uniquely liable, a comedy that always effects at last the redemption of that solipsism by showing it – to the sufficiently percipient – to have been self-conscious all along.

Frank O'Connor, in the best of all reminiscences of Yeats,[49] has

captured this side of the poet best and recognized that it sometimes approached, in the overelaborateness of intrigue and
manipulation to which it often tempted Yeats, a kind of delusion:
"Perhaps it was the worldliness of the unworldly which helps to
keep them sane by making them feel cynical and subtle." But he
recognized, too, far better than most, that Yeats's awareness of
the world around him was much sharper than it pleased him to
have people think:

> I was grateful for his pin-point awareness, so different from
> A. E.'s dim benevolence. He had a sort of sideway glance
> from around his spectacles – as if he were looking at you
> round his pose – that was full of knowingness, though I only
> suspected how much he really saw. That vagueness, that
> inability to find the cigarettes or remember the names of
> people he didn't want to remember, was a protective psy-
> chological weakness, probably developed during the timid-
> ity of boyhood. He was really diabolically observant, or so
> I think, and even when I bored him, I was aware that it was
> I who was boring him, not somebody else, and that he
> would remember it for me.

It is O'Connor, too, who retails an anecdote that wonderfully
captures the deliberate happiness of Yeats's comic pose at its gay-
est and most teasing: Yeats telling about himself a story whose
preposterousness he and his hearer both recognize, but telling it
as if he himself does not, and with full – and, in the event, justified – confidence that his interlocutor will do nothing so grace-
less as to call him on it. The friend was F. R. Higgins, a longtime
croney – coeditor with Yeats of *Broadside,* a founding member
with Yeats of the Irish Academy, and for years Yeats's colleague
(as managing director) of the Abbey Theatre. Higgins was a
trusted friend who surely knew as well as anyone of Yeats's notorious inaptitude, either as listener or performer, for the art of
music. Yeats was, in fact, tone deaf, and Dublin and London
laughed often at humorous accounts of Yeats's gaffes at concerts
and recitals or (better yet) his own ludicrous attempts at singing
traditional folk songs or settings of his poems. Many such stories
are told, most amusingly, by Yeats himself, in his *Autobiography.*
At any rate, the poet one day told Higgins of his meeting, years

earlier, an old peasant woman reputed to be gifted with the second sight. She had never met or, indeed, heard of Yeats before, but once she was put into her trance, she passed her fingers over his face and said, "Poet." Then, a moment later, having mused further, added, "*Great* poet." Yeats stands silent; interested, yet skeptical and aloof, until a moment later, "Musician," she said at last. "And then," said Yeats – picture him leaning forward in his chair, eyebrows raised for emphasis, a delighted smile playing about his face – "and *then* I knew she was genuine!"

CONCLUSION

ESOTERIC COMEDY AND "MAKING THE UNCONSCIOUS CONSCIOUS"

> Is not this nostalgia of innocence precisely the characteristic of the man whose dedicated career is the exploration of the hitherto unknown and unconscious, who is by the very nature of his voyage travelling farther and farther away from unconsciousness; and would not the same man despise most those who have started, cannot go back, and yet dare not go forward?
>
> – W. H. Auden, *The Enchafèd Flood*

> A very small part of acting is that which takes place on the stage . . . when anyone is conscious of himself as acting, something like a sense of humour is present.
>
> – T. S. Eliot, "Rhetoric and Poetic Drama"

> I . . . will watch with amusement the emergence of the philosophy of my own poetry, the unconscious becoming conscious.
>
> – Yeats, letter to Dorothy Wellesley

THIS STUDY BEGAN, as my introduction noted, in an apprehension that there was something "protomodernist" about *Sartor Resartus,* the *Apologia,* and *A Vision,* preeminently their self-conscious difficulty and their devious, ironic, and almost endlessly suggestive transactions with the conventions of genre and address they seem to invoke. A signal difference, though, is that whereas the masterpieces of modernism mantle themselves in an armor of "art," these esoteric comedies are unemphatic about their own artfulness and retain about them – even amid transcendental rhapsodizing, theological disquisition, and playful spiritualizing – some ambiguous but obstinate trace of the actual. *Sartor Resartus* parodies a nonfiction genre, and though any "active reader" will see quickly enough that the book is not "non-fiction," still, "art" might not immediately seem the right name for what it undertakes. The *Apologia* and *A Vision,* too, never intermit an insistence that all their artfulness is firmly subdued to the service of "what really happened."

The masterworks of modernism, by contrast, are so insistently, self-consciously, and categorically "art" as to make of the insistence a constant provocation. But the preoccupation of "the men of 1914" with art, with a rhetoric of "control" and "mastery," generated an irony beyond their power to master or control. The provocations they fomented as rebels became, in the hands of overeager disciples, articles of an inflexible dogma of evasion. Eliot's "impersonality," Pound's "technique," Joyce's God-like artist paring his fingernails sponsored doctrines according to which "sincerity" was a concern only of the naïve, authorial intention a fallacy, the biography of the artist an irrelevance and a distraction, to be ignored on principle. Art, said I. A. Richards, was "pseudo-statement," and in his wake the founding orthodoxy of English departments everywhere held that art "should not mean / But be" – an injunction, no one noticed, that disregards itself.[1]

"Pseudo-statement" and "Fictionalism"

As Sanford Schwartz demonstrates in *The Matrix of Modernism* (1985), modernism emerged from a philosophical and intellectual milieu much taken with what Hans Vaihinger called "fictionalism," that is, the view that reality is constituted by the mind, rather than objectively perceived by it, and that all abstractions, conceptualizations, theories, and so on are no more than variously useful "fictions" rather than accounts of "truth."[2] "Pseudo-statement" is a locution entirely characteristic of this recognition, but by the time it had been formulated, the makers of modernism (Eliot and Pound, at least; Joyce is a trickier case) were already moving toward commitments transcending mere art, commitments that talk of "fictions" would compromise. Eliot, for example, deals respectfully with Richards's "pseudo-statement" statement in his 1929 "Dante" essay, but five years later the whole argument of *After Strange Gods* (1934) implicitly classes any such view of art's function as among the "heresies" of our time. (Wyndham Lewis's *Men Without Art* [1934], in

Conclusion

which Eliot's epithet is "The Pseudoist," was surely catalytic for Eliot on this question.) Eliot's new commitment to something greater than art involved art's demotion to the status merely of a "superior amusement." ("The poetry does not matter.")³ Not so Pound, whose post-Great War political anger required that poetry be committed above all else. It is one of the sharper ironies of Pound's sadly ironic career that the scandal surrounding the award of the 1948 Bollingen Prize to *The Pisan Cantos* probably did more than anything else to establish as orthodox, at least in the universities, the New Critical estheticism that irrevocably disjoins the work from the allegiances of its author – yet all of Pound's writing from *Mauberley* on had been founded on an increasingly vehement repudiation of any such suggestion.

If works like *The Waste Land,* the *Cantos,* and *Ulysses* have been readily regarded (and domesticated) as art, *Sartor Resartus,* the *Apologia,* and *A Vision* have, conversely, been taken too much at face value – if not quite as nonfiction, still as books whose matter can be excerpted from the presentation without overmuch regard for their art. On the whole, the latter seems the preferable fate, insofar as it at least acknowledges, however inadequately, that the difficulties these works present are not to be negotiated via reduction to "pseudo-statement." I have tried here to read these books with a heightened sense of their artfulness, but in a way that I hope augments, rather than reduces, awareness of what their authors had at stake in them. But I recognize that my "modernist" reading of these books, especially the *Apologia* and *A Vision,* sometimes seems to suggest that these authors do not mean what they say, that Newman's Catholicism was a fiction Newman regarded and exploited as a fiction, that Yeats's spiritualism was a sort of game Yeats was amused to play. It is easy enough to agree that anything people say, think, or believe is a fiction, but there nevertheless remain some fictions that we do mean, that will suffer themselves to be "deconstructed" but not (as the wiser deconstructionists know) to be disowned. There are fictions that are past cure: They belong to us, and for better or worse, we to them.

To agitate just such fictions is the common project of esoteric comedy and modernist poetry and fiction. Their contrasting fates – esoteric comedy inadequately understood, modernism understood too well – are linked by their common effort to engage the

219

reader in a sense of difficulty and enigma by making the activity of reading itself difficult and problematic. Each risks, in different ways, what used to be called "the fallacy of imitative form" in order to pose, in the most immediate way possible, the problem of how literature works, how it means, how it persuades or compels, how we experience its power even as we remain conscious of its artificiality. We laugh at the rube in *Tom Jones,* who, at a performance of *Hamlet,* thinks the Ghost is real; but we would not go to the theater ourselves if its illusion did not exercise some not entirely dissimilar power over us. By committing themselves so insistently to disclosures that are scarcely entertainable as "true," these texts force on their readers the perplexing experience of alternately undergoing and resisting appeals simultaneously too compelling to dismiss and too bizarre to accept. We are kept in a state of contradiction like the one Yeats describes as characterizing his relations with the spirit communicators who dictated the raw materials of *A Vision:* He could not help but take them and their pronouncements "literally," he says, when "overwhelmed by miracle as all men must be when in the midst of it," but adds, as if reassuringly, that in every such instance, "my reason has soon recovered." (Observe the irony of Yeats's speaking here as if such recoveries of reason were a welcome relief from miracle, when his single complaint about miracle is always its transiency, its inevitable, and too speedy, "wither[ing] into the truth.")[4] In reading these books we, too, experience a tension between our susceptibility (and our desire) to be "overwhelmed" and our "reason" that resists such engulfment.

These works thus share with modernism the project of inciting reader and writer alike to the exercise of a function most Romantic and Victorian theorists of literature regard as inimical to either esthetic creation or appreciation, namely the function of an alert and vigilant critical intelligence. The values and the sorts of "reading" DeQuincey separates under the headings "the literature of knowledge" and "the literature of power"[5] the modernist and the esoteric comedian aim to bring together and hold in tension; they test one against the other and find, against the grain of their time, that at the disposition of an ironic, self-conscious, and tough-minded wit, knowledge and power may rather enlarge than diminish each other. And they mean not merely to attest this discovery themselves, but to make the experience of it real to the

Conclusion

reader. The "self-activity" commended in *Sartor Resartus* ("the best effect of any book"), the "embodied forms" that model the *Apologia*'s rhetorical aims, Yeats's insistence on the fictiveness of everything, and then on the fiction become flesh, are both expounded and enacted in these texts, in a fashion that requires our participation. "A certain inarticulate Self-consciousness dwells dimly in us," writes Teufelsdröckh, "which only our Works can render articulate";[6] and clearly "the proper art of reading" can be such a species of "Work." The difficult prose of Carlyle, Newman, and Yeats aims to make reading itself not the passive reception of arguments that it usually is, but a kind of activity, or "self-activity," and a kind of experience. The active reader not only is witness to an authorial self-consciousness in the text, but is made conscious and self-conscious of the work of reading as cognate with the work being read.

Self-consciousness

An apprehension of the uses of a studied and cultivated self-consciousness (not only in reading) seems to me finally the most importantly protomodernist characteristic of the esoteric comedy of Carlyle, Newman, and Yeats. Carlyle's declension, after *Sartor Resartus,* into his "anti-self-consciousness theory" is one of the signal events of Victorian culture, an index of the degree to which "self," having usurped the space where "soul" used to be, was a central and disturbing issue for Carlyle's era. Since Locke, all problems had tended to pose themselves as psychological; Wesleyan ardor – which often seems an effort to disprove, by dint of saintly and selfless example, the nasty account of human motives rendered by Thomas Hobbes – had inspired English "conscience" to a neo-Puritan self-scrutiny arguably more profound, and certainly more widespread, than any it had previously experienced; while Bentham (a sanitized Hobbes) had made rational "self-interest" the basis of all well-being, both private and public.

Victorian respectability thus stood perilously astride a widening fissure, with one foot seeking purchase on the self-abnegation of Evangelical moralism, the other on the prudential self-interest of bourgeois liberalism. Nor can any thinking person, indeed, any reader of Dickens, have escaped noticing that the Victorian compromise tended to apportion the self-interest to those with interests to protect and the self-abnegation to those with little more than their "selves" to renounce – a class arrangement whose analogue within each class assigned the obligations of selflessness to women, whence the curious mix of vibrancy and vapidity in the heroines of so many Victorian novels. Between them, Evangelical moralism and utilitarian liberalism summed up the alternatives available to anyone conscious of "self" as a moral problem; the one had to lead either to neurosis or to hypocrisy, the other to rationalized greed. The pain of this dilemma is attested by the extremity of the later Carlyle's response to it: Where all consciousness must be false consciousness, better to have no consciousness at all.

Within the terms of such conflicts, the resolution offered by the "wordly asceticism" of the Calvinist work ethic had at least the merit of comprehensiveness, and Carlyle's "Work" differs from its Reformation originals only insofar as its coloration is darker and more desperate. While sixteenth- and seventeenth-century Protestantism did at least genuinely believe in God and salvation, Carlyle's project amounts to (incurring the obligations of) a theodicy without (assuming any of the benefits of) a God: This is what is so ironic, so desperate, and so extremely Victorian about it. Such contradictions could be sustained only at the cost of massive denial, and for Carlyle, "self" – because its energy and intelligence are obstinately alive to the contradictions – is synecdoche for all that must be denied. Any effort to think through such problems, because it is necessarily conscious and purposeful, is thereby also necessarily tainted by the motives of "self" and can thus only aggravate what it had sought to relieve – a dilemma Freud diagnoses as the "moral masochism" attending a "negative therapeutic reaction" in which "a 'moral' factor, a sense of guilt" impels the superego to blame and punish the ego precisely for its motions toward cure.[7] Just this is what Carlylean "conscience" does, by identifying the "self" as the source of every low, appetitive, manipulative motive and locating innocence and happiness in an irrecoverable condition of unconsciousness.

From such dilemmas, Carlyle supposed, the only escape lay in some honorable narcosis, an oblivion of "self" *("Selbst-tödtung")* secured by immersion in a transpersonal "Work." An instructive contrast is with Samuel Johnson, prototypically Victorian in his sense of "self" as a source of moral trouble. But Johnson judged that the pain and conflictedness that self-consciousness brings were of the moral essence of the human fate, and he regarded as either delusion or cowardice any suggestion that "self" could be evaded. Carlyle insists, in defiance of his better knowledge, that it can, then demands that it must. If thy self offend thee, pluck it out: Stupefy it with "Work," condemn it to "Silence," humble it with "Hero-Worship." These are strategies of rendering unto Caesar so nearly all the energy of consciousness as to leave for "God" only a depleted shell, a vessel emptied of its contents.

But Teufelsdröckh knows better, and so do Newman and Yeats. It is a suggestive irony about Carlyle that he could celebrate self-consciousness only by not quite recognizing that that was what he was doing. The contradiction offered by Teufelsdröckhian example to Carlylean precept seems unconscious – a state of affairs Carlylean precept would differ from Teufelsdröckhian example in defending. But as long as he is possessed of the Teufelsdröckhian *daimon,* Carlyle joins Newman and Yeats as an exemplary figure of a resourceful and confident selfhood, undaunted by inner divisions and accusations – seemingly innocent even of any such possibility – sustaining and sustained by an empowering, rather than a disabling, self-consciousness. Under the aegis of that radical, protodeconstructionist wit, the "Descendental" Teufelsdröckh, Carlyle appears not as advocate of *Selbst-tödtung* and "anti-self-consciousness," but as celebrant of the energy and power of the self to master its burdens, for whom (as Carlyle writes in "Characteristics" [1831], his principal diatribe against self-consciousness and intellectualism), "self-consciousness is the symptom merely; nay, it is also the attempt towards cure" (*Works,* 28:20) – a formulation that strikingly anticipates the Freudian axiom that every neurosis is also an attempt at recovery.[8]

So although Mill identified Carlyle as the avatar of the nineteenth century's "anti-self-consciousness theory,"[9] as esoteric comedian, Carlyle (with Newman and Yeats) exemplifies the impulse, from Hegel to Freud, to make self-consciousness the key to all human projects, part of the problem, yes, but part of the solution, too. Esoteric comedy exemplifies the strain of Romanticism that sought, in Geoffrey Hartman's words, "to draw the antidote to self-consciousness from consciousness itself, not to escape from or limit knowledge, but to convert it into an energy finer than intellectual."[10] The last phrase, "finer than intellectual," resonates with the thought of the esoteric comedians – one recalls Carlyle's persistent anti-intellectualism, Newman's sense of the dangers of "that universal solvent," the "wild, living intellect of man," Yeats's search for effects "too subtle for the intellect"[11] – but reminds us that their seeming anti-intellectualism aims to sublimate and transcend, rather than degrade, intellect and its works. Even Carlyle, the most "anti-intellectual" of the three, could affirm, in "Characteristics," that "Thought must needs be Doubt and Inquiry before it can again be Affirmation and Sacred Precept" (*Works,* 28:32); and the essay ends with proto-Yeatsian disdain for the defeatism of "hysterical women" and confident assertions of the "heroic joy" of the tasks ahead (*Works,* 28:42–3). Carlyle, or rather Teufelsdröckh, never doubts that "the Man makes the Circumstances, and spiritually as well as economically is the artificer of his own fortune" (*Works,* 28:229).

The Self as "Fictile" and "Fingent"

I said in my introduction that esoteric comedy offered a strategy of deliverance from what Arnold called

> . . . this strange disease of modern life,
> With its sick hurry, its divided aims,
> Its heads o'ertaxed, its palsied hearts . . . [12]

If the intellectual crises of Victorian culture ensued from a materialist world view that seemed to expose immemorial belief systems as mere fictions, esoteric comedy answers that the new world picture is a "fiction" too and that the fictions we live by, both private and collective, remain in our power to manage. The esoteric comedians respond to the problem of self-consciousness with the cognate insistence that the self that projects all other fictions is itself (in Carlyle's words) "fictile" and "fingent," simultaneously creature and creator of the world it shapes and is shaped by: "self-born," as Yeats has it, "self-begotten" and "self-delighting."[13] Carlyle's Teufelsdröckh mask and Newman's manipulation of voices and tones prefigure a modern literature that will require the concept of persona, a literature whose sense of the self as fictive attains one of its richest elaborations in Yeats's theory of "the mask."

Notoriously, the sense of the self as "fictile" and "fingent" complicates the problem of self-consciousness in a late Protestant age obsessed with sincerity. The period from Carlyle's youth to Yeats's maturity saw the emergence of an urban culture in which manners became more refined but also more superficial, an affair of masks, poses, and a sense of the self as a quasi-theatrical presentation, a repertoire of roles alterable to suit circumstances, which might change several times a day.[14] Against a backdrop of increasing bourgeoisification, self-consciousness diminishes from a Titanic curse (Childe Harold) to the stuff of comic pathos (J. Alfred Prufrock) – though for some writers that diminution makes it more of a laceration, not less: Arnold, for example, whose Empedocles experiences the classic "Know thyself" as the highest human imperative, but also (conflictedly) the most anguishing human burden. Arnold deplores "the sick fatigue, the languid doubt" in which the self multiples into "a hundred different lives," the "frivolous" modern condition in which "distractions" prompt a man to "change his own identity" in "capricious play" that estranges him from "his genuine self."[15]

If Arnold's "genuine self" or "best self" is a "buried life" he yearns to disinter, self-consciousness is the guilty burden he longs to bury. (Empedocles invokes the trope of the "buried self" moments before burying himself in the volcano.) The conflictedness of this central problem of Arnold's poetry is sublimated in the idealizations worked out in Arnold's prose: That "Hellenism" whose "spontaneity of consciousness" Arnold prefers to the "Hebraism" that tends to cultivate "strictness of conscience" acts to palliate the strictures of Arnold's own "Hebraic" obsession with "self." Arnold nowhere comes closer to esoteric comedy than when he urges the "free play" of the "Hellenic" attitude:

> And as the force which encourages us to stand staunch and fast by the rule and ground we have is Hebraism, so the force which encourages us to go back upon this rule, and to try the very ground on which we appear to stand, is Hellenism – a turn for giving our consciousness free play and enlarging its range.[16]

This pattern of poetry confessing anxieties to which solutions are later found in prose recurs in Arnold's most important ephebe, T. S. Eliot. If Prufrock is burdened by a self-consciousness (and a self) that he yearns, vainly, to escape, Eliot distances himself from his creature in his doctrine of "impersonality":

> The point of view which I am struggling to attack is perhaps related to the metaphysical theory of the substantial unity of the soul: for my meaning is, that the poet has, not a "personality" to express, but a particular medium, which is only a medium and not a personality, in which impressions and experiences combine in peculiar and unexpected ways.[17]

In Eliot as in Arnold the tension between the "genuine" or "buried" self and the multiple and distracted selves of the social performer is acute. The unitary self is both a lamented paradise lost, to which return is longed for but interdicted, and a hell from which escape is a vain but unremitting wish; Arnold's "free play" that acts "to try the very ground on which we appear to stand," Eliot's "escape" from (or "surrender" or "sacrifice" or "extinction" of) mere "personality" in favor of "something which is more valuable" are sublimations of an experience of selfhood – "the dialogue of the mind with itself," the preparation of "a face to meet the faces that you meet" – that these poets elsewhere protest bitterly.[18]

Psychologists of Apocalypse

I risk this digression on Arnold and Eliot to suggest some of the subtler ways that the burden of self-consciousness is experienced, and negotiated, in our period. I have argued that Carlyle could find the largest possibilities of liberation in himself only through the mask of Teufelsdröckh and that his reversion to "anti-self-consciousness" is a victory of his post-Calvinist conscience over his protomodern sense of nature and society as fictions projected by a no less "fictile" self. (A vestigial Calvinism is the one thing Carlyle has in common with Arnold and Eliot – and it is the key to the ambivalence common to all three, that the apprehension of the self as "fictile" and "fingent" incites both grandiose projects of liberation and anxieties of guilty fatedness.)[19] Carlyle's fictive self-projection via the Teufelsdröckhian mask – what it gains for him and what forgoing it costs him – is a perfect emblem of everything at stake in the apprehension of the self as "fictile" and "fingent." The self as the agent of its own deliverance is presented with "thaumaturgic" opportunities, but also enormous burdens. The sovereignty of mind over the world can ensue only from its sovereignty over itself; and the apocalyptic program of esoteric comedy is necessarily, first, a program for the management of the self.

Carlyle, Newman, and Yeats are thus *psychologists* of apocalypse: Like Wordsworth in the *Immortality Ode* or Coleridge in *Dejection,* they are concerned with the problematic of disposing of one's own state of mind. They are heirs of the "internalized quest" of "the greater Romantic lyric" or "crisis poem,"[20] as well as of the earnest style of moralizing from "human nature" (i.e., psychology) from Hobbes and Locke to Johnson and Hume – indeed, of the modern tendency since Luther to transpose problems of morals into problems of morale. Carlyle's quasi-religious rhetoric of "conversion" figures a psychological progress, a "developmental" transit from "Everlasting Nay" to "Everlasting Yea." Likewise, Newman's distinction between "notional" and "real assent" is fundamentally a psychological distinction, and the "illative sense" a psychological phenomenon. Yeats's talk of "masks" and "poses," and even his phasal and cyclical theory of universal history and the career of the individual soul, arise from a lifetime's struggle for self-possession and encode his sense of the volatility of the self and what he variously calls its "moods" or "passions." Carlyle, Newman, and Yeats are prophets of what a later age would solicit (e.g., Auden) or denigrate (e.g., Orwell) as "change of heart,"[21] and the distinctive note of their esoteric comedy is to present this transformation not as a visitation the self must passively await, but as a volitional operation within the power of the self to compel – an apprehension aligning them with the "modern" development Philip Rieff has called "The Emergence of Psychological Man."[22]

Esoteric Comedy and the Modern

But if modernity agrees that the burdens and opportunities of self-consciousness and the management of the self are of the essence of the human problem, the coloration of the problem has darkened drastically since 1914. A phrase I used a few pages ago,

227

"from Hegel to Freud," graphs the transformation of self-consciousness from a high, collective spiritual destiny to a last-ditch therapy for the alienated sufferer in an age of anxiety. Modernity did not work out as Carlyle, Newman, and Yeats, or anyone else, had supposed it might, and so their protomodern kind of comic self-consciousness can only seem one of the many quaint premodern optimisms swept away in the deluge of 1914 and after. To the moderns, Carlyle and Newman are old clothes, while Yeats's deliberate anachronism in pursuing his *Vision* project against the grain of "disillusioned" modernity is tolerated for the sake of the poetry, rather than admired as enacting (like modernism itself) a protest against modernity.

In short, angst, not comedy, has seemed the distinctively modern, and modernist, note, an angst founded on the wreck of all Victorian hopes and impatient of all Victorian yea saying. For moderns, T. S. Eliot explains, the quest was necessarily "*through* suffering" and "*in* suffering." "Everything else was cheerfulness, optimism, and hopefulness; and these words stood for a great deal of what one hated in the nineteenth century."[23] Yeats himself emphasized the abyss between his own attachment to "traditional sanctity and loveliness" and the modernist insistence on "hitherto ignored ugliness" ("a man fishing behind a gas works, the vulgarity of a single Dublin day prolonged through 700 pages").[24] Between himself and the modernists, Yeats insisted on differences so fundamental as to sustain (or require) a whole theory of history. How, then, claim something protomodern for esoteric comedy? The most ambitious works of modern art and literature typically press the penchant for "ugliness" toward ironic conflations of the comic and the serious, the high and the low, the sublime and the ridiculous, the tragic and the *buffo,* with motives that run the gamut from *contemptus mundi* (Eliot) to *amor mundi* (Joyce) to combinations impossible to untangle (Beckett). But the distinctively modern black comedy, or comedy of the absurd, seems as different as anything could be from esoteric comedy – an effect that is, of course, entirely deliberate.

Self-consciousness and the *Eiron*

Yet for all the differences, continuous between esoteric comedy and modern and modernist literature is an authorial comic self-consciousness that seems intrinsic to the posture of "the artist" in a mass culture. Esoteric comedy's appeal to a special sort of reader, to an elite audience within the general audience, is part of the emergence of a notion of "high culture" and of the artist as culture hero that, in the 1890s and after, will flower into a self-conscious avant-garde. As Roger Henkle demonstrates, the late-nineteenth-century "aesthetic movement" (a proto-avant-garde), was thoroughly tinctured with a self-consciously "comic" spirit, from Meredith, who identifies comedy as expression and measure of high and refined civilization generally, to Wilde (an idol of the young Yeats) and Beerbohm.[25] After 1914, comedy turns black and absurd, and the artist becomes more than ever a figure alienated from the culture at large, occupying a position and committed to projects that require a pose to sustain, a self-conscious pose – and as T.S. Eliot remarks, "whenever anyone is conscious of himself as acting, something like a sense of humour is present."

It is particularly valuable to have this testimony from T. S. Eliot, the artist more than any other definitive of "modern" despair, the poet who managed (as Orwell wryly observed) "to achieve the difficult feat of making modern life out to be worse than it is."[26] Eliot's despair is certainly "serious," yet even Eliot's somberest works evince a self-conscious jokiness, as if to keep seriousness free of the charge of *self*-seriousness. Consider the comic-pathetic note of "Prufrock" or the occasional arch grotesquerie with which *The Waste Land* mocks its own melodrama ("I think we are in rats' alley / Where the dead men lost their bones").[27] Asked whether the notes to *The Waste Land* were "a lark or serious," Eliot replied "that they were serious, and not more of a skit than some things in the poem itself."[28] At Harvard in 1932, Eliot vented his impatience with learned exegetes inquiring the "meaning" of *Ash-Wednesday* and threatened that future editions of the poem would bear an epigraph from *Don Juan:*

> I don't pretend that I quite understand
> My own meaning when I would be *very* fine,
>   But the fact is that I have nothing planned
> Except perhaps to be a moment merry . . .

At a later lecture he confessed the sardonic wish that a poet "could have at least the satisfaction of having a part to play in society as worthy as that of the music-hall comedian."[29]

Esoteric Comedies

A similar ironic diffidence lurks behind the poker face with which Joyce greeted his lionization after 1920, when, having achieved fame and fortune as one sort of artist, he immediately transformed himself into something altogether different and more difficult, moving from "Flaubertian" naturalism to an idiosyncratic art of verbal performance in a nonsense language entirely his own. In the course of his oeuvre, the figure of the artist changes from Ibsenesque, "heaven ascending" culture hero (Stephen Dedalus), to a portrait of the artist as not-an-artist (Leopold Bloom), to jokester, con man, cad (Shem the Penman).[30] Consider, likewise, Pound's mission as "guide to kulchur": the grandiose ambition announced, and mocked, in Uncle Remus orthography. Pound's conflicted relation to his own project is even more evident in his letters, where the "Pogo" patois becomes a mania; but elsewhere, too, Pound compounds arrogance and self-depreciation: in *Propertius* and *Mauberley,* particularly, where these conflicts emerge as themes. A like arrogance-diffidence attends the *Cantos,* the most ambitious poem of the century, in which the author appears as "Old Ez" and "ego scriptor cantilenae" ("cantilena" = "chatter"). Pound's incarceration in St. Elizabeth's solemnized a dialectic evident in his career years earlier, and never far from the surface in any of our great moderns, by which the artist-as-culture-hero becomes the culture-hero-as-crank. It is our century's version of the genius-madness topos.

I adduce Joyce, Pound, and Eliot as centrally important modernist writers, but the point could be illustrated from almost any modern artist in any medium: for instance, the incorporation into the visual arts of refuse, from Picasso's collages to Schnabel's broken crockery; the line from Stravinsky's dissonances to Stockhausen's cacophonies to Cage's zen symphonies for AM radios. But to stick to writers in English, the baby talking of Gertrude Stein and other early-modern women writers (Laura Riding, Stevie Smith), not to mention Hemingway; Stevens's blackbirds, his Crispin, his man on the dump; Williams's making so much depend on a wheelbarrow in a barnyard; Faulkner's crackers and cretins; Auden's "silly like us" and his Caliban; the desolate Beckett-scape of talking heads in garbage cans; Mailer's "white negro," his hipster, the Promethean clowning of his advertisements for himself; the whoopee-cushion wit of Pynchon (who else would name a hero "Slothrop"?) – all assert the claims of the low, the plain, the ugly, the vulgar against any canon of beauty or significance that would exclude them. And involved in such claims is a figure we have seen before, a figure that comprehends the self-consciousness of esoteric comedy and the very different kinds of comic self-consciousness of 1914 and after, the figure of the *eiron*.

The *eiron* is a low-seeming figure; his name gives us the word "irony," and he is thus the representative protagonist of what Frye calls an "ironic age" whose literature is peopled with figures "inferior in power or intelligence to ourselves, so that we have the sense of looking down on a scene of bondage, frustration, or absurdity." That, of course, is "our" age and "our" literature. Frye finds that an "ironic" age typically follows a "low mimetic" one, in which literature represents the audience's world pretty much as the audience itself sees it, and that sounds recognizably like the Victorian age. (Frye even notes "a great increase, in the low mimetic period of future hopes, of a sense of Messianic powers as coming from 'underneath' or through esoteric and hermetic traditions" – and that formulation seems to touch some of the bases of esoteric comedy.)[31] These remarks seem to focus the rupture between esoteric comedy and modern angst on the issue of the power writers (and readers) have or can imagine having in the world. Where esoteric comedy entertains high hopes of (in Carlyle's phrase) the "thaumaturgic art of Thought," the disillusioned moderns seem to offer counsels of despair.

Yet despite the tones of despair, failure, impotence, and futility so frequent in modernism, a deep and paradoxical part of its appeal is the promise of new mastery and power implied in its technical innovations and its challenges to familiar ways of seeing and understanding. The enormous ambitions of writers like Joyce, Pound, and Eliot are kin to the thaumaturgics of esoteric comedy; and the subversiveness of such enterprises increasingly impels the artist to extremities that inspire (and increasingly are calculated to inspire) the public to shock, disbelief, and cries of hoax – the now *démodé* routine of the *succès de scandale*. As the ambitions of the artist become more grandiose, their realizations become increasingly such as to suggest at first glance absurdity, incompetence, ugliness, and thumbing of the nose at all "high" or even merely respectable notions of art. To conflate culture-hero aspirations with eccentric and clownish presentations and self-presentations is a characteristically modern note and one, I think, best understood in connection with the transformation in England of the laughable "humour character" into an "amiable" *eiron* figure exemplifying something of great human value.

Stuart Tave traces the first stage of this transformation through the changing response to such characters as Falstaff and Don Quixote. Formerly seen as laughable and ridiculous figures whose foibles encourage a proper "superiority feeling," in the eighteenth century they begin to be viewed as exemplifying human qualities it would be a shame to lose. By 1750, Falstaff emerges as flawed and weak, yet fundamentally good-natured and "good-humoured," while Quixote is on his way to becoming "The Man of La Mancha," not the delusional lunatic, but an attractive idealist, Everyman as Dreamer of Impossible Dreams. The transformation of the ridiculous "humour character" into the "amiable" figure of the "Whimsical" is completed in Fielding's Parson Adams and Sterne's Uncle Toby.[32]

But in esoteric comedy, the humor-character-become-amiable develops further, to the humor-character-become-judge or -critic of the society at large, whose norms his humor transgresses. It is a development in line with other manifestations, after the French Revolution, in which "low" or humble figures – from Wordsworth's rustics and Dickens's urban *lumpen* to Beckett's derelicts or Pynchon's superannuated sophomores – reproach the culture that surrounds them. Emblematic here is Yeats, setting the Fool among the personae of his late work, along with the Saint and the Hero (Yeats's fools are legion: Crazy Jane, the Wild Old Wicked Man, Tom the Lunatic, etc.), but in all three, the "low" figure who turns out to have great moral force, the *eiron,* looms large. *Sartor Resartus* orchestrates the contending voices of two characters, the one an unaffiliated German philosopher, present address unknown, the other a nameless Fleet Street hack. In the *Apologia* and *A Vision,* the effect is the more striking because Newman and Yeats write *in propria persona,* and thus take upon themselves the absurdity they know their audiences will ascribe to their esoteric interests: Newman fiercely parodies the parodies of himself circulating in popular journalism, while Yeats smilingly reports his transactions with the beyond as if oblivious of the raised eyebrows of his hearers.

The *eiron*-become-judge seems to me a feature definitive of modern comic consciousness since the French Revolution. As in so much else, the French Revolution marked a divide in the ethos of comedy. George McFadden distinguishes the "classic" from the "romantic" comic ethos by observing that the romantic "always tends to be critical of the ethos that underlies customary response, at least in the sense of reflecting upon it, whereas the classic tends to accept that ethos implicitly."[33] This shift is indicated in the transformation of the "humour character," a figure we laugh at in favor of the societal norm, to the figure of the modern *eiron,* with whose alienation from the norm we sympathize *against* society. To summarize, in the seventeenth century the "humour character" is a vehicle by which authors represent properly laughable and contemptible human failings in behalf of general morality; in the eighteenth century, the "whimsical" is a vehicle by which authors rehabilitate certain styles of eccentricity for societal acceptance, sympathy, and love; in the nineteenth century and later, eccentricity becomes an ironic vantage from which to criticize and "correct" the culture at large, "the ethos that underlies customary response."

In esoteric comedy, such eccentricity is pervasive and nothing if not self-conscious: In *Sartor Resartus,* The Editor complains endlessly about Teufelsdröckh's "humour," thus advertising it lest any reader miss it; Newman acknowledges that "what I have been saying will, with many men, be doing credit to my imagination at the expense of my judgment" and rejoins "'Hippoclides doesn't care;' I am not setting myself up as a pattern of good sense or of anything else."[34] And Yeats goes genially on about spirits and smells and noises in the upper stories of his house. These personae, these *eiron* figures, conduct themselves with all the obstinacy, insouciance, and comic self-assurance attaching to the "humour character." Against any canon of common sense that might be urged against them, they persist in their folly, defying our laughter with so contrary a mix of lightheartedness and passion as to present, each in his own way, a complexly impressive spectacle, whose peculiar power springs from a paradoxical compound of self-absorption and self-consciousness, at once indifferent to their audiences and intensely (and comically) aware of their audiences. Their conviction and self-possession exhibit that quasi-"megalomania" Freud identifies as what primitives and children have in common with the characterological type he examines in his 1914 paper "On Narcissism":

> an over-estimation of the power of wishes and mental processes, the "omnipotence of thoughts," a belief in the magical virtue of words and a method of dealing with the outer world – the art of "magic" – which appears to be a logical application of these grandiose premises.[35]

This might seem almost a prescription for creating a "humour character," but it also describes the pose of an esoteric comedian. In the former case, the point would be our alienation from a character whose rigidity is laughable, in ways we ourselves (we hope) are not. Bergson accounts for *le rire* as a response to human behavior that is "mechanical" and therefore rigid and unchangeable; we laugh at (what the English would call) the "humour character," whose responses and actions are reliably, under the stress of no matter what exigency, always the same. Like all earlier accounts of the "humour character," Bergson's is a variation on the "superiority theory": We laugh at someone whose powers of response and action are narrower than our own.

But Freud's connection of "humour" with "narcissism" turns Bergson's formulation upside-down, in ways fruitfully suggestive for esoteric comedy and for the self-consciousness of the artist generally in modern culture. The "narcissist" is like the "humour character" in being self-absorbed, resistant to influences that might prompt departure from eccentric behavior into something more like the "norm," and viewed unsympathetically, this sort of persistence in folly can be made to seem (in Bergson's language) "mechanical" and therefore laughable. But Freud sees that there can be something attractive about such figures: They remain self-assured and self-possessed under stresses that might bend us "normal" people quite out of shape. Freud characterizes narcissism as "insusceptibility to influence," and in a world of

Conclusion

pressures and strains, the narcissist's resoluteness appears as a kind of strength. The esoteric comedian presents just such an image of the fool persisting in folly and argues his case with such wit, humor, and intellectual-imaginative audacity as to present at last a most attractive figure of integrity and self-possession against the claims of a world whose coercions we "normal" folk may all too frequently and too compliantly obey.

The strangely compelling power that the spectacle of such self-absorption exercises, Freud calls a "charm," and he explains it this way:

> It seems very evident that one person's narcissism has a great attraction for those others who have renounced part of their own narcissism and are seeking after object-love; the charm of a child lies to a great extent in his narcissism, his self-sufficiency and inaccessibility, just as does the charm of certain animals which seem not to concern themselves about us, such as cats and large beasts of prey. In literature, indeed, even the great criminal and the humorist compel our interest by the narcissistic self-importance with which they manage to keep at arm's length everything which would diminish the importance of their ego. It is as if we envied them their power of retaining a blissful state of mind – an unassailable libido-position which we ourselves have long since abandoned.[36]

The principle of such an effect is the reverse of what Bergson describes: not detachment, in behalf of the norm, from the eccentricity of the "humour character," but *identification* with the "humour character" *against* the norm, *against* "the ethos that underlies customary response." Thus does the "humour character " evolve at last into the *eiron,* the seeming fool who triumphs over the conventional wisdom that would exclude, silence, dismiss, or laugh at him. Evident here is the comic "obstinacy" in pursuit of an idea of "freedom" that George McFadden, in his suggestive formulation of a modern comic ethos, finds a persistent feature of the comic in all its protean diversity.

The other quality McFadden identifies as definitive of the comic is "an enhanced sense of the self."[37] Freud's persistent references to children, primitives, and even animals suggest that what characterizes the "narcissist" is a condition of low differentiation between self and other, an incomplete "fall" into the selfhood of high ego definition – a formulation, incidentally, that owes much to the subject–object distinction so fundamental to Romantic ways of thinking about Imagination and Its Discontents. The "charm" of the narcissist is not an active property, but more like a reflexive one: The narcissist exhibits less a power of charming than an exemplary susceptibility to being charmed, which very much resembles the egoless condition Victorians wistfully ascribe to innocence and that colors so profoundly their idealizations of children and childhood. On the other hand, Freud's calling this un-self-conscious condition "narcissism" registers the paradox that "self" is necessarily its matrix and that the narcissist's un-self-conscious charm is a function not of abnegation of self, but of absorption in it.

Just such a charm of happy and potent self-absorption is the effect of esoteric comedy: the "inaccessibility," the "self-sufficiency," the "self-importance" of the esoteric comedian are impressive in their apparent obliviousness of their audience. But for Carlyle, Newman, and Yeats, this charm is anything but un-self-conscious: They are shrewdly aware of their audience, and their seeming obliviousness is also a kind of defiance and, at the same time a kind of appeal. The poses of crankery, eccentricity, and foolishness that Carlyle, Newman, and Yeats so grandiosely strike are the ironic tribute their self-possession pays to their age's distrust of any self-aggrandizing gesture, and it is never so self-consciously ironic as in its seeming earnestness and un-self-consciousness, its air of blandly treating esoteric matters as if they were affairs of everyday, as if unaware that the age will take them for folly. It is the enigmatic power of their various ways of playing the fool that they exert their "charm" over those who take the pose at face value, who see only "the fool," as well as over those who see the irony and self-consciousness, who see the "playing" – or perhaps it would be better to speak not of two different classes of readers, but of two orders of response in our own reading, analogous to the alternations Yeats describes between being "overwhelmed" and the recoveries of "reason." Freud's word "narcissism" suggests this fusion or mediation, this

236

co-presence, of states – the "visionary gleam" of innocence together with the ironic acuities of self-consciousness – whose disjuncture is central to the Victorian as to the Freudian understanding of melancholy.

In the passage above, Freud implies a self-conscious complement to the charmed and charming narcissism of such un-self-conscious innocents as children and cats in those more imposing figures met with "in literature . . . the great criminal and the humorist." Freud examines this latter type of self-conscious narcissism in his 1928 essay "Humour":

> . . . humour has in it a liberating element. . . . Obviously, what is fine about it is the triumph of narcissism, the ego's victorious assertion of its own invulnerability. It refuses to be hurt by the arrows of reality or to be compelled to suffer. It insists that it is impervious to wounds dealt by the outside world, in fact, that these are merely occasions for affording it pleasure. . . . Humour is not resigned; it is rebellious. It signifies the triumph not only of the ego, but of the pleasure principle.[38]

Despite its masochistic sound, this captures something essential of the esoteric comedian's project – something of its ironic idealism, too, when Freud speaks of "the arrows of reality," because Freud knows that the most wounding of these are not contrivances of steel and feathers, but mind-forged phantasms of the psyche. Carlyle's "thaumaturgic art of Thought," Newman's "Economy," Yeats's "miracle" are victorious rebellions, assertions of invulnerability, refusals of suffering or resignation, of just this humorous sort – even, perhaps, victorious only insofar as they are humorous in this way: Think how short-lived is Carlyle's avowedly "everlasting" affirmation, how ominous are Newman's dark and pointedly contrafactual hints about "the absence of God," how often and how utterly Yeats's "antithetical" poses are disrupted by "primary" lust and rage. The darker area void of such humor is Freud's usual terrain: If he grants less to humor and entertains more modest hopes of escape from suffering, that is perhaps only to say that he is more a "modernist" than Carlyle, Newman, or Yeats. But the esoteric comedian's self-conscious enterprise, a sort of sympathetic magic of selfhood, resembles Freud's and modernism's in locating its most durable consolations in apprehensions that must be called profoundly ironic and in a presumption that the work of understanding exacts an unremittingly self-conscious application of intelligence and imagination to the difficult and fatedly human project Freud called "making the unconscious conscious."[39]

NOTES

INTRODUCTION

1. For example, in the January 1943 *Horizon* George Orwell introduces a review of a book about Yeats's occultism with a breezy reference to "*A Vision,* a privately printed book which I have never
   read . . . " (*The Collected Essays, Journalism and Letters of George
   Orwell,* 4 vols., ed. Sonia Orwell and Ian Angus [New York, 1968],
   2:272). Orwell evidently does not even know that the privately
   printed edition of 1926 (but dated 1925) had been revised and
   republished by mainstream publishers in England in 1937 and
   America in 1938.
2. John Holloway, *The Victorian Sage* (New York, 1965), 9.
3. Northrop Frye, *Anatomy of Criticism* (Princeton, N.J., 1965), 303.
4. Thomas Carlyle, *Sartor Resartus,* ed. C. F. Harrold (New York,
   1937), 319. The question of *Sartor'*s genre has been debated by critics and scholars ever since it first appeared, and by publishers' readers even before it appeared. For a survey of the history of the genre
   question in *Sartor,* see Gerry Brookes, *The Rhetorical Form of Carlyle's "Sartor Resartus"* (Berkeley, Calif., 1972), 1–15.
5. On the genre question in the *Apologia,* see Walter E. Houghton,
   The Art of Newman's "Apologia" (1945; rpt. Folcroft, Penn., 1970),
   68–9; Francis X. Connolly, "The *Apologia:* History, Rhetoric, and
   Literature," in *Newman's "Apologia": A Classic Reconsidered,* ed.
   Vincent Ferrer Blehl and Francis X. Connolly (New York, 1964),
   105–11.
6. Frye, *Anatomy of Criticism,* 313.
7. Ibid., 307, 323.
8. Ibid., 309–11.
9. Cf. Yeats on Berkeley: "Descartes, Locke, and Newton took away
   the world and gave us its excrement instead. Berkeley restored the
   world . . . Berkeley has brought back the world that only exists
   because it shines and sounds. A child, smothering its laughter

because the elders are standing round, has opened once more the great box of toys" (*Explorations* [New York, 1962], 325).

10. *A Tale of a Tub,* Sec. 2, in *Prose Works of Jonathan Swift,* ed. Herbert Davis (Oxford, 1965), 1:47.

11. George Meredith, "An Essay on Comedy," in *Comedy,* ed. Wylie Sypher (Garden City, N.Y. 1956), 49.

12. *The New Organon,* Sec. 1, Subsec. 56, in *Francis Bacon: A Selection of His Works,* ed. Sidney Warhaft (New York, 1965), 343–4: "But the course I propose for the discovery of sciences is such as leaves but little to the acuteness and strength of wits, but places all wits and understandings nearly on a level. For as in the drawing of a straight line or a perfect circle much depends on the steadiness and practice of the hand, if it be done by aim of hand only, but if with the aid of a rule or compass, little or nothing, so is it exactly with my plan."

13. William Blake, Letter to Reverened Dr. Trusler (August 23, 1799), *Poetry and Prose of William Blake,* ed. David V. Erdman with commentary by Harold Bloom (New York, 1965), 676.

14. W. B. Yeats, *A Vision* (New York, 1937; rpt. New York, 1956), 25.

15. C. F. Harrold, *John Henry Newman: An Expository and Critical Study of His Mind, Thought, and Art* (1945; rpt. Hamden, Conn., 1966), 308.

16. *Two Note Books of Thomas Carlyle,* ed. Charles Eliot Norton (New York, 1898), 170.

17. See Newman's letter to Hope Scott, May 2, 1864: "I have never been in such stress of brain and such pain of heart, – and I have both trials together. Say some good prayers for me. . . . I have been constantly in tears, and constantly crying out with distress. I am sure I never could say what I am saying in cold blood." Quoted in Wilfred Ward, *The Life of John Henry Cardinal Newman,* 2 vols. (London, 1913), 2:25.

18. W. B. Yeats, "Upon a House Shaken by the Land Agitation" (1910), in *The Variorum Edition of the Poems of W. B. Yeats,* ed. Peter Allt and Russell K. Alspach (New York, 1957), 264.

19. I am indebted here to Hugh Kenner's witty pages on *A Tale of a Tub* in *The Stoic Comedians* (Berkeley, Calif., 1962), 37–50.

20. "Date Line," in *Literary Essays of Ezra Pound,* ed. T. S. Eliot, (New York, 1968), 75.

21. *William Wordsworth: Selected Poems and Prefaces,* ed. Jack Stillinger (Boston, 1965), 446.

22. They thus share the motives of secular and psychological apocalypse identified in a book that takes its title from a key chapter of

Sartor Resartus, M. H. Abrams's *Natural Supernaturalism: Tradition and Revolution in Romantic Literature* (New York, 1971). Especially relevant to this study are Parts 2, 3, 4, and 6.

23. *Selected Poetry and Prose of Percy Bysshe Shelley,* ed. Carlos Baker (New York, 1951), 519.

24. Yeats, "The Apparitions" (1938), in *Variorum Poems,* 624.

25. John Henry Newman, *Apologia Pro Vita Sua,* ed. Martin J. Svaglic (New York, 1967), 12.

26. Yeats, "Coole Park and Ballylee, 1931," in *Variorum Poems,* 491.

27. Roger B. Henkle has argued (*Comedy and Culture: England 1820–1900* [Princeton, N.J., 1980], 20–39) that after the Napoleonic Wars, the volatility and social dislocations of middle-class urban life promoted a new and disturbing sense of the self as fluid, as a congeries of different roles and masks elicited in different social situations. The esoteric comedian's penchant for self-parody, i.e., for an ironic, artificial, and unstable self-presentation, is an instance of this phenomenon. Henkle demonstrates that this new sense of the self was initially disturbing enough to bring comic treatments of it up short but that as the century wore on it became a comic principle of the social satire of Butler, Meredith, Wilde, and Beerbohm; this formulation, too, illuminates the evident difference between Carlyle's anxiety about his self-multiplying (and -disguising) procedure in *Sartor Resartus* and the more assured irony and self-parody (even *in propria persona*) of Newman and Yeats. But as "esoteric comedian," each of the three – even Carlyle, for all his conflictedness about "self" – responds to the contemporary assault on the self with nonchalance, as if to see in what most readers regard as a dilemma and an anxiety a problem too puny to disarray the strong imagination. I discuss these matters more fully in connection with self-consciousness in the conclusion to this book.

28. At issue here is not, of course, the admiration of Addison and Steele for Milton. Their papers on Milton in the *Spectator* not only installed the cult of Milton among the genteel middle class, but (arguably) provided the model of high-culture appropriation for the bourgeois age that concludes with T. S. Eliot. The point is that the *style* of the Addison–Steele presentation of Milton was such as to encourage reverence for Milton, but not imitation of him.

29. *The Spirit of the Age* (1825), in *Selected Essays of William Hazlitt,* ed. Geoffrey Keynes (New York, 1930), 740.

30. Letter to Richard Woodhouse (October 27, 1818), in *John Keats: Selected Poems and Letters,* ed. Douglas Bush (Boston, 1959), 279.

31. Walter Jackson Bate, *Samuel Johnson* (New York, 1977), 493–4.

32. *The Task,* l. 26, in *The Poetical Works of William Cowper,* ed. H. S. Milford (London, 1926), 165; *Charity,* ll. 491–512, in ibid., 86.

33. Thomas Hobbes, *Leviathan,* ed. C. B. Macpherson, Part 1, Chap. 6, (Baltimore, Md., 1968), 125. Hobbes's famous definition of laughter as a *"Sudden Glory"* should be read in juxtaposition with his immediately preceding remarks on *"Glory"* and *"Vain-glory."*

34. Stuart Tave, *The Amiable Humorist* (Chicago, 1960).

35. Newman, *Apologia,* 18.

36. Blake, *Auguries of Innocence,* ll. 103–4, in *Poetry and Prose,* 483.

37. Robert Bernard Martin, *The Triumph of Wit* (London, 1974), 38, 100.

38. Ibid., 19–24.

39. Meredith, "An Essay on Comedy," 47, 33, 48.

40. Lionel Trilling, *The Opposing Self* (New York, 1959), x.

41. Quoted by L. A. G. Strong in *W. B. Yeats: Interviews and Recollections,* ed. E. H. Mikhail (London, 1977), 152. Elsewhere Yeats ascribes this aphorism to "some Frenchman"; see "Other Matters," from "On the Boiler" (1939), in *Explorations* (New York, 1962), 449.

42. Bacon, *New Organon,* Sec. 1, Subsec. 129, 374.

43. "Memorial Verses, April, 1850," ll. 43–6, in *The Poems of Matthew Arnold* ed. Kenneth Allott (London, 1965), 228.

44. Carlyle, *Sartor Resartus,* 184, 183.

45. Both Northrop Frye (*Anatomy of Criticism,* 286–7) and George McFadden (*Discovering the Comic* [Princeton, N.J., 1982], 35, 244) identify discursive elaboration as a common feature of comedy, though Frye's observation is characteristically transtemporal, or platonic, whereas McFadden's professes to be describing a particularly "modern" kind of comedy. Both cite Shaw – McFadden uses Shaw's word "discussion," Frye prefers "symposium" – and Shaw himself, notably, adapts the technique from Ibsen, a writer not usually regarded as comic. For Shaw, Frye, and McFadden "discussion" or "symposium" permits a kind of intellectual playing out of ideas and possbilities that allows for reversals and shifting points of view whose effect is comic, in a way that certainly comports with what I see happening in esoteric comedy. Roger Henkle makes a cognate point, but relying on the psychoanalytic notions of "elab-

oration," "working through," and "play" as articulated by Ernst Kris (Henkle, *Comedy and Culture*, 14–15; referring to Ernst Kris, *Psychoanalytic Explorations in Art* [1952; rpt. New York, 1965], 185).

46. "On Heroes, Hero-Worship, and the Heroic in History" (1840), in *The Centenary Edition of the Works of Thomas Carlyle*, 30 vols., ed. H. D. Traill (London, 1896–99), 5:80; Newman, *Apologia*, 23, 36–7, 241–2, 299–301; *Estrangement* (1909), in *The Autobiography of William Butler Yeats* (New York, 1967), 326.

47. Carlyle, *Sartor Resartus*, 219. The phrase appears on the second page of *The Symbolist Movement in Literature* by Yeats's friend Arthur Symons (ed. Richard Ellmann [New York, 1958]). Symons dedicated the book to Yeats; for Yeats's influence on its composition, see Richard Ellmann's introduction (xi–xiii). Newman generates an uncannily similar formulation in his typological account of pre-Christian history as an "Economy" that "concealed yet suggested" the revelation it prefigured (*Apologia*, 36). Here the consonance of esoteric comedy with older typological traditions of apocalyptic reading and writing is especially evident.

48. Meredith, "An Essay on Comedy," 39.

49. Frye, *Anatomy of Criticism*, 43.

50. Carlyle, *The French Revolution*, Book 1 Chap. 2, in *Works*, 2:6.

51. Yeats, "Meru," in *Variorum Poems*, 563.

52. Roland Barthes, "The Structuralist Activity," in *The Structuralists from Marx to Lévi-Strauss*, ed. R. DeGeorge and F. DeGeorge (Garden City, N.Y. 1972), 153.

53. T. S. Eliot, *Knowledge and Experience in the Philosophy of F. H. Bradley*, ed. Anne C. Bolgan (New York, 1964), 163–4. On the pervasive "fictionalism" of early modern philosophy, see Sanford Schwartz, *The Matrix of Modernism: Pound, Eliot, and Early Twentieth-Century Thought* (Princeton, N.J., 1985), 12–49.

54. *Selected Poetry and Prose of Shelley*, 516, 519.

55. Tave, *Amiable Humorist*, 238. Carlyle's essays on Richter: "Jean Paul Friedrich Richter" (1827), in *Works* 27:117–30; "Jean Paul Friedrich Richter" (1827), in ibid., 26:1–25; "Jean Paul Friedrich Richter Again" (1830), in ibid., 27:96–159.

56. *Autobiography of William Butler Yeats*, 144.

57. Yeats, *A Vision*, 116. For Newman and Phase 25, see 172–6. The parallel passages of the 1925 edition are virtually identical; George Mills Harper and Walter K. Hood, ed., *A Critical Edition of Yeats's "A Vision" (1925)* (London, 1978), 49, 106–10.

1. THE "THAUMATURGIC ART OF THOUGHT"

1. With the exception of some letters to Emerson, all references to writings by Carlyle are included in the text. References to *Sartor Resartus* are to the edition by Charles Frederick Harrold (New York, 1937). References to Carlyle's other writings are keyed to the following abbreviations:

> *Letters:* *Collected Letters of Thomas and Jane Welsh Carlyle*, ed. Charles Richard Saunders and Kenneth J. Fielding (Durham, N.C., 1970–).
> *TNB:* *Two Note Books of Thomas Carlyle*, ed. Charles Eliot Norton (New York, 1898).
> *Works:* *The Centenary Edition of the Works of Thomas Carlyle*, 30 vols., ed. H. D. Traill (London, 1896–9).

2. John Stuart Mill, *The Autobiography and Other Writings*, ed. Jack Stillinger (Boston, 1969), 85.

3. Eric Bentley, *A Century of Hero-Worship* (Boston, 1957), 65–6; George Levine, *The Boundaries of Fiction: Carlyle, Macaulay, Newman* (Princeton, N.J., 1968), 46; Philip Rosenberg, *The Seventh Hero: Carlyle and the Theory of Radical Activism* (Cambridge, Mass., 1974), 106.

4. For a penetrating, if narrow, discussion of the self-consciously difficult style of *Sartor*, see Jerry A. Dibble, *The Pythia's Drunken Song: Thomas Carlyle's "Sartor Resartus" and the Style Problem in German Idealist Philosopy* (The Hague, 1978). Dibble argues that the possible uses of a deliberately different style for the presentation of difficult matter, and with the ambition of changing the reader's mind on long-settled questions, were suggested to Carlyle by the rhetorical strategies of Kant and Fichte.

5. *The Correspondence of Emerson and Carlyle*, ed. Joseph Slater (New York, 1964), 99. On Emerson's reactions to *Sartor Resartus*, see Kenneth Mark Harris, *Carlyle and Emerson: Their Long Debate* (Cambridge, Mass., 1978), 38–42.

6. See Miriam Milford Hunt Thrall, *Rebellious "Fraser's": Nol Yorke's Magazine in the Days of Maginn, Thackeray, and Carlyle* (New York, 1934).

7. *Correspondence of Emerson and Carlyle*, 147, 157. For the "Irish Bishop," see Swift's letter of November 27, 1726, to Pope, written shortly after the anonymous and sensational appearance of *Gulliver's Travels:* "A Bishop here said, that Book was full of improbable lies, and for his part, he hardly believed a word of it; and so much

for Gulliver" (*Correspondence of Jonathan Swift*, 5 vols., ed. Harold Williams [Oxford, 1963–5], 3:189).

8. On this point, see G. B. Tennyson, *"Sartor" Called "Resartus": The Genesis, Structure, and Style of Thomas Carlyle's First Major Work* (Princeton, N.J., 1965), 152n. The teufelsdreck-asafoetida joke makes "Diogenes Teufelsdröckh" suggest (among other meanings) "Godly Laxative," which makes the bearer of the new word about "Clothes," wrappings in which to protect the outward body, the bearer also of a name that suggests turning the innards of the body out. Patrick Brantlinger has discovered (in Engels) that a common cheap fabric of the time, made from rags and quite flimsy, was called "devil's dust" and suggests that this might have been another component of the professor's name ("Teufelsdröckh Resartus," *English Language Notes* 9[March 1972]:191–3).

9. On this "present tense" fiction, see Tennyson, *"Sartor" Called "Resartus,"* 256–7.

10. The Editor is, of course, more than Teufelsdröckh's stooge in *Sartor Resartus,* as virtually everyone (except Dibble; see *Pythia's Drunken Song,* 5) agrees. As I said in my introduction, The Editor is a projection of aspects of Carlyle's own personality; I have suggested that The Editor's impatience with Teufelsdröckh suggestively resembles Carlyle's with Goethe; and I will argue later in this chapter that the emergence of the late, "reactionary" Carlyle amounts to the victory of The Editor over the Teufelsdröckh in himself. Albert J. LaValley has succinctly summarized The Editor's functions as not only a satirical representative of British common sense, but also "as a bridge between Germany and the English public; [The Editor] can really be an image of the Carlyle who found these German authors difficult and had to struggle to understand them as he interpreted them to the public. But most interestingly, the role of editor functions as a means of really qualifying Teufelsdröckh's philosophy: it both implements Carlyle's Voltaire-like bent of skepticism and incorporates it into the total vision"(*Carlyle and the Idea of the Modern: Studies in Carlyle's Prophetic Literature and Its Relation to Blake, Nietzsche, Marx and Others* [New Haven, Conn., 1968], 93). I endorse these remarks; indeed, I extend them in numerous places below; but I am concerned here with esoteric comedy, which is to say with how an "active" but uninstructed reader – the sort of reader Carlyle might have hoped to address, a reader without information about the (originally anonymous) author, his psychology, or the eventual course of his career – might have responded to The Editor as an ambiguously satirical device in an unusually complicated text.

245

11. Max Weber, *The Protestant Ethic and the Spirit of Capitalism,* trans. Talcott Parsons (New York, 1958), 115.
12. "Ode, Inscribed to W. H. Channing," in *Selected Writings of Ralph Waldo Emerson,* ed. Brooks Atkinson (New York, 1940), 770; "Philosophical Manifesto of the Historical School of Law," in *Writings of the Young Marx on Philosophy and Society,* ed. Lloyd D. Easton and Kurt H. Guddat (Garden City, N.Y., 1967), 98.
13. Although Carlyle dismisses "Hegelism" in knowledgeable-sounding tones in his letters (cf. *Sartor Resartus,* 15, 69), there is no evidence that he ever read a word of Hegel. Hegel is unmentioned, for example, in the *Two Note Books,* which record Carlyle's excited response to Kant. See Charles Frederick Harrold, *Carlyle and German Thought 1819–1834* (New Haven, Conn., 1934), 12, 75; and Dibble, *Pythia's Drunken Song,* 57–75. On Carlyle's unwitting affinities with Hegel, see LaValley, *Carlyle and the Idea of the Modern,* 222–25.
14. Raymond Williams, *Culture and Society* (Garden City, N.Y., 1960), 84. On the affinities between Carlyle and the contemporary "cause-and-effect" science he affected to despise, see Frank M. Turner, "Victorian Scientific Naturalism and Thomas Carlyle," *Victorian Studies* 18 (March 1975): 325–43.
15. Carlyle's reservations about Goethe seem as little noticed now as in Carlyle's own day; see Rosemary D. Ashton, "Carlyle's Apprenticeship: His Early German Criticism and His Relationship with Goethe," *Modern Language Review* 71 (1976): 1–18.
16. Carlyle's dogged common sense qualifies, with neat symmetry, *Sartor*'s account both of "Metaphor" and of "Symbol": Teufelsdröckh appends to his "metaphorical paragraph on Metaphors" acknowledgment that there are "sham Metaphors," too far-fetched to compel assent (73–4); likewise, his discussion of "Symbols" distinguishes, as an afterthought, between "intrinsic" and "extrinsic" symbols, i.e., between those grounded in nature and those grounded in mere custom, or history (222–6).
17. The vestigial Calvinism of Carlyle's temperament has been evident since Carlyle's own time. J. A. Froude called him a "Calvinist without the theology" (*Thomas Carlyle: The First Forty Years of His Life,* 2 vols. [New York, 1882], 2:2), and the theme has engaged many a commentator since. Harrold considers it in *Carlyle and German Thought,* 25–30, 235–7, and further examines its implications for Carlyle's social and political thinking in "The Nature of Carlyle's Calvinism," *Studies in Philology* 33 (July 1936): 475–86. The best study of the conflictedness Carlyle's Calvinism generates in his writings is A. Abbott Ikeler, *Puritan Temper and Transcen-*

246

Notes to pp. 77–86

dental Faith: Carlyle's Literary Vision (Columbus, Ohio, 1972). On Carlylean "Work" as a version of the Calvinist "work ethic," see Eloise M. Behnken, *Thomas Carlyle: Calvinist Without the Theology* (Columbia, Mo., 1978).

Carlyle's Calvinism seems a sad affair. One wonders what a man whose life could be changed by reading writers as different as Gibbon and Goethe might have made of Freud or Max Weber; it is pleasant to imagine that Carlyle might have learned from Weber's pages on the psychology of Calvinism what he evidently did not learn from Hazlitt's in "On Cant and Hypocrisy" or Mill's in Chapter 3 of *On Liberty,* which Mill may have written with Carlyle in mind. (For another consideration of Carlyle vis-à-vis Weber, see Rosenberg, *The Seventh Hero,* 70–6).

18. "The Eighteenth Brumaire of Louis Bonaparte," in *Marx and Engels: Basic Writings on Politics and Philosophy,* ed. Lewis S. Feuer (Garden City, N.Y., 1959), 320.

19. On Carlyle's early desire for fame, see Fred Kaplan, *Thomas Carlyle: A Biography* (Ithaca, N.Y., 1983), 39.

20. Sigmund Freud, *The Ego and the Id,* ed. and trans. James Strachey (New York, 1960), 39.

21. On Carlyle's masks in *Sartor Resartus,* see LaValley, "Discovery of a Voice," in *Carlyle and the Idea of the Modern,* 17–44, and Levine, *Boundaries of Fiction,* 19–24, 29–32.

22. The style of Carlyle ("the Rembrandt of English prose," Logan Pearsall Smith called him) has been often and well discussed. The most thorough discussion of the style of *Sartor* is Tennyson, *"Sartor" Called "Resartus";* but see also Dibble, *Pythia's Drunken Song,* and Levine, *Boundaries of Fiction,* 42–51. Levine acutely diagnoses the late Carlyle's pathologies of thought and expression in "The Use and Abuse of Carlylese," in *The Art of Victorian Prose,* ed. George Levine and William Madden (New York, 1968), 101–26; and Tennyson bases a provocative discussion of "Carlylese" on the ways in which it has been parodied in "Parody as Style: Carlyle and His Parodists," in *Carlyle and His Contemporaries: Essays in Honor of Charles Richard Saunders,* ed. John Clubbe (Durham, N.C., 1978), 298–316.

23. Jeffrey's strictures on the "Burns" essay are quoted in D. A. Wilson, *Carlyle to "The French Revolution"* (New York, 1924), 65–7, 73.

24. Another suggestive coincidence: Among the passages Jeffrey cut was one employing the "clothes-make-the-man" topos, which Jeffrey thought trite. Was "Thoughts on Clothes" motivated in part by a desire to demonstrate a power to find original possiblities in what others would dismiss as a threadbare cliché?

25. The degree to which *Sartor* is "fictional" is a perennial issue in the century-and-a-half-long debate about the book's genre (see, again, pp. 4–6 and note 4 to the Introduction). Until recently the question was pursued in a merely taxonomic spirit, and its relevance to *Sartor*'s motives, meanings, and methods began to be explored only a generation ago, by Morse Peckham in *Beyond the Tragic Vision* (New York, 1962) and G. B. Tennyson in *"Sartor" Called "Resartus"* (1965). George Levine's treatment of this question in *Boundaries of Fiction* (1968) remains definitive. The relation of Carlyle's art to that of the novel has also become a subject of fruitful inquiry. Barry Qualls devotes a chapter of his book on the Victorian novel to Carlyle (*The Secular Pilgrims of Victorian Fiction* [New York, 1982], 17–42), and Janet Ray Edwards compares Carlyle as fictionist with Thackeray ("Carlyle and the Fictions of Belief: *Sartor Resartus* to *Past and Present*," in *Carlyle and His Contemporaries*, ed. Clubbe, 91–111). How Carlyle's Calvinism, with its distrust of fiction, affected his writing and thought is a leitmotif in most of the above; it is a central theme in Ikeler, *Puritan Temper and Transcendental Faith*.

26. John D. Rosenberg, *Carlyle and the Burden of History* (Cambridge, Mass., 1985), 7–11.

27. Peckham, *Beyond the Tragic Vision*, 180–2; Tennyson, *"Sartor" Called "Resartus,"* 173–85. Others who argue or assume The Editor's "conversion" include LaValley, *Carlyle and the Idea of the Modern*, 117–19; Masao Miyoshi, *The Divided Self in Victorian Literature* (New York, 1969), 144; and Walter L. Reed, "The Pattern of Conversion in *Sartor Resartus*," *ELH* 38 (1971): 311–31.

28. Levine, *Boundaries of Fiction*, 61–6; Hazard Adams, *Philosophy of the Literary Symbolic* (Tallahassee, Fla., 1983), 82–9. Cf. the closing pages of Patrick Brantlinger, "'Romance,' 'Biography,' and the Making of *Sartor Resartus*," *Philological Quarterly* 52 (1973): 108–18.

29. James P. Farrell ("Carlyle: The Politics of Apocalypse," in *Sources for Reinterpretation: The Use of Nineteeth-Century Literary Documents – Essays in Honor of C. L. Cline* [Austin, Tex., 1975], 81–94) argues for *Sartor*'s acquiescence to or accommodation of politics, even to the disadvantage of its apocalyptic (transpolitical) ambitions, but finds that this compromise lends the book a "tragic" coloring. In my view, Carlyle's immanentism conflates or identifies apocalypse with politics and projects (in *Sartor* at least) a fundamental hopefulness about the consequences, whence "comedy." I will agree in calling the despair that came to Carlyle later "tragic," of course.

2. "HIPPOCLIDES DOESN'T CARE"

1. All page references in the text are to Martin J. Svaglic's Oxford edition of the *Apologia* and materials related to the controversy between Newman and Kingsley (New York, 1967). Page references keyed to *Grammar* are to Charles F. Harrold's edition of Newman's *An Essay in Aid of a Grammar of Assent* (New York, 1947).

2. For an illuminating discussion of the *Apologia* with reference to Newman's troubled relations with the Roman hierarchy, see John Coulson, *Newman and the Common Tradition: A Study in the Language of Church and Society* (Oxford, 1970), especially Chap. 8, "Apologia for a Silent Church," 132–49.

3. On the collision of faith and skepticism following the publication of Mill's *On Liberty* and Darwin's *Origin of Species* in 1859 and of *Essays and Reviews* in 1860 (i.e., in the years immediately preceding publication of the *Apologia*), see Walter E. Houghton, *The Victorian Frame of Mind 1830–1870* (New Haven, Conn., 1957), 426–8; G. M. Young, *Victorian England: Portrait of an Age* (1936; rpt. New York, 1960), 102, 108–14.

4. On Newman's "Englishness" in the *Apologia,* see Thomas Vargish, *Newman: The Contemplation of Mind* (Oxford, 1970), 178.

5. Matthew Arnold, *The Complete Prose Works,* 11 vols., ed. R. H. Super (Ann Arbor, Mich., 1960), 1:26–7. Arnold, of course, admired Newman enormously, even though he judged that Newman had "adopted, for the doubts and difficulties which beset men's minds to-day, a solution which, to speak frankly, is impossible" ("Emerson" [1885], in *Discourses in America* [London, 1912], 139). Arnold's reverence for Newman and his engagement with Newman's writings are demonstrated by David J. DeLaura, *Hebrew and Hellene in Victorian England: Newman, Arnold, and Pater* (Austin, Tex., 1969).

6. George Levine, *The Boundaries of Fiction: Carlyle, Macaulay, Newman* (Princeton, N.J., 1968), 252. Newman's way of disowning an earlier self is illustrated in what Charles Frederick Harrold calls his "Preface to One's Dead Self," the 1877 preface the Catholic Newman wrote for a new edition of his preconversion *Via Media* (C. F. Harrold, *John Henry Newman: An Expository and Critical Study of His Mind, Thought, and Art* [1945; rpt. Hamden, Conn., 1966], 217–22). Disowning one or more of his earlier selves in the *Apologia* would have seemed to many a welcome and conciliatory gesture; Newman's refusal to do so cannot have been indeliberate.

7. That Newman's irony correctly forecasts the responses of such readers is borne out by Vincent Ferrer Blehl's survey, "Early Crit-

icism of the *Apologia*" (in *Newman's "Apologia": A Classic Recon-sidered,* ed. V. F. Blehl and F. X. Connolly [New York, 1964], 47–63):

> A careful scrutiny of the fifty or sixty reviews of the *Apologia* reveals that the reaction was not at all uniform, but exceedingly complex, subtle, and nuanced. Those who conceded that Newman's sincerity had been vindicated generally did not agree with his doctrinal views. Some paid a polite tribute to his honesty as a thinker and a theologian but proceeded to qualify that judgment, in some instances, to such an extent that one finds it difficult to understand how the reviewer could have been fully honest in asserting his belief in Newman's sincerity. There were those who straightforwardly affirmed that Newman was sincere, but who, with confident self-assurance declared that he was deluded, deranged, a skeptic, emotionally unbalanced, over-imaginative or in need of the external support and security that only the Catholic Church could give. His conversion to Catholicism, however irrational, was said to be perfectly understandable in psychological terms. Others, though a minority, thought that Newman had not vindicated himself against Kingsley's charge. Still others thought that however sincere Newman might be as an individual, he had nonetheless joined a church which by common agreement was shifty, cunning and unsolicitous for truth. This viewpoint summarizes the problem that confronted nearly every reviewer in greater or less degree. If Newman were sincere and if he had a commanding intellect, how was one to "explain" his conversion to Catholicism? (48–9)

Blehl substantiates his summary with citations that cover the full range of possible responses to Newman. Representative for our purposes are the High Church admonition of the *Quarterly Review* ("never is [Newman] more a controversialist than when he avoids controversy" [Blehl, "Early Criticism," 52]), the contempt of the Congregationalist and Baptist *British Quarterly Review* (Newman had "pounced" on Kingsley "with all the animus of a vulture"; he is "a wary, subtle, and far-seeing antagonist on all questions of this nature; but, unconsciously to himself, he has supplied, if not a full vindication of the language of Professor Kingsley, certainly a very natural, and almost sufficient, excuse for the use of it" [ibid., 53]) and of the Low Church *Christian Observer* ("an utter want of reverence of truth for truth's sake ... a union of presumptuous self-confidence, diseased fancy, and mental blindness" [ibid., 53–4]). For a useful survey of late-nineteenth- and early-twentieth-century opinion on the *Apologia,* see Harrold, *Newman,* 312–17.

Among the serendipitous curiosa that access to open stacks has brought me in the course of this project is a book by an author named Walter Walsh, called *The Secret History of the Oxford Movement* (London, Church Association, Swan Sonnenschein and Co., 1899). The copy I have used boasts on its title page, "Sixth Edition. Forty-Second Thousand," and includes a "New Preface Containing a Reply to Critics." Under "Newman" in the index are such heads as these:

> does not wish the names of his party known,
> expects to be called a papist,
> eats his "dirty words,"
> his use of "irony,"
> "thought the Church of Rome was right,"
> has a "secret longing love of Rome,"
> writes: – "I love the Church of Rome too well,"

I should add that the book seems neither stupid nor sensationalistic, but a genuine and measured expression of Protestant indignation with everything that the Tractarian Movement represented.

And it still goes on: as recently as 1969 Sheed and Ward (of all people) published a book by G. Egner called *Apologia Pro Charles Kingsley.*

8. See Robin Selby, *The Principle of Reserve in the Writings of John Henry Cardinal Newman* (New York, 1975), for the theological background and for a brilliant account of the place of "Reserve" in Newman's psychology of faith. Selby's study does not consider "Reserve" in relation to the qualities of Newman's writing, but G. B. Tennyson has placed it at the center of a "Tractarian Aesthetics," which he derives from John Keble's Latin *Lectures on Poetry* (1831–41; in *Praelectiones,* trans. E. K. Francis [Oxford, 1912]); Newman's "Poetry, with Reference to Aristotle's *Poetics*" (1829), in *Essays Historical and Critical,* 2 vols. (London, 1871), 1: 1–26, and "Literature" (1858), in *The Idea of a University,* ed. C. F. Harrold (New York, 1947), 234–56; Isaac Williams's *Tract 80,* "On Reserve in Communicating Religious Knowledge," in *Tracts for the Times, by Members of the University of Oxford,* 6 vols. (London, 1839–40), 4: n.p., and Keble's *Tract 89,* "On the Mysticism Attributed to the Early Fathers of the Church," in ibid., 6: n.p. Tennyson sees this esthetic as producing "high" effects of style and eloquence

and figure; I cannot claim his authority for my extrapolation of a "comic" version of it. See G. B. Tennyson, "Tractarian Aesthetics: Analogy and Reserve in Keble and Newman," *Victorian Newsletter* 55 (Spring 1979): 8–10; cf. Tennyson, "The Sacramental Imagination," in *Nature and the Victorian Imagination,* ed. U. C. Kneopflmacher and G. B. Tennyson (Berkeley, Calif., 1977), 370–90.

9. John Henry Newman, *Essay on the Development of Christian Doctrine* (New York, 1927), Sec. 6, Subsec. 1, 207–8, and 245–7.

10. For a still-interesting discussion (after forty years) comparing Newman's epistemology with Coleridge's, see D. G. James, *The Romantic Comedy* (London, 1948), 155–270.

11. William Empson, *Some Versions of Pastoral* (New York, 1974), 250.

12. Newman, "Poetry, with Reference to Aristotle's *Poetics,*" in *Essays,* 1: 9, 23. For a useful discussion of this essay's place in Newman's thinking, see Robert A. Colby, "The Poetical Structure of Newman's *Apologia,*" in *Apologia Pro Vita Sua,* ed. David J. DeLaura (New York, 1968), 455–6. James discusses Newman's contrast of poetry with science in "The Mission of St. Benedict" and "The Benedictine Schools" and relates it to Newman's epistemology (*Romantic Comedy,* 253–8). J. S. Lawry traces "correspondences between Newman's general apology for poetry and his general theory of assent" in a provocative article that helps us see how Newman's project involves an esthetic as well as a psychology of faith ("Notes Toward a Syntax for Assent in Newman's *Apologia,*" *Renascence* 25 [Spring 1973]: 129–45).

13. Huxley remarked that a primer of skepticism could be compiled from Newman's writings; the *locus classicus* for this view of Newman is Leslie Stephen, "Newman's Theory of Belief," in *An Agnostic's Apology and Other Essays* (London, 1893), 168–341. Newman's "skepticism" is usually charged against him by nonbelievers, but a Christian, pro-Newman version of the case is presented by James, *Romantic Comedy,* 162–6, 213–14. The most penetrating treatment of these issues I know of is J. M. Cameron, "Newman and the Empiricist Tradition," in *The Rediscovery of Newman,* ed. John Coulson and A. M. Allchin (London, 1967), 76–96: "Bacon aside, it is characteristic of British empiricism that it is preoccupied, almost obsessively, with epistemology" (76). This elision of Bacon enables Cameron to effect a dazzling, surprising, even Newman-esque conflation of empiricism (especially Hume's) with idealism, a conflation whose tensions Cameron traces in Newman's writings. Newman's position, he argues, though untenable philo-

sophically, enabled Newman to play out the tensions of the age with unique comprehensiveness: "Empiricism is an experience that has to be lived through if one is to grasp the mentality of the modern educated man. Newman has had this experience, and this is one of the reasons why what he writes strikes so sympathetically upon the ear, and why so much Catholic writing of that time, and later, grates" (ibid., 95). But Newman's "seemingly sceptic method" is not merely a kind of appeal to something that the anxious modern can share; it is also a (comic) provocation to those who prefer other skepticisms – as David J. DeLaura has noted: "Newman puzzled and irritated rationalist critics like Leslie Stephen and T. H. Huxley by breathtakingly conceding the basis of the sceptical case . . . while continuing to draw orthodox conclusions from the fact of doubt itself" ("Newman's *Apologia* as Prophecy," in *Apologia,* ed. DeLaura, 499).

14. I do not mean to suggest that the lion of the *Apologia* becomes altogether a lamb in the *Grammar of Assent.* The *Grammar* offers provocations of its own, ably surveyed by Philip Synder, "Newman's Way with the Reader in *A Grammar of Assent," Victorian Newsletter* 56 (Fall 1977): 1–6; Snyder argues that Newman assigns the reader the role of sympathetic listener, then narrows his address to provoke a "confrontation" between the reader's "permanent self" and "Newman-created self." For an account of the "argument of the *Grammar of Assent,* and . . . how its principles are exemplified in the *Apologia,*" see Jonathan Robinson, "The *Apologia* and the *Grammar of Assent,*" in *Newman's "Apologia,"* ed. Blehl and Connolly, 145–64.

15. John Henry Newman, *Letters and Correspondence to 1845,* 2 vols., ed. Anne Mozley (London, 1890), 1: 21.

16. Newman seems the perfect case to instantiate the aphorism that style is the man. No commentator on the *Apologia* fails to mention Newman's literary style; among the many discussions of this well-discussed subject I can mention only a few here as making points of special relevance to my own argument. Walter Houghton emphasizes the "difficulty" of Newman's style as index of the "difficulty" of Newman's project (*Art of Newman's "Apologia"* [1945; rpt. Folcroft, Pa., 1970], 50–7) and acknowledges that "no biography so concrete and human as the *Apologia* was ever so difficult to read" (89). William E. Buckler remarks the difference between the *Apologia*'s impetuosity and the more sedate style of all Newman's other work and comments that "the speed with which [the *Apologia*] was written, if one recalls the pain with which Newman

habitually wrote, becomes almost a dimension of its character"
("The *Apologia* as Human Experience," in *Newman's "Apologia,"*
ed. Blehl and Connolly, 67), an observation suggesting that what I
have called Newman's comedy of "Reserve" was in part an effect
of the rush of events and the pressure under which the *Apologia*
was composed. David J. DeLaura has discussed "Newman and the
Victorian Cult of Style" (*Victorian Newsletter* 51 [Spring 1977]: 6–
10) and its impact on Pater (*Hebrew and Hellene*, 329–38), whence
its transmission to Yeats and Joyce. The subtlest discussion of
Newman's style as a register or measure of his response to experience is Levine, *Boundaries of Fiction*, 245–58.

17. Selby, *Principle of Reserve*, 25. The first passage quoted is from a
letter of Newman's to James Stephen, dated March 16, 1835; the
second from a letter to William Wilberforce, March 10, 1835.

18. Selby, *Principle of Reserve*, 62.

19. I am not the first reader to be teased by the notion that Nietzsche
and Newman represent complementary treatments of the same tangle of problems. In the October 1924 *Criterion*, Ramon Fernandez
published an essay called "The Experience of Newman," which
elicited a response from Frederic Manning ("French Criticism of
Newman," January 1926 *Criterion*) complaining that Fernandez
read Newman with too modern eyes and thus made him seem
anachronistically Nietzschean. Fernandez replied ("Reply to Manning," October 1926 *Criterion*), with something of Newman's own
comic provocativeness, that he regarded Newman as, indeed,
"more modern than Nietzsche" (656). What Jacques Derrida
intends by "infinite interpretation" is to cut us off from just the
sorts of sponsoring authority Newman wishes to affirm – an action
meant, of course, not to deny us a consolation, but to liberate us
from a burden, so that our own interpretations can claim for themselves that they are self-born, self-begotten. Newman's sense of
human difference, individuality, and (indeed) isolation is sufficiently acute that appeals to "authority" can incur no threat, no
"anxiety" from its influence.

20. John Henry Newman, *Sermons Chiefly on the Theory of Religious
Belief* (London, 1843), 70. Cf. Vargish, *Contemplation of Mind*,
179–80: "If we approach the *Apologia* as an account of a man's
search for God, we are bound to be disappointed: faith in God had
possessed Newman almost from the beginning ... [the *Apologia*]
shows us a man seeking not faith in God, but a source of information about God, a means of drawing nearer, a communion. ...
[The *Apologia*] provides us with a kind of personal epistemology in

which the inquirer attempts to discover not spiritual truth but the voice which can utter it."

21. Newman's 1859 "Proof of Theism" has been edited (with commentary) by Adrian J. Boekraad and Henry Tristram, *The Argument from Conscience to the Existence of God, According to J. H. Newman* (Louvain, 1961).

22. The most thorough and compelling recent statement of the neo-Thomist case against Newman that I know is Harold L. Weatherby's *Cardinal Newman in His Age: His Place in English Theology and Literature* (Nashville, Tenn., 1973). For a sympathetic account of Newman's modernism, see Coulson, *Newman and the Common Tradition;* for Newman as precursor of the Second Vatican Council, see Christopher Hollis, *Newman and the Modern World* (New York, 1968). For a brief account of Newman's place in Catholic modernism, see Harrold, *Newman,* 357–69.

23. On Newman's residual Protestantism, see David Newsome, "The Evangelical Sources of Newman's Power," in *The Rediscovery of Newman,* ed. Coulson and Allchin, 11–30: Newman's conviction of the solitude of the soul evinces "an implicit Protestantism, for it recognizes no mediator between God and the individual soul. But what it really is, is Newmanism" (22). Orthodox Catholic criticism of Newman often amounts to the charge that "Newmanism" is crypto-Protestant, but Newsome mounts, very persuasively, an argument cognate with J. M. Cameron's in the same volume (see note 13 above) that Newman's very inconsistencies are what lend his appeal such comprehensiveness.

24. Cf. Lytton Strachey: "When Newman was a child, he 'wished that he could believe the Arabian Nights were true'. When he came to be a man, his wish seems to have been granted" ("Cardinal Manning," in *Eminent Victorians* [1918; rpt. New York, 1963], 33).

25. A. Dwight Culler, Introduction to John Henry Newman, *Apologia Pro Vita Sua* (Boston, 1956), ix.

26. John Henry Newman, *Autobiographical Writings,* ed. Henry Tristram (London, 1956), 248. Newman adverts frequently in the *Autobiographical Writings* (see, e.g., p. 82) to his disinclination to "enthusiasm" and its role in his youthful move away from evangelicalism. In a letter he writes, "All my life I have complained of ἀδυναμία, as I have called it. I mean a strange imprisonment, as if a chain were round my limbs and my faculties, hindering me doing more than a certain maximum – a sort of moral tether. People have said 'Why don't you *speak* louder? You speak, as far as you go, with such evident ease, you certainly can do more if you wish and try –'

I can only answer, 'I can't.' I am kept in my circle by my moral
tether, which pulls me up abruptly" (*Letters and Diaries of John
Henry Newman,* ed. C. S. Dessain [Oxford, 1961–], 15: 242).
27. Herodotus, *History,* trans. Rev. William Beloe (New York, 1828),
Chap. 6, 126–9.
28. John Henry Newman, "Literature," in *Idea of a University,* ed.
Harrold, 244.
29. Wilfred Ward, *The Life of John Henry Cardinal Newman,* 2 vols.
(London, 1913), 2: 349–50.

3. "BECAUSE THERE IS SAFETY IN DERISION"

1. With only a few exceptions, all references to writings by Yeats are
included in the text, keyed to the following abbreviations:

    A: *The Autobiography of William Butler Yeats* (New York,
    1967)
    AV-A: *A Critical Edition of Yeats's "A Vision" (1925),* ed.
    George Mills Harper and Walter Kelly Hood (London,
    1978); page references are to Yeats's text (reproduced in
    facsimile from the 1925 *A Vision*); italic page numbers
    refer to the editors' critical apparatus
    AV-B: *A Vision* (1937; rpt. New York, 1956)
    E: *Explorations* (New York, 1962)
    E & I: *Essays and Introductions* (New York, 1961)
    M: *Mythologies* (New York, 1974)
    Memoirs: *Memoirs,* ed. Denis Donoghue (New York, 1972)
    Plays: *Collected Plays of W. B. Yeats* (New York, 1953)
    V: *The Variorum Edition of the Poems of W. B. Yeats,* ed.
    Peter Allt and Russell K. Alspach (New York, 1957)

2. E. H. Mikhail, ed., *W. B. Yeats: Interviews and Recollections* (London, 1977), 263.
3. Ibid., 152.
4. My discussion owes much to Hazard Adams's brief but penetrating
essay, "Some Yeatsian Versions of Comedy," in *In Excited Reverie,* ed. A. N. Jeffares and K. G. W. Cross (New York, 1965), 152–70.
5. Robert Graves, "These Be Your Gods, O Israel," in *On Poetry: Collected Talks and Essays* (Garden City, N.Y., 1969), 132.
6. Stephen Spender, *World Within World* (New York, n.d.), 151. On
the preceding page Spender records some of Yeats's more bizarre
political pronouncements, emitted by the poet "in a half-humourous, half-prophetic vein." Spender observes that "it is difficult to
understand how seriously to take such a prophecy," but immedi-

ately hastens to concede that "what is clear, though, is that spiritualism as a revolutionary force is an important in its power to influence the world as politics, psychology, or science." A similar respectful bafflement animates Spender's review of the 1937 *A Vision* in the *Criterion* 17 (April 1938): 536–7.

7. *Letters of Virginia Woolf,* ed. Nigel Nicolson and Joanne Trautman (New York, 1975–80), 4: 253.

8. Mikhail, ed., *Interviews and Recollections,* 205, 33, 136, 143. On Wilde, the "forty-nine articles," and the "Twenty Commandments," see Richard Ellmann, "Oscar at Oxford," *New York Review of Books,* March 29, 1984, 24.

9. Mikhail, ed., *Interviews and Recollections,* 97, 176, 296.

10. Joseph Hone, *W. B. Yeats: 1865–1939* (New York, 1962), 84.

11. W. R. Rodgers, "W. B. Yeats: A Dublin Portrait," in *In Excited Reverie,* ed. Jeffares and Cross, 5. The utterance of Rodgers's "Austin Clarke" nicely communicates, in fuller quotation, the specifically Irish flavor of the young Yeats's literary milieu:

> "I think," said he ["Austin Clarke"], "that it is a great pity that the poet, like the soldier and the clergyman and many others, hasn't got some specific dress, or at least part of a dress, to distinguish him from, say, the business man. As a young poet I wore an enormous bow tie – it was of shimmering gold and green, and I was very proud of it. Well, the reason I wore that bow tie was because in Dublin all the poets wore a bow tie. Yeats from the Abbey Theatre, appearing there frequently, had a magnificent black tie, which we would copy in other colours. When I got to London, I found that poets no longer wore any specific sign or symbol of their art. They were all dressed in hard stiff white collars, like business men. It was the time of the Georgian school, and I think it would have been better for the Georgian poets if they had worn flowing ties. It might have saved them from the terrible rush and pressure of the modern world. It might have protected their art. Look what happened to the Georgian school. I attribute that solely to the fact that they did not wear flowing ties like the Irsh poets!"

12. George Moore, "Yeats, Lady Gregory, and Synge," *English Review,* 16 (January 1914): 172.

13. The Great War, which obtruded politics and history on so many who had hitherto ignored them, had the opposite effect on Yeats: It silenced his "political" utterance. His Anglo-Irish loyalties were

too conflicted to negotiate; for while England cast itself in the war as savior of civilization, Ireland regarded it as the long-awaited imperial debacle that would give the smaller subject nations their opportunity. On Yeats's disillusion with the Irish nationalist movement, see Dudley Young, *Out of Ireland: The Poetry of W. B. Yeats* (Cheadle, 1975), 35–41. For a fuller account of this "change of mask," see Richard Ellmann, *Yeats: The Man and the Masks* (New York, n.d.), 185–219; cf. Geoffrey Hartman, *Beyond Formalism: Literary Essays 1958–1970* (New Haven, Conn., 1970), 249–52.

14. For Yeats's telling of this story, see *Memoirs*, 23–4, and *A*, 122–3. Yeats's skepticism in his occult "researches" has been noted by many commentators. Yeats's generation was the first to attempt to study supernatural phenomena scientifically, and Alex Zwerdling reports that "the writings of men like Osty, Richet, J. W. Dunne, Myers, and Ochorowicz were familiar to Yeats" (*Yeats and the Heroic Ideal* [New York, 1965], 154). On Yeats's reading of such authors, see Austin Warren, "William Butler Yeats: The Religion of a Poet" (1942), in *The Permanence of Yeats*, ed. James Hall and Martin Steinmann (1950; rpt. New York, 1961), 200–12. Ellmann *(Man and the Masks)* narrates Yeats's involvement with Madame Blavatsky's Theosophist Lodge (Chap. 5, 70–85) and the Hermetic Students of the Golden Dawn (Chap. 7, 86–98). The definitive work on Yeats's spiritualism is George Mills Harper, *Yeats's Golden Dawn* (London, 1974), and George Mills Harper, ed., *Yeats and the Occult* (Toronto, 1975).

15. Quoted by W. Y. Tindall, "The Symbolism of W. B. Yeats" (1945), in *The Permanence of Yeats*, ed. Hall and Steinmann, 238.

16. Arthur Symons, *The Symbolist Movement in Literature* (1899), ed. Richard Ellmann (New York, 1958), 2; Thomas Carlyle, "Symbols," in *Sartor Resartus*, ed. C. F. Harrold (New York, 1937), 219.

17. Ellmann, *Man and the Masks*, 3.

18. Symons, *Symbolist Movement*, 21. It would be unfair to leave the impression that Symons's interest in the otherworldly is altogether innocent of irony. Villier de l'Isle Adam's "buffoonery" is a leitmotif of Symons's essay on him ("the idealist is never more the idealist than in his buffooneries" [ibid., 25]), and at moments Symons suggests possibilities of making estheticism and occultism yield satire that may well have had something to do, whichever way the currents of influence ran, with Yeats's "esoteric comedy": "Satire, with [de l'Isle Adam], is the revenge of beauty upon ugliness, the persecution of the ugly; it is not merely social satire, it is a satire on the material universe. Thus it is the only laughter of our time which is fundamental, as fundamental as that of Swift or Rabelais.

And this lacerating laughter of the idealist is never surer in its aim than when it turns the arms of science against itself" (ibid., 27).

19. James Joyce, *Ulysses,* ed. Hans Walter Gabler (New York, 1986), 178.

20. W. B. Yeats, *The Poems: A New Edition,* ed. Richard J. Finneran (New York, 1983), 595. No less insouciant, but somewhat fussier, was an earlier version of this note that worried over the peripheral distractions of the tendency of John Aherne and Owen Aherne to intertransmogrify: "I now consider that *John* Aherne is either the original *Owen* Aherne or some near relation of the man that was." (*V,* 821). No such anxiety over detail troubles the serenity of the final version.

21. See Richard J. Finneran, "On Editing Yeats: The Text of *A Vision* (1937)," *Texas Studies in Literature and Language* 19 (Spring 1977): 119–34, and *Editing Yeats's Poems* (New York, 1983), 6–8. For a succinct and authoritative narrative of Yeats's labors revising *A Vision,* see Connie K. Hood, "The Remaking of *A Vision,*" in *Yeats: An Annual of Critical and Textual Studies,* ed. Richard J. Finneran (Ithaca, N.Y., 1983), no. 1, 33–67.

22. T. R. Henn, *The Lonely Tower* (London, 1965), 192.

23. Edmund Wilson, "Yeats's Guide to the Soul" (review of 1925 text of *A Vision*), *New Republic* 57 (January 16, 1929): 251; Wilson, *Axel's Castle* (New York, 1931), 57.

24. "The Seven Sacred Trances," unsigned prefatory essay apparently by one or both of the editors, *The Permanence of Yeats,* ed. Hall and Steinmann, 1.

25. For the reader who wants an introduction to Yeats's "system," Ellmann is the best guide, in *Man and the Masks,* 220–39, and *The Identity of Yeats* (New York, 1964), 149–70. Northrop Frye considers *A Vision* as a thesaurus of Yeatsian (and trans-Yeatsian) themes and symbols in "The Rising of the Moon: A Study of *A Vision,*" in *An Honoured Guest,* ed. Denis Donoghue and J. R. Mulryne (New York, 1966), 9–33. Helen Hennessy Vendler, *Yeats's "Vision" and the Later Plays* (Cambridge, Mass., 1963), approaches it as Yeats's model for the creative processes of his poetry, and Harold Bloom does the same, though psychologizing where Vendler estheticizes, in *Yeats* (New York, 1969), 210–91. For Frye, Vendler, and Bloom, the "problem of Yeats's beliefs" that so preoccupied critics between Richards's *Science and Poetry* (1926) and the fifties is a dead letter, though Bloom communicates better than the others a sense of all that Yeats had at stake in it. For Frye and Bloom, *A Packet for Ezra Pound* is an occasion for joking asides of their own, while Vendler's otherwise exhuastive chapter-by-chapter account of *A Vision* elides

it altogether. These critics exemplify the late period of New Criticism, which accepted Yeatsian esoterica as "pseudo-statement" with much more composure than Richards could ever muster. Since the 1970s, critics have been readier, again, to take Yeats's "beliefs" at something closer to Yeats's own valuation. For a survey of the history of critical response to the "problem of Yeats's beliefs" (and an especially acute analysis of Ellmann's role in it), as well as an example of the newer trend, see James Lovic Allen, "Belief vs. Faith in the Credo of Yeats," *Journal of Modern Literature* 4 (1975): 692–716. Other examples include Barbara L. Croft, *"Stylistic Arrangements": A Study of William Butler Yeats's 'A Vision'* (Lewisburg, Penn., 1987), and the work associated with George Mills Harper – not only his two studies, *Yeats's Golden Dawn* (London, 1974) and *The Making of Yeats's 'A Vision': A Study of the Automatic Script*, 2 vols. (Carbondale, Ill., 1987), and his facsimile (edited with Walter Kelly Hood) *Critical Edition of Yeats's "A Vision" (1925)* (London, 1978), but also the essays gathered in his *Yeats and the Occult*. Harper's motive is apparently to get the story of Yeats's occultism registered in the terms in which Yeats himself understood it and to keep questions of "belief" from eclipsing others no less important. James Olney most satisfactorily mediates between the *episteme* of "our" modernity and Yeats's way of putting things, and takes seriously (but not näively) the question of its "truth value," in *The Rhizome and the Flower: The Perennial Philosophy, Yeats and Jung* (Berkeley, Calif., 1980), an inquiry into the roots of Yeats's (and Jung's) esoterica in the Pre-Socratics and Plato.

26. Hugh Kenner, *The Stoic Comedians* (Berkeley, Calif., 1962), 37–50.

27. Ellmann, *Identity of Yeats*, 239. On Yeats's relations with Pound, see Richard Ellmann, *Eminent Domain: Yeats Among Wilde, Joyce, Pound, Eliot and Auden* (New York, 1967), 57–87.

28. Ezra Pound Interview, *Writers at Work: The Paris Review Interviews, 2nd Series* (New York, 1963), 63. Pound is remembering not *A Vision* and its preface, but *The King of the Great Clock Tower* (1934). Yeats's courtly and amusing preface is reprinted in *V*, 855–6. George Mills Harper conjectures that some revisions to the 1937 text may have been prompted by Pound's criticisms (*The Making of Yeats's 'A Vision,'* 2: 416–17).

29. Persuading birds to improve their manner of life evidently exercised over Yeats himself the fascination of what's difficult. He kept birds as pets, and Lennox Robinson reports that "it distressed him

that they would use their bathwater for drinking purposes and [he] sought vainly from a bird fancier for a cure for this deplorable habit" (Robinson, "William Butler Yeats: Peronality," in *In Excited Reverie,* ed. Jeffares and Cross, 16). Yeats frequently cites the nesting instincts of birds as disproving Locke's dismissal of innate ideas (e.g., *A,* 112, 177, 181, 182).

30. The provenance assigned this woodcut within the 1937 text of *A Vision* (none was offered in the 1925 text) is John Aherne, who enclosed it in his letter printed toward the close of the introduction. In actuality, Yeats commissioned it from Edmund Dulac and was delighted with the way it came out; he even wrote Dulac that he doubted "if Laurie [the publisher of the 1925 *A Vision*] would have taken the book but for the amusing deceit that your designs make possible" *(AV-A, 1).* Henn notes (*The Lonely Tower,* 192) that "it looks like an authentic woodcut" and reports that "a beard was added to disguise the resemblance of the finished block to Yeats himself." John Aherne observes in his letter to Yeats that John Duddon, whom he gently chides for his literal-mindedness, "discovers a resemblance between your face and that of Giraldus in the *Speculum*" *(AV-B,* 54).

31. This possibility gains support four pages away *(AV-B,* 54), where John Aherne remembers Yeats as having remarked that this and two other poems were based on "hearsay." In a 1919 pamphlet, "A People's Theatre," Yeats attributes authorship of the poem to "a certain friend of mine" (*E,* 259), unnamed but clearly identifiable (at least to the instructed) as Michael Robartes.

My reading of the conclusion of "The Phases of the Moon" owes much to Hugh Kenner, "The Sacred Book of the Arts," *Gnomon: Essays on Contemporary Literature* (New York, 1958), 27–8.

32. *Letters of W. B. Yeats,* ed. Allan Wade (New York, 1955), 781.

33. Certainly just for sheer size, leaving the other obvious difficulties aside, the task must have afforded enormous scope to the "Frustrators" Yeats speaks of who bedevilled his efforts. "Exposition in sleep came to an end in 1920," Yeats explains in *A Packet for Ezra Pound,* "and I began an exhaustive study of some fifty copy-books of automatic script, and of a much smaller number of books recording what had come in sleep. . . . I had already a small concordance in a large manuscript book, but now made a much larger, arranged like a card index" *(AV-B,* 17–18). George M. Harper and Walter Kelly Hood reckon that Yeats and his wife undertook a total of 450 sessions of automatic writing during which responses were gathered to 8,672 questions, of which material, 3,627 pages have been pre-

served. Another 164 sessions of "sleeps and meditations" produced material of which 270 pages have been preserved (*AV-A*, xix–xxi). Harper promises that one day all of this material will be published; in the meanwhile he has provided an eye-opening narrative digest in *The Making of Yeats's 'A Vision'*.

34. W. B. Yeats, Introduction to *The Oxford Book of Modern Verse 1892–1935*, ed. Yeats (Oxford, 1937), xxxiv.

35. Ellmann, *Man and the Masks*, 171.

36. The argument that I am making about Yeats's confidence applies also to his political poetry; it was not until late 1920 (in the *New Statesman* and *Dial*) that Yeats published his Easter Rising poems, "Easter, 1916," "Sixteen Dead Men," and "The Rose Tree." All had been composed years earlier, but prudence had kept them unpublished, available only to the poet's friends. I have seen it suggested that Yeats decided to publish in 1920 because it seemed by then "safe": nonsense. As Conor Cruise O'Brien remarks in his superb essay "Passion and Cunning," these poems appeared at the height of the Black-and-Tan terror: "To publish these poems in this context was a political act, and a bold one: probably the boldest of Yeats's career" (in *In Excited Reverie*, ed. Jeffares and Cross, 239).

37. I. A. Richards, *Principles of Literary Criticism* (New York, [1925]), 266; *Science and Poetry* (New York, 1926), 85–6, 87–8.

38. Theodore Spencer's review in the *New Republic* (October 10, 1928) is reprinted in A. Norman Jeffares, ed., *W. B. Yeats: The Critical Heritage* (Boston, 1977), 287–90; for Wilson, see note 23 above; William Empson, *Seven Types of Ambiguity* (1930; rpt. New York, 1947), 189; F. R. Leavis, *New Bearings in English Poetry* (London, 1932), 49.

39. T. S. Eliot, *After Strange Gods* (London, 1934), 47. In speaking this way of the "right" and the "wrong" supernatural worlds, Eliot is of course suggesting something far more irksome to Richards than it would ever be to Yeats. Elsewhere, Eliot implies a response subtler than Richards's to such "modern heretics" as Yeats: "The essential of any important heresy is not simply that it is wrong: it is that it is partly right" (ibid., 19). As for Richards, it would be unfair not to acknowledge that as time went on, his esteem for Yeats increased enormously. In a 1935 reprint of *Science and Poetry,* Richards adds a footnote to the very passage Eliot had quoted just the year before: "Who could have foreseen before *The Tower* Mr. Yeats's development into the greatest poet of our age or the miracles in *Songs for Music Perhaps?*" (*Poetries and Sciences* [London], 1970, 72n).

40. *Letters of W. B. Yeats*, 742.

41. There is a suggestive identity of interests here between the "instruc-

tors" and their medium, Mrs. Yeats, an identity of interests Yeats was not above teasing; for a time he thought of publishing the revised *A Vision* with this dedication: "TO MY WIFE who created this system which bores her, who made possible these pages she will never read, and who has accepted this dedication on the condition that I write nothing but verse for a year" (quoted in Ellmann, *Man and the Masks*, 262n). In the event, as we have seen, he had mercy on Mrs. Yeats and, in effect, dedicated the book instead to Ezra Pound.

42. Hone, *W. B. Yeats,* 476.

43. Ellmann, *Man and the Masks,* 282.

44. A. E. (George Russell), Review of *A Vision* (1925), *Irish Statesman* 5 (February 1926): 714–16; reprinted in Jeffares, ed., *Critical Heritage,* 269.

45. For example, the essays collected in 1950 in *The Permanence of Yeats* often read almost like a casebook on this issue. The strongest indictment of Yeats's "determinism" in the collection is D. S. Savage, "The Aestheticism of W. B. Yeats" (1945), 173–94, especially 185–6; Yeats is acquitted of the charge by Allen Tate ("Yeats's Romanticism: Notes and Suggestions" [1942], 97–105), Cleanth Brooks ("Yeats: The Poet as Myth-Maker" [1938], 60–84, especially 71), and Martin Dauwen Zabel ("Yeats: The Book and the Image" [1940, 1943], 315–26). The issue is raised, but noncommittally, by Austin Warren ("W. B. Yeats: The Religion of a Poet" [1942]), 200–12, and by Graham Hough, *The Last Romantics* (1947; rpt. London, 1961), 243.

46. On Yeats's sense of history, see Thomas R. Whitaker, *Swan and Shadow: Yeats's Dialogue with History* (Chapel Hill, N.C., 1964); for the historical reading behind *A Vision,* see Chap. 5, "Dove or Swan," 76–96. On "determinism," Whitaker provides a novel twist: Whereas most "constructions" of the issue oppose historical necessity to individual (free) will, Whitaker assumes that the real danger of unfreedom for Yeats lay in that most tempting simulacrum of freedom, solipsism, and that what saved him was his "dialogue" with the not-self of history.

47. To Edith Shackleton Heald, February 21, 1938; *Letters of W. B. Yeats,* 905.

48. As Alex Zwerdling suggests in *Yeats and the Heroic Ideal,* 176–8. Zwerdling, in effect, revives the view (without using the word) that Yeats's system is "deterministic," but in such a fashion as to yield tragedy rather than totalitarian nightmare; clearly, though, it is a tragedy (and a heroism) Zwerdling is not happy with: Yeats's "thirteenth cycle," *pace* Ellmann, "scarcely makes [Yeats's] system a

very optimistic one, since the knowledge of this ultimate reality is denied to man and 'has kept the secret.' . . . Perversely, the Yeatsian hero looks on the inevitable destruction of what is valuable and beautiful in life as in some way right and good. . . . The false 'resolution' of the antithesis between mortal and immortal thus leads ultimately to an exaltation of man himself, for its pessimistic message is a test of heroic resiliency."

49. Mikhail, ed., *Interviews and Recollections,* 266, 261–2.

CONCLUSION

1. I. A. Richards, "Poetry and Beliefs," Chap. 6 of *Science and Poetry* (New York, 1926), 66–79; Archibald MacLeish, "Ars Poetica," in *The Oxford Book of American Verse,* ed. F. O. Matthiessen (New York, 1950), 894.

2. Sanford Schwartz, *The Matrix of Modernism: Pound, Eliot, and Early Twentieth-Century Thought* (Princeton, N.J., 1985), 12–49.

3. T. S. Eliot, Preface to the 1928 edition of *The Sacred Wood* (rpt. New York, 1950), viii; "East Coker," Sec. 2, in *Collected Poems 1909–1962* (New York, 1963), 184.

4. W. B. Yeats, *A Vision* (New York, 1937; rpt. New York, 1956), 25; "The Coming of Wisdom with Time" (1910), in *The Variorum Edition of the Poems of W. B. Yeats,* ed. Peter Allt and Russell K. Alspach (New York, 1957), 261.

5. "The Literature of Knowledge and the Literature of Power" (1848), in *Selected Writings of Thomas DeQuincey,* ed. Philip Van Doren Stern (New York, 1937), 1096–1105.

6. Thomas Carlyle, *Sartor Resartus,* ed. C. F. Harrold (New York, 1937), 162.

7. Sigmund Freud, *The Ego and the Id* (1923), ed. James Strachey (New York, 1960), 38–40; see also Freud's paper "The Economic Problem in Masochism" (1924), in *General Psychological Theory,* ed. Philip Rieff (New York, 1963), 190–201. Freud's account of guilt and neurosis, according to which the superego punishes the ego for the transgressive impulses of the id, squares almost too neatly with Carlyle's conflicted psychology of "Work" and *"Selbsttödtung."*

8. See, e.g., Sigmund Freud, "On the Mechanism of Paranoia" (1911), in *General Psychological Theory,* ed. Rieff 41; "The Analogy," Part 3, Sec. 1, Subsec. 3 of *Moses and Monotheism* (1939; rpt. New York, 1967), 97.

9. John Stuart Mill, *The Autobiography and Other Writings,* ed. Jack Stillinger (Boston, 1969), 85.

10. Geoffrey Hartman, "Romanticism and Anti-Self-Consciousness," in *Beyond Formalism: Literary Essays 1958–1970* (New Haven, Conn., 1970), 300. An index of the tentativeness of Hartman's essay is that Hegel figures only as a "Cf." in a footnote, Freud not at all.

11. John Henry Newman, *Apologia*, ed. Martin Svaglic (New York, 1967), 218; W. B. Yeats, "The Symbolism of Poetry" (1900), in *Essays and Introductions* (New York, 1961), 155.

12. "The Scholar-Gipsy," ll. 203–5, in *The Poems of Matthew Arnold*, ed. Kenneth Allott (London, 1965), 342.

13. *The Centenary Edition of the Works of Thomas Carlyle*, 30 vols., ed. H. D. Traill (London, 1896–9), 2: 6; Yeats, "Stream and Sun at Glendalough" (1932), in *Variorum Poems*, 507; "Colonus' Praise" (1927), in ibid., 446; "A Prayer for My Daughter" (1919), in ibid., 405.

14. Roger B. Henkle, in *Comedy and Culture: England 1820–1900* (Princeton, N.J., 1980), a study of comic fiction from Bulwer to Wilde and Beerbohm, argues the emergence of this new sensibility and traces the development of a social comedy responsive to it. Henkle finds that this emergent sensibility causes moral distress in the beginning of his chosen period, as writers shrink from a view of life that threatens to dissolve the unitary self of Protestant conscience into an ensemble of social roles; but as the period progresses, writers increasingly see in this state of affairs an opportunity rather than a danger. Although Henkle's writers and their "comedy" are different from mine, his argument is suggestive for the various responses to the problem of self-consciousness evinced by Carlyle, Newman, and Yeats.

15. "The Scholar-Gipsy" (1852–3), ll. 164, 169, in *Poems of Arnold*, 340; "The Buried Life" (1849–52), ll. 31–6, in ibid., 272.

16. Matthew Arnold, *Culture and Anarchy*, ed. J. Dover Wilson (Cambridge, 1960), 150–1. David J. DeLaura finds a direct influence of the *Apologia* on Arnold's distinction between "Hebrew" and "Hellene" in *Hebrew and Hellene in Victorian England: Newman, Arnold, Pater* (Austin, Tex., 1969), 72–5. DeLaura here traces resemblances between the ideas or thought of the two writers, but I would add (what is implicit in DeLaura's earlier pages on "The Oriel Inheritance" [*Hebrew and Hellene*, 5–26] that Newman's influence was surely an affair as much of style as of content and may well have acted on Arnold less by precept than by example. The playfulness and wit of Newman's esoteric comedy, the "exuberant and joyous energy" of which Newman boasts and which he so often exemplifies in the *Apologia*, doubtless provided a model of

that "free play" and "spontaneity of consciousness" Arnold commends in the quoted passage.

17. T. S. Eliot, "Tradition and the Individual Talent" (1919), in *Selected Essays* (New York, 1960), 9.

18. Eliot, "Tradition and the Individual Talent," 6–7, 10; Arnold, Preface to the first edition of *Poems* (1853), in *Poems of Arnold*, 591; Eliot, "The Love Song of J. Alfred Prufrock" (1910), in *Collected Poems 1909–1962*, 4. For a fuller discussion of these issues in Eliot see my essay, "The Success and Failure of T. S. Eliot," *Sewanee Review* 96 (Winter 1988): 55–76.

19. Roger Henkle cites Ernst Kris's account of "play" and "elaboration" as a model for comic imagination. According to Kris, comedy often proceeds through three phases, from (1) a transgressive, id-driven, destructive "play" that amounts to a kind of revenge on or rebellion against the world as it is, through (2) a more self-conscious and "artful" working out, or "elaboration," of these impulses, to (3) a phase of retraction, in which the id-driven energies are checked and corrected by the reascendant superego, in a motion of atonement for the original transgression (*Comedy and Culture*, 15–6, 47–9). This account squares with my reading of *Sartor Resartus*, according to which the extreme radicalism of the "Descendental" Book 1 is revised into something altogether more conventionally and preachily "Transcendental" in Books 2 and 3. A similar argument might be made concerning the relation of the *Apologia* to the *Grammar of Assent*, written two years later and explaining as accommodatingly as Newman could issues he was pleased to leave baffling in the earlier book.

20. See M. H. Abrams, "Structure and Style in the Greater Romantic Lyric," in *From Sensibility to Romanticism*, ed. Frederick W. Hilles and Harold Bloom (New York, 1965), 527–60; for Harold Bloom's "revision" of the "greater Romantic lyric" into the "crisis poem," see "The Internalization of Quest Romance," in *The Ringers in the Tower* (Chicago, 1971), 12–35.

21. "Sir, No Man's Enemy" (1929), in *The English Auden: Poems, Essays, and Dramatic Writings 1927–1939*, ed. Edward Mendelson (New York, 1977), 36; "Inside the Whale" (1940), in *The Collected Essays, Journalism and Letters of George Orwell*, 4 vols., ed. Sonia Orwell and Ian Angus (New York, 1968), 1: 507.

22. This phrase is the title of the concluding chapter of Rieff's *Freud: The Mind of the Moralist* (1959; rpt. Garden City, N.Y., 1961), 361–92.

23. Eliot, "Dante" (1929), in *Selected Essays*, 223.

24. Yeats, "Coole Park and Ballylee, 1931," in *Variorum Poems*, 491;

A Critical Edition of Yeats's "A Vision" (1925), ed. George Mills Harper and Walter Kelly Hood (London, 1978), 210, 211–2. Yeats cut these observations on his younger contemporaries from the 1937 text of *A Vision.*

25. On high culture and avant-garde, see Henkle, *Comedy and Culture,* Chap. 6, "Meredith and Butler: Comedy as Lyric, High Culture and the Bourgeois Trap," 238–95; and Chap. 7, "Wilde and Beerbohm: The Wit of the Avant-Garde, the Charm of Failure," 296–352. On the artist as culture hero, see Frank Kermode, "The Artist in Isolation," Chap. 1 of *Romantic Image* (New York, 1957), 1–23. On mass bourgeois culture as the necessary backdrop for the emergence of the avant-garde, see Renato Poggioli, *The Theory of the Avant-Garde,* trans. Gerald Fitzberald (Cambridge, Mass., 1968), and Peter Bürger, *The Theory of the Avant-Garde* (Minneapolis, Minn., 1984).

26. George Orwell, "Inside the Whale" (1940), *Collected Essays, Journalism and Letters,* 1: 507.

27. Eliot, *The Waste Land* (1922), in *Collected Poems 1909–1962,* 57.

28. The question was asked by Arnold Bennett in 1923; cited in Hugh Kenner, *The Invisible Poet: T. S. Eliot* (New York, 1959), 181.

29. T. S. Eliot, *The Use of Poetry and the Use of Criticism* (London, 1964), 30–1, 154.

30. See my "Joyce the Irresponsible," *Sewanee Review* 94 (Summer 1986): 450–70; and "Joyce: Autobiography, History, Narrative," *Kenyon Review* 10, 2 (Spring 1988): 91–109.

31. Northrop Frye, *Anatomy of Criticism* (Princeton, N.J., 1957), 34, 321.

32. I am summarizing Chapters 6 and 7 of Stuart Tave's *The Amiable Humorist* (Chicago, 1960); on Falstaff, see 121–39; on Quixote, 151–63; on Parson Adams, 140–51; on Uncle Toby, 148–51. "Whimsical," tellingly, began as a term of abuse used against Richard Steele; Steele (in the *Theatre* [1720]) turned it into a term of approbation by characterizing the "Whimsical" as one who "governs himself according to his own Understanding, in Disobedience to that of others, who are more in fashion than himself" (Tave, *Amiable Humorist,* 101–2) – a representative episode in the transformation of the "humour character" into the "amiable" *eiron.*

33. George McFadden, *Discovering the Comic* (Princeton, N.J., 1982), 49.

34. Newman, *Apologia,* 39.

35. Freud, "On Narcissism: An Introduction" (1914), in *General Psychological Theory,* ed. Rieff, 58.

36. Ibid., 70. This formulation exemplifies the modern transformation

of comic theory, revising the classical "superiority theory" from a moralism of virtuous self-regard to a psychology of self-preservation. The closest version of this in English (and nearly contemporary with Freud's) is Kenneth Burke's view of comedy as a "corrective," a "frame of acceptance" or "strategy for living" that helps the imperiled self "discount" some threat of diminishment or humiliation (*Attitudes Toward History* [1937; rpt. Boston, 1961], 39–44, 166–75).

Though both McFadden and Henkle link Freud's "On Narcissism" with their various ideas of the comic, neither makes much of it. My own effort here to connect it with the peculiar ironic self-consciousness of the modern avant-garde artist is perhaps a "comic" version of Harold Bloom's darker story of the "strong" poet's necessary "narcissism"; see Bloom, "Freud's Concepts of Defense and the Poetic Will," *Agon: Towards a Theory of Revisionism* (New York, 1982), 119–44.

37. McFadden, *Discovering the Comic.* "Obstinacy" and "freedom" are prominent themes throughout the book, but see especially 11–20. The phrase "enhanced sense of the self" (48) comes in a discussion headed "Self and Character in the Comic" (46–48). McFadden cites Freud on narcissism (20–1), but I cannot claim that he would endorse my account of the transformation of "humour character" into *eiron* – or, indeed, my account of "esoteric comedy," though he observes that "discovering the comic" is an enterprise that must proceed "sometimes in the strangest places" (254).

38. Sigmund Freud, "Humour" (1928), in *Character and Culture,* ed. Philip Rieff (New York, 1963), 265.

39. I give the phrase as it is invariably quoted in English, though I cannot find it in that form in any of the translations of Freud that I have been able to check. The phrase is apparently misremembered from Freud's *Introductory Lectures on Psychoanalysis,* lectures 27 ("Transference") and 28 ("Analytic Therapy"), which in the most up-to-date translation, by James Strachey (New York, 1977), speak of therapy as "the replacing of what is unconscious by what is conscious, the translation of what is unconscious into what is conscious" (435) and as an activity that "transforms what is unconscious into what is conscious" (455).

INDEX

Abrams, M. H., 240–1 n22, 266 n20
Adams, Brooks, 210
Adams, Hazard, 92, 248 n28, 256 n4
Adams, Henry, 210
Addison, Joseph, 19, 241 n28
A. E. (George Russell), 209, 214
Allen, James Lovic, 260 n25
"amiable humour," 20–5, 232–3, 267
  n32
Arnold, Matthew, 25, 113–14, 224–6
Ashton, Rosemary D., 246 n15
Auden, W. H., 158, 176, 227, 230

Bacon, Francis, 9, 25, 28, 194, 240 n12,
  252 n13
Barthes, Roland, 27–8
Bate, Walter Jackson, 20
Beckett, Samuel, 228, 230, 232
Beerbohm, Max, 17, 162, 229, 241
  n27
Behnken, Eloise M., 247 n17
Bentham, Jeremy, 221
Bentley, Eric, 34
Bergson, Henri, 234–5
Berkeley, Bishop George, 6, 136, 157,
  239 n9
Blackmur, R. P., 176
Blake, William, 10, 19, 21, 22, 160,
  164
Blavatsky, Helena Petrovna, 164
Blehl, Vincent Ferrer, 249–50 n7
Bloom, Harold, 19, 31, 177, 209–10,
  259 n25, 266 n20, 268 n36
Boehme, Jacob, 164
Borges, Jorge Luis, 10, 41
Brancusi, Constantin, 211
Brantlinger, Patrick, 245 n9, 248 n28
Brookes, Gerry, 239 n4

Brooks, Cleanth, 176, 263 n45
Browning, Robert, 179
Buckler, William, E., 253–4 n16
Burke, Kenneth, 62, 189, 268 n36
Butler, Bishop Joseph, 133
Butler, Samuel, 241 n27
Byron, George Gordon, 6th baron, 20,
  225, 229

Cage, John, 230
Calvin, John, 30
Cameron, J. M., 252–3 n13
Carlyle, Thomas, 1–31, 33–95, 130–2,
  146, 165, 221–7, 228, 231, 232–3,
  236–7; and Calvinism, 69, 77, 82,
  131, 222, 226–7, 246–7 n17, 248
  n25; works: "Characteristics," 69,
  223, 224; The French Revolution, 39,
  89; Heroes and Hero-Worship, 31, 131;
  Past and Present, 39; Sartor Resartus,
  1–31, 33–95, 130–2, 217–8, 219,
  221, 232–3; see also "difficulty,"
  fictiveness, figuration, genre, parody,
  self and self-consciousness, self-
  referentiality, style, "textuality"
Cervantes Saavedra, Miguel de, 13
Clarke, Austin, 162
Clough, Arthur Hugh, 148
Coburn, Alvin Langdon, 165
Colby, Robert A., 252 n12
Coleridge, Samuel Taylor, 75, 132,
  227, 252 n10
comedy, 25–9, 228–38
Connolly, Francis, X., 239 n5
Cosgrave, William Thomas, 212
Coulson, John, 249 n2, 255 n22
Cowper, William, 20
Croft, Barbara L., 260 n25

269

Index

Index

Kant, Immanuel, 74, 244 n4
Kaplan, Fred, 247 n19
Keats, John, 19, 132, 180, 193
Keble, John, 121, 251 n8
Kelly, P. J., 160
Kenner, Hugh, 180, 240 n19, 261 n31
Kingsley, Charles, 21, 32, 98–110,
    117–19, 121–2, 124, 126, 128, 129,
    132, 134–6, 138, 143, 148
Kingsmill, Hugh, 161
Kris, Ernst, 242–3 n45, 266 n19

Landor, Walter Savage, 193
LaValley, Albert J., 245 n10, 246 n13
Lawry, J. S., 252 n12
Leavis, F. R., 205
Levine, George, 34, 92, 120–1, 247
    n22, 248 n25, 248 n28, 254 n16
Lewis, Wyndham, 166, 176, 206, 211,
    218
Locke, John, 19, 221, 227, 239 n9, 261
    n29
Luther, Martin, 17, 30, 77, 227

MacNeice, Louis, 159–60
Mailer, Norman, 230
Manning, Frederic, 254 n19
Markiewicz, Constance, 198–9
Martin, Robert Bernard, 22–3
Marx, Karl, 70, 74, 78, 210
McFadden, George, 233, 235, 242 n45,
    268 n36, 236 n37
Meredith, George, 9, 23, 26, 229, 241
    n27
Mill, John Stuart, 34, 78, 223, 247 n17
Milton, John, 19–20, 241 n28
Miyoshi, Masao, 248 n27
modernism, 8–15, 217–21, 227–33,
    237–8
Montesquieu, Charles Louis de
    Secondat, Baron de la Brede et de,
    49–51
Moore, George, 162–4, 206
Murray, Gilbert, 165

New Criticism, 2, 206, 259–60 n25
Newman, John Henry, 1–31, 97–153,
    221, 223, 224, 227, 228, 232–3,
    236–7; and "Economy," 104–9, 117,
    121–2, 129–43, 243 n47; and
    "Reserve," 119–22, 251 n8, 254 n16;
    works: Apologia Pro Vita Sua, 1–31,
    97–153, 217–18, 219, 221, 232–3;

*Essay on the Development of Christian
    Doctrine,* 127; *Grammar of Assent,* 134,
    137–8; "Literature," 139 251 n8;
    Lyra Apostolica, 120, 123; "Poetry,
    With Reference to Aristotle's
    Poetics," 134, 142, 251 n8; "Present
    Position of Catholics in England,"
    102, 113; *see also* fictiveness,
    figuration, genre, parody, self and
    self-consciousness, self-referentiality,
    style
Newsome, David, 255 n23
Newton, Isaac, 60, 239 n9
Nichols, Beverley, 160
Nietzsche, Friedrich, 140, 254 n19

O'Brien, Conor Cruise, 262 n36
O'Connor, Frank, 156, 214–15
Olney, James, 260 n25
Orwell, George, 227, 229, 239 n1

parody, 13–17; in Carlyle, 42–7, 51,
    83, 89, 90–1; in Newman, 98–106,
    110–19, 123–5, 128–43; in Yeats,
    166–7, 173–4, 178–82
Pascal, Blaise, 17
Pater, Walter, 165
Peckham, Morse, 91, 248 n25, 248 n27
Picasso, Pablo, 230
Pope, Alexander, 19–20
Pound, Ezra, 8–9, 13, 166,180, 204,
    210, 218–19, 230, 231, 260 n28, 263
    n41
"pseudo-statement," 176, 206, 218–21,
    260 n25
Pynchon, Thomas, 231, 232

Qualls, Barry, 248 n25

Reed, Walter L., 248 n27
Richards, I. A., 176, 204–6, 218, 259–
    60 n25, 262 n39
Richter, Jean Paul Friedrich, 30
Riding, Laura, 230
Rieff, Philip, 227
Robinson, Jonathan, 253 n14
Robinson, Lennox, 261 n29
Rodgers, W. R., 162, 257 n11
Rosenberg, John D., 248 n26
Rosenberg, Philip, 34, 74
Ruskin, John, 165
Russell, George, *see* A. E.

271

Index